D0126815

TWELVE

LARGE PRINT

Also by Al Franken

I'm Good Enough, I'm Smart Enough, and Doggone It,
People Like Me! Daily Affirmations by Stuart Smalley

Rush Limbaugh Is a Big Fat Idiot:
And Other Observations

Why Not Me? The Inside Story of the Making
and Unmaking of the Franken Presidency

Oh, the Things I Know! A Guide to Success, or,
Failing That, Happiness

Lies: And the Lying Liars Who Tell Them:
A Fair and Balanced Look at the Right

The Truth (with Jokes)

AL FRANKEN
GIANT *of the* SENATE

by AL FRANKEN

TWELVE

LARGE PRINT

Twelve
Hachette Book Group
1290 Avenue of the Americas, New York, NY 10104
twelvebooks.com
twitter.com/twelvebooks

First Hardcover Edition: May 2017

Twelve is an imprint of Grand Central Publishing. The Twelve name and logo
are trademarks of Hachette Book Group, Inc.

The publisher is not responsible for websites (or their content) that are
not owned by the publisher.

The Hachette Speakers Bureau provides a wide range of authors for speaking events.
To find out more, go to www.hachettespeakersbureau.com or
call (866) 376-6591.

Library of Congress Control Number: 2017932020

ISBNs: 978-1-4555-4041-9 (hardcover), 978-1-4555-7120-8 (large print),
978-1-5387-5998-1 (signed edition), 978-1-4555-4043-3 (ebook),
978-1-4789-1255-2 (audiobook, downloadable),
978-1-4789-1256-9 (audiobook, cd)

Printed in the United States of America

LSC-C

10   9   8   7   6   5   4   3   2   1

Contents

To Paul and Sheila

Based on actual events

Foreword

An Optimist's Guide to Politics

In the eight years since I came to Washington, probably the question I've been asked more than any other is some version of this: "Is being a United States senator as much fun as working on *Saturday Night Live*?"

The answer has always been NO!!! Why would it be?

When people ask me my favorite moment from my fifteen seasons at *SNL*, I always tell them it's all the late Tuesday nights or very early Wednesday mornings when the show got written on the seventeenth floor of 30 Rock, when I was rolling on the floor laughing at a line that Dan Aykroyd or Gilda Radner or my partner Tom Davis just came up with or a character that Dana Carvey or Chris Farley just invented. Nothing could be more fun.

That said, I've always told people that representing my home state of Minnesota in the U.S. Senate is, without a doubt, the *best* job I've ever had. I get to wake up every morning and go to work on behalf of five and a half million people—taking their best ideas to Washington, fighting for what they need to make a better life, and improving their lives in real, tangible ways.

Which would often prompt them to ask, "Are you talking about the same U.S. Senate that is one of the two bodies in today's U.S. Congress? And isn't today's Congress just an unrelenting horror show?"

The answer is YES!!! Today's Congress is a polarized, dysfunctional body, rendered helpless by partisanship, more focused on scoring short-term political points than on solving our nation's urgent problems. In short, the Washington of the past decade has been awash in nincompoopery.[USS*]

And *that* was before Trump.

Watching Donald J. Trump take the oath of office to become the 45th president of the United States was perhaps the most depressing moment I've had since I

---

* A note on style from the author: Because I'm a United States senator, I can't use the word "bull———." Even though Washington is indeed awash in bullshit. So throughout this volume, whenever you see a very mild oath like "Fiddlesticks!" (or some gentle name-calling like "numbskull" or "dimwit," or some old-timey synonym for "bull———" like "poppycock" or "flim-flummery"), followed by the letters "USS" in superscript, that means I've replaced something far more plainspoken with a less offensive phrase or expression. The "USS" stands for "United States Senate," the body in which I now serve. I feel I have a duty to both my colleagues and my constituents to make at least a token effort to preserve its dignity and decorum. I wish I could say the same for that dunderhead[USS] Ted Cruz.

entered politics, although that record has been repeatedly surpassed since January 20. The heartless and counterproductive Muslim ban; the barrage of racist and/or corrupt and/or unqualified staff appointments and Cabinet nominees; the unhinged tweets attacking anyone who opposes his agenda; the constant, constant, constant lying—Trump's presidency so far has been one shock to the system after another.

And while we're still finding out exactly how bad, and exactly what specific *kind* of bad, President Trump will be, it seems very likely that things in Washington are going to get worse before they get better.

Indeed, people have stopped asking me whether I'm having fun in my new career. These days, the question I get more than any other is some version of this: "What the hell do we do now?"

We're all going to have to figure out the answer together. But, as unpleasant as my job is going to be in the coming months and years, I'm still glad to have the chance to be part of the fight. And, really, while nobody could have prepared for the grim reality of a Trump presidency, when I look back at my own political journey, I can't help but feel like I'm as prepared as anyone could be for this moment.

* * *

This book is the story of that journey.

It's the story of a midwestern Jewish boy of humble

roots (the first in his family to own a pasta maker) who, after a thirty-five-year career in comedy, moved back home to challenge an incumbent senator.* It's the story of how a satirist who had spent a good part of his career heaping scorn and ridicule upon conservative Republican officeholders developed a solid working relationship with (many of) his Republican colleagues. It's the story of how a novice politician learned not just how to win an election, but how to be good at serving in office: how to find common ground when possible, but also stand his ground when powerful interests come after the middle class. It's the story of how, after spending a lifetime learning how to be funny, I learned how not to be funny.

This book will be different from other books written by U.S. senators. For instance, I'm not going to write stuff like, "Mitch McConnell and I may disagree, but when we're off the clock, we're the best of friends—sometimes we go to dinner and Mitch will laugh so hard that milk shoots out of his nose." No, I'm not going to be writing clichés like that.

Instead, I'm going to tell you what it's really been like to go from writing political satire to actually being in politics. I'm going to tell you how Washington really

---

* Don't worry. Former senator Norm Coleman landed on his feet and continues to serve the people of Minnesota as a paid lobbyist for the government of Saudi Arabia.

works. And I'm going to tell you what I've learned about the direction of our country and our prospects for the future.

Is what I do more fun than *Saturday Night Live*? Not by a long shot. But this book will tell you why, despite all the hugely disheartening moments I've experienced since I got into politics, I still think I have the best job in the world (some days) and why, despite the rise of Trump, I'm still (kind of) optimistic about our future (most of the time [albeit certainly less than I was a few months ago]).

—Al Franken
Washington, D.C.

Chapter 1

Why I'm a Democrat

I was born in the house I built myself with my own two hands.

I'm sorry. That's not true. I got that from my official Senate website. We really should change that.

Let me start over.

My dad, Joe Franken, was born in New York City in 1908. When he was sixteen years old, *his* dad, Otto, a German immigrant, died of tuberculosis. So Dad went to work and never ended up graduating from high school. In 1955, when I was four years old, Dad moved us from New Jersey out to a little town in southern Minnesota called Albert Lea to open a quilting factory.* The factory failed within two years, and

---

* A quilting factory doesn't make quilts. It makes quilted fabric that is very often used in garments. For example, in the lining of winter coats. Hence Minnesota.

our family moved up to St. Louis Park, a suburb of Minneapolis.

When I was a teenager, I asked Dad, "Why Albert Lea?"

"Well, your grandfather* wanted to open a factory in the Midwest. And the railroad went through Albert Lea."

"And why did the factory fail?"

"The railroad went *through* Albert Lea, but it wouldn't *stop*."

Dad wasn't a good businessman. But he was a great dad. And we were a very close family.

Most evenings, Mom, Dad, my brother, Owen, and I would sit together eating dinner on tray tables watching Huntley-Brinkley or Walter Cronkite. And because we grew up during the civil rights movement in the early '60s, we learned some important lessons while we did.

Civil rights, our parents taught us, are about basic justice. And when the news would be full of southern sheriffs turning firehoses, dogs, and nightsticks on demonstrators, my dad would point to the TV and

---

* Mom's dad, Simon Kunst, came to America in 1904 at the age of sixteen from Grodno, which is a city in Belarus or Lithuania or Poland or Russia, depending on which one was persecuting the Jews of Grodno at any given time. Simon had a quilting factory near New York City. For more about quilting, see the previous footnote.

he'd say in his gravelly New York voice, "No Jew can be for that!"

Until 1964, Dad had been a liberal Republican.* And Mom was a Democrat. I took after my dad, so until I was thirteen, I was a Republican, too.

But Dad switched parties when the Republicans nominated Barry Goldwater, a guy who had voted against the 1964 Civil Rights Act.† LBJ was right when he told an aide that Democrats would lose the South for a generation when he signed that bill. But he got my dad. And, therefore, me.

In Minneapolis, Dad made a modest living as a printing salesman, and Mom supplemented our family's income by working as a real estate agent. The Frankens never struck it rich—I spent my Wonder Years in a two-bedroom, one-bath house. But I considered myself the luckiest kid in the world. Because I was. I was growing up middle-class in St. Louis Park, in Minnesota, and in America at the height of the middle class in America. I believed I could do anything I wanted (except possibly open a quilting factory—I had learned that lesson the hard way).

---

* Those used to exist.

† On this subject, some conservative commentators will say that a higher percentage of Republican senators voted for the Civil Rights Act than Democrats. That's true. But the Democrats who voted against it were southerners. Today, not one Democratic U.S. senator comes from the Deep South.

For most of my childhood, I thought I was going to be a scientist of some sort. When the Soviet Union launched Sputnik in 1957, my parents, like the rest of America, were terrified. The Soviets had nuclear weapons and now were ahead of us in space. So my parents marched me and Owen into our living room, sat us down, and said, "You boys are going to study math and science so we can beat the Soviets!"

I thought that was a lot of pressure to put on a six-year-old. But Owen and I were obedient sons, so we studied math and science. And we were good at it. Owen was the first in our family to go to college. He went to MIT, graduating with a degree in physics, and then became a photographer.

I went to Harvard, and became a comedian. My poor parents.

But we still beat the Soviets. You're welcome.

* * *

I met my wife, Franni, during our first week of college. When our daughter, Thomasin, was six years old, her first-grade teacher assigned the kids to write about how their parents met. This was before parents met on Tinder (or Grindr, for that matter). I told her, "I met Mommy at a freshman mixer—that's a dance. And I saw her across the room, organizing a group of girls to leave. And I liked the way she was taking charge. Also, she was just beautiful. So I asked her to dance and we had a dance. And then I got her a ginger ale. And then I escorted her to her dorm and asked her for a date."

My daughter wrote it this way: "My dad asked my mom to dance, bought her a drink, and took her home."

Franni's family was not as lucky as mine. When Franni was eighteen months old, her father, a decorated World War II veteran, died in a one-car accident returning home from his shift at the paper mill near Portland, Maine. My mother-in-law, Fran,* was widowed at age twenty-nine with five little kids. The oldest, Kathy, was seven. The youngest, Bootsie, was three months old.

Fran heroically raised her kids on Social Security survivor benefits and her paycheck from working in the produce department of the nearby supermarket. Sometimes they had the heat cut off. Or the phone turned off. Sometimes—often—there wasn't enough to eat.

While my childhood could be fairly described as carefree, Franni's was almost entirely carefree-free. She started working at age eleven, and every penny went to keep her family above water.

---

* Franni's a Jr.

But they made it. All four girls went to college on combinations of Pell Grants and scholarships. My brother-in-law went into the Coast Guard, where he became an electrical engineer.

When Bootsie was old enough to go to high school, Fran got herself a $300 GI loan to enroll at the University of Maine. She got three more loans and graduated with a teaching degree. Because she taught Title I kids—poor kids—all her loans were forgiven. Every member of Franni's family made it to the middle class. And they did it because of Social Security, Pell Grants, the GI Bill, and Title I of the Elementary and Secondary Education Act.

They tell you in this country that you have to pull yourself up by your bootstraps. And we all believe that. But first you've got to have the boots. And the federal government gave Franni's family the boots.

* * *

When I think about the values that motivate me to this day—the values that brought me (in a very, very, extremely roundabout way) to politics—I think back to my childhood, and to Franni's. I think about the economic security that was the birthright of middle-class families like mine, and the opportunity that was available for families like Franni's who wanted to work their way up into the middle class.

That, as I wrote in this year's Senate Patriotic Essay Contest,* is what America means to me.

And that's how it's supposed to be for every kid in America. You're not supposed to have to be rich or lucky to have a chance to do great things. Opportunity is supposed to be for everyone.

And that's why I'm a Democrat.

You see, Democrats are still the party of civil rights (and with each passing year, Republicans seem less and less interested in competing for that title). But Democrats aren't just the party of equality for all—we're the party of opportunity for all. We're the ones who want to give people the boots. We're the ones who stand for the middle class and for those aspiring to it—not just because it's the fair thing to do, but because it's the smart thing to do. It's how our country has always worked best.

My friend and political hero Paul Wellstone, who once held the seat that I now hold in the United States Senate, had a great way of putting this. He said, "We all do better when we all do better."

So simple, so profound. "We all do better when we all do better." It's almost like a haiku, if I knew what a haiku was.

Which I don't.

---

* First prize: a twenty-five-dollar savings bond, plus you get your picture taken with Mitch McConnell.

Chapter 2

How I Became a Comedian

I wrote my first show in second grade. One afternoon, the girls in Mrs. Morrison's class surprised the boys by presenting a little revue for us that we all considered very corny. It included, I swear, "I'm a Little Teapot."

So I got the boys together and we wrote a scathing parody of the girls' show. A few days later, we told Mrs. Morrison and the girls we had a surprise for *them* in the AV room. During the show, some of the girls cried.

Mrs. Morrison was a wonderful teacher, so she turned that sow's ear into a silk purse: "Why not have Alan write a show that the boys and girls can do together for your parents?" I have a vague memory of just one sketch for that show. It was a Civil War sketch where the joke was anachronisms. While nurses were attending to wounded soldiers, they all heard the news of Lincoln's assassination on the radio.

Not funny? I was SEVEN!

* * *

As much as Mom and Dad wanted me and Owen to go to college and win the Cold War, the fact that I chose to become a comedian had everything to do with them.

My mother was my first audience. She was a stay-at-home mom until I went to kindergarten, so when I was little, we'd spend the day together, and I'd love to make her laugh. This is a little embarrassing, but here it is. When I was three years old, Mom would have me do my impression of Jackie Gleason's signature "And away we go!" for company. My guess is there may be something not entirely healthy there, but I'll save that for my next book, *The Sorrow and the Gavel: The Sad Inner Lives of U.S. Senators.*

Dad loved comedy, and I loved watching it with him and Owen and Mom in the TV room. His absolute favorite was Buddy Hackett.

Now, Dad inhaled a pipe all his adult life. When I was a kid, if Dad got on a laughing jag, he'd start coughing at some point and inevitably end up coughing up phlegm into the clean, neatly pressed white handkerchief he always carried in his right front pocket. So if Johnny Carson said, "Ladies and gentlemen, Mr. Buddy Hackett!" Mom would get up and leave the room. But the phlegm didn't bother me and Owen.

Throughout grade school and junior high, I continued to be a good student and something of a comedian. I wasn't the "class clown" so much as a sly, observational comic. If I found a teacher, like Mr. Knutsen in sixth grade, who dug my stuff, I'd play to the teacher. If I didn't like the teacher, like my eighth-grade civics teacher, also named Mr. Knutsen, I'd work the room at his expense. I think he sent me to stand in the hall about a dozen times during the school year.

After ninth grade, Mom and Dad threw me a curve. Owen was now at MIT, and was therefore the Franken family expert on college. He told my parents that the students at MIT were wonks and nerds, and that I should go to Harvard. Owen also said that I should switch out of the St. Louis Park public school system and go to Blake, a country day private school in an adjacent suburb, because the wonks and nerds at MIT who had gone to private school were better prepared.

I didn't hear about this conversation until years later. All I knew at the time was what Dad told me, which was, "You're going to take a test to go to a school for smart kids."

Ever obedient, I said, "Okay." A few days later, Dad

drove me to the beautiful Blake campus, where I took the test.

A couple weeks later, Dad told me, "You passed the test to get into the school for smart kids."

I spent the next three years at Blake.* All in all, I had a pretty good experience, even if I was permanently scarred by going to an all-boys school. But, again, I'll save that for a heartwrenching chapter in *The Sorrow and the Gavel*, "Escape from the Cloakroom."

It turned out that there were a lot of really smart kids at Blake and some not so smart, kind of like St. Louis Park High School, where you didn't have to pay a lot of money, and could interact on a daily basis with members of the opposite sex during a crucial developmental period of your life. Still, I found my way.

Blake had all the elements of a British boarding school in a novel or movie, except we were just a

---

* You may be asking, "I thought your dad had a modest income. How are you going to a hoity-toity prep school?" Good question, reader. Here's the deal. My grandmother, Clara Franken, Otto's widow, continued to live in her apartment near the Polo Grounds in upper Manhattan and was an astoundingly frugal hausfrau. Every Sunday morning at nine, Grandma would call us in Minnesota. Dad would answer, "Guten Morgen, Liebschen." The call would end abruptly when the operator informed them that three minutes were up. When we visited Grandma, she always wore the same old-lady dress, and baked us the best apple pie. She also saved everything (including, for some reason, shoeboxes full of worthless canceled postage stamps), invested wisely in the stock market, and left my parents enough money for Owen's and my education.

bunch of goofy midwestern kids who went home at night. But the stuffy vestiges of an outdated model for schooling boys gave a number of us something to rebel against. Or, at the very least, to make fun of.

* * *

Tom Davis was a year behind me at Blake. I didn't meet him until he did an announcement with a group of other boys one morning in chapel. I don't remember what it was for—probably a meeting of the Glee Club or something. (I'm kicking myself for not taking notes during my childhood.) All I remember is thinking, "That guy's really funny!"

I made it a point to go up to Tom and introduce myself. The comedy team of Franken and Davis was born.

Chapel became our stage. We did announcements for practically every organization in school, borrowing moves from comics we both loved: Johnny Carson, Soupy Sales, Jack Benny, Peter Sellers, Woody Allen, the Smothers Brothers, George Carlin, Godfrey Cambridge, Bob Newhart, Richard Pryor, and Laurel and Hardy. We traded off being the straight man and the funny guy. We did a lot of physical comedy and threw in not-so-veiled barbs aimed at the school. But mainly we just did goofy stuff, like parodies of the hit movie *Cool Hand Luke* ("Anyone who doesn't go to homecoming spends a night in the box!").

We'd write in each other's basements. Well, in

my house it was a basement. In Tom's house it was a finished family room. At the time, Tom's dad, Don Davis, was a handsome midlevel executive at 3M. Tom's beautiful, sweet mom, Jean Davis, the former Jean Johnson, had been the 1950 Queen of the Lakes. Besides Tom, Don and Jean Davis had another son, Bob, who was three years younger. So that was Don, Jean, Tom, and Bob.

Jean loved hearing me and Tom laughing from down in their finished basement. "Oh, you boys are so funny!" she'd say, and bring us some treats.

But as the middle '60s turned into the late '60s, things started getting tense around the Davis household. Don, as Tom himself described him in his memoir *Thirty-Nine Years of Short-Term Memory Loss*, was "a lifelong kneejerk Republican" and "the uptight son of an alcoholic." In fact, Don's father, Tom's grandfather, drank himself to death. As Tom grew his hair and discovered pot, rock and roll, and girls, all the ingredients were there for the classic Oedipal battle common to so many suburban baby boomers.

Don didn't like Franken and Davis one bit. So Tom started spending more and more time at my house. Once Tom returned to his home after a couple days with the Frankens to find a newspaper clipping taped to his bedroom wall. The headline:

STUDENT TAKES LSD, CUTS OFF OWN PENIS

Things were getting a little tense at school as well. Our chapel material got edgier, to the point where we were ruffling some feathers. So we turned our attention to pep fests that were parodies of pep fests—hanging the other team in effigy and repeatedly clubbing the dummy in the crotch with a baseball bat. The football coach, Mr. Mezzenga, seemed to like it, though I'm not sure he was taking it at the same ironic level that the team and the rest of the students were.[*]

Meanwhile, Tom and I discovered a comedy revue theater in Minneapolis called Dudley Riggs's Brave New Workshop. We saw actual adults onstage doing pretty much what we wanted to do—make audiences laugh.

We started hanging out at the Workshop, getting to know the performers and the impresario, Dudley Riggs, a former vaudevillian and circus performer. Dudley took a liking to us and suggested we come to an open stage night and do ten minutes. So we did.

We led off with a local newscast on the night of the day of World War III:

AL: Tragedy, death, catastrophe highlight tonight's news at ten! I'm Ray Thompson, substituting

---

[*] Forty years later, during my first campaign for Senate, my long, easily decontextualized history of metacomedy would turn out to be something of a problem.

for the deceased Chet Newholm. And now with
the weather, meteorologist Bob Carlson.
TOM: Well, don't grab those umbrellas just yet…
temperatures up to six thousand degrees tonight.
Winds gusting at five hundred miles per hour
with occasional firestorms. Back to you, Ray.
AL: The stock market closed today—for good.

We got solid laughs, and Dudley told us he "saw
sparks." By the summer we were doing one show a
week at the Workshop. Also, we got paid! (A little.)
Tom and I were professional comedians!

* * *

At the end of that summer I went off to college, still
intent, I thought, on pursuing a career in science. In
the back of my mind, show business didn't seem like
a secure career choice for someone from Minnesota,
though Bob Dylan had been kind of tearing it up in
the '60s there. And unlike Bob Dylan, the poor loser,
I had gotten into Harvard. (I guess Dylan didn't test
well.)

Unfortunately, by the end of my first semester of
college, I could tell I wasn't cut out to be a scientist.
Even though we had just beaten them to the moon,
the Soviets were still something of a problem—but I
knew my heart wasn't in it.

Franni encouraged me to go to the counseling

office, where I was given an extensive personality test, the Minnesota Multiphasic Personality Inventory, to see what career I was psychologically suited for.*

The results were very interesting. The number one career match for Alan Franken was "jazz musician." Number two was "camp counselor." Coming in dead last? "Scientist."

Since I didn't play a musical instrument and had never been to an overnight summer camp, I decided the one-two combo pointed to either "jazz camp counselor," which sounded like an unimaginable bummer, or "comedian," a career that was not on the Minnesota Multiphasic list, but which I had been preparing for pretty much all my life.

Years later, Dana Carvey said to me, "There's no reason to be a comedian unless you absolutely have to be." He didn't mean that comedians weren't *able* to do any other job. It's just that, to be a comedian, comedy has to be the thing you absolutely *have* to do. Like a jazz musician *has* to be a jazz musician. (And maybe

---

* How do I remember what test I took? Because it consisted of five hundred statements, to which you answered "yes" or "no," and I remember exactly one: "I have never had any black-tarry bowel movements." When I recently entered "black-tarry bowel movements" into Google, the first item that popped up was an article about the Minnesota Multiphasic Personality Inventory. In addition to questioning the validity of the test, the article said that this was the one question that everyone who takes the test remembers. And, sorry: I can't tell you *how* I answered, because I don't remember. I certainly haven't had any recently.

some camp counselors just *have* to be camp counselors.) It wasn't until that stupid Minnesota Multiphasic that I felt like I had permission to pursue the career I actually *had* to pursue.

Now, this was the early '70s, and there was this war in Southeast Asia. I got a 2-S student deferment, which kept me out of the draft until graduation. In its wisdom, the government felt it was important for me to continue my studies so I could pursue my chosen profession—comedian—and keep America strong. I ended up majoring in behavioral sciences—sociology, anthropology, and psychology—which has actually been helpful in the Senate (and might have been useful in Vietnam).

Summers, I worked with Tom at Dudley's by night, and by day for the St. Louis Park Street Department, where I worked on a crew with two other college guys. Our job was to mow weeds around water towers and other public buildings with industrial-sized mowers.

Though Tom was an avid reader, he was at best an indifferent student. After two years at the University of the Pacific, including a sophomore year during which he traveled through India and Nepal to study smoking hashish, he dropped out and became a cast member at Dudley's and a wonderfully inventive and hilarious improvisational comedian. Still, we'd do our two-man shows during the summer. One night, I got a horrible migraine after working all day in the sun.

We went on with the show, but I had to bolt backstage to throw up, leaving Tom to improvise for a minute or two. The audience figured out what was going on because I looked horrible, and at the end of the show they gave us a standing ovation.

Dudley watched the show from the back of the house and came backstage afterward to commend us. I was lying facedown on a couch, but Tom asked him, "What would have happened if Al had thrown up onstage?"

"Oh, they would have all walked out," he said with the total assurance of a showbiz veteran who had seen everything.

Between my junior and senior years, Tom and I hitchhiked from Minneapolis to L.A. (kids, don't do this) to perform at the Comedy Store. Our twenty minutes killed, and suddenly we were on the radar of our contemporaries—struggling comedians trying to get a break.

During my senior year, Tom came out to Cambridge and stayed in my dorm room. He smoked pot, played Frisbee, and didn't go to classes, and thus was often mistaken for a student. On weekends, Tom and I would drive two or three marginally more prosperous students down to Manhattan in exchange for gas money and perform at the Improvisation with comedians like Jay Leno, Robert Klein, and Andy Kaufman.

In 1973, Franni and I graduated, and the three of us

drove out to Hollywood. Tom and I played the Comedy Store (where Franni worked as a cocktail waitress) and a few other clubs around L.A. Occasionally we'd go on the road and play colleges in the Midwest for five hundred bucks a gig.

One spring we did a show at Huron State in South Dakota. As we drove up to the student union, we noticed there were no cars. They had booked us during spring break. There were a grand total of seven students remaining on campus who couldn't make it home for the break. Six were African American guys from the East Coast. Tom asked them why there were six of them, and one said wryly, "In case one of us fouls out."

The other kid was a very depressed junior who had been caught smoking pot during his sophomore year and as punishment was confined to campus for the remainder of his college career, except for summers. Tom and I did our show for the seven bummed-out students and a custodian. They were actually a pretty good audience.

We were doing a lot of political material back in those days, including lots and lots of Nixon stuff. I'd play Nixon to Tom's David Eisenhower,* and then Tom would play Nixon to my Henry Kissinger. We

---

* For younger readers, David Eisenhower was President Dwight Eisenhower's grandson and Nixon's son-in-law, married to Nixon's daughter

ate a lot of rice and beans and did odd jobs. During Christmas season, we'd alternate playing Santa and Winnie-the-Pooh at a Sears in North Hollywood (Sears had declined to let us play Nixon).

* * *

When you're starting out in comedy, you meet a lot of other people doing the same thing, and you influence each other. A comedy writer friend of ours, Matt Neuman, grew up in New York and had collected hours of Bob and Ray on reel-to-reel audiotape. Bob Elliott and Ray Goulding were a radio comedy team in New York from the 1950s through the '80s who developed a cult following of generations of fans, from Groucho Marx to Johnny Carson to David Letterman. Tom and I had seen Bob and Ray a few times on *The Tonight Show* and were fans ourselves.

Listening to hours of these Bob and Ray tapes, Tom and I heard both what we had been trying to do and what we wanted to become. Like them, neither of us were exclusively the straight man nor the funny guy. They were dry, and gently subversive, committed to their characters—various gasbags, self-serving idiots, and absurdly banal authorities. Tom and I would sit with Matt, smoking dope and laughing our

Julie. For older readers, sorry for making you dart your eyes to the bottom of the page.

asses off at Bob's mild-mannered reporter Wally Ballou, who promoted himself as "radio's highly regarded
Wally Ballou, winner of eleven diction awards, two
of which are cuff links." On shows like "Widen Your
Horizons" with sponsors like "Einbinder Flypaper, the
name you've gradually grown to trust over three generations," Bob would interview Ray, an expert on how
to floss, who would point out that to floss properly
you don't actually have to have one hand inside your
mouth.

When I first got to the Senate, I discovered that
Kansas senator Pat Roberts, a very funny archconser-
vative (but one you can work with) and fifteen years
my senior, is a huge Bob and Ray fan. One day, early
on, I brought over a CD I'd made from some of Matt's
tapes to Pat's office, and we laughed and laughed. I
never asked Pat if he had ever listened to them while
smoking dope. Frankly, it's none of my damn business.

Franni and I had smoked pot in college, but Tom
introduced us to LSD and the Grateful Dead—I think
in the reverse order. We'd drive around California in
our Volkswagen bus following the Dead—so we were
in danger of being a cliché. Years later, though, I'd
bond with Vermont senator Pat Leahy, chairman of
the Senate Judiciary Committee, over our love of the
Dead. I didn't even have to ask Leahy whether he had
ever dropped acid. After all, he started his career as a
prosecutor.

So, Tom and I were Deadheads, and Bob-and-Ray-heads.

We were beginning to get noticed. And I'll always remember the moment I knew we'd made it.

It was December 1974, and we were offered the chance to be part of a show at Harrah's Casino in Reno called *The Boob Tube Revue*. No, that wasn't the moment. *The Boob Tube Revue* was pretty awful. What? You could tell from the name it was awful? Still, the awful show was popular, and Franken and Davis were something of a hit in Reno.

One night, management decided to throw a party to honor the cast of *The Boob Tube Revue*. And that's where I saw it: an enormous platter holding a gigantic mound of jumbo shrimp.

Let me explain: For my dad, the worst part of moving to Minnesota in 1955 was that he loved seafood—especially clams, softshell crabs, lobster, and shrimp. In the 1950s and '60s, you simply could not get fresh seafood in Minnesota. Every summer, we'd all drive to New York to visit my uncle Erwin and his family, and the biggest treat for me was the seafood. I remember thinking, "I'll know I'll have made it when I can eat as much shrimp as I want."

That evening in Reno, I probably ate three dozen jumbo shrimp. So as far as I was concerned, I had made it well before Tom and I got hired for *Saturday Night Live*.

Chapter 3

Saturday Night Live
(Not the Drug Part)

In the spring of 1975, a William Morris agent named Herb Karp saw Franken and Davis at the Comedy Store and asked us to put together a writing sample.

We knew we weren't right for the few comedy-variety shows on TV at that time. *The Carol Burnett Show* was terrific, but from another generation. *The Sonny and Cher Comedy Hour*, though slightly superior to *The Boob Tube Revue*, was, well, dreck. So Tom and I wrote a fourteen-page submission for a hypothetical show we'd like to work for. It included a news segment (our World War III newscast), a sketch about a bad variety show, a commercial parody, and the script for a short conceptual film. Even now, almost fifty years later, I still harbor the faint hope that someone, some-where, will someday do a show like that.

A few months later, a thirty-year-old producer

named Lorne Michaels read our writing sample for a new late-night show he was putting together. We got the word that we'd been hired from Herb late on a Friday afternoon after playing basketball with some other unemployed comedians in Hollywood: "Be at 30 Rockefeller Plaza on Monday."

Of the writers hired for the original *SNL* staff, Tom and I were the only ones Lorne hadn't met. Dick Ebersol, then the network exec in charge of late night, wanted to hire another team, who were from New York, in order to save NBC the airfare. But Lorne insisted on us.

Tom and I came as a team, and since this was our first job in TV, NBC got a waiver from the Writers Guild to allow them to pay us as a single apprentice writer. We couldn't have been happier.

When we arrived on Monday, July 7, 1975, the first colleague we met was Mike O'Donoghue, already legendary for his hilariously dark work as a founding writer of the *National Lampoon*. As the three of us waited for clearance at the elevator bank, Mike sized us up and asked Tom and me what we were being paid. We told him we were sharing three hundred and fifty bucks a week. Mike snickered. "I spend that much to shine my cats' shoes." Tom and I were delighted.

We soon met some of the other writers, including Chevy Chase and Garrett Morris, who were yet to be named cast members. At that point, Dan Aykroyd and Gilda Radner, whom Lorne knew from

Toronto, and Laraine Newman, who had performed at the Groundlings, an improv-based theater in L.A., were the only cast members. A week or so later, John Belushi, a Second City vet, arrived at the audition as his Samurai character and blew the room away. John and Jane Curtin, who came from the Proposition in Boston, yet another improv-based theater, rounded out the Not Ready for Prime Time Players.

Lorne had bargained with NBC for a long preproduction period. Part of the idea was to give us time to write a lot and start forging a common sensibility as a staff. During preproduction, Tom and I would meet periodically with Lorne in his office to go over something we'd written. He'd always ask us the same question: "Is this the best piece you've ever written?" We'd say no, and then Lorne would tell us to keep working on it until it was.

Finally, one of us, and I'm guessing it was Tom, figured out that not *everything* you write can be the *best* thing you've ever written. Lorne dropped that particular gambit after that, but over the years, every so often we would write the best thing we'd ever written.

Tom and I got the sense that Lorne was looking out for us. He himself had started in Toronto as part of a team, Hart and Lorne, and I think he appreciated the bond between us. Around the show, Tom and I were "the Boys." Even if just one of us walked into the room, someone would say, "The Boys are here."

The first show was scheduled for October 11, 1975. As the premiere approached, I grew increasingly confident that we were all on board a giant hit. It was the first time that baby boomers had been allowed to do TV, and the people around me were among the most talented writers and comedians of our generation.

When I look back on that youthful arrogance, I laugh. This was our first real job in show business. Hits almost never happen. But Tom and I had gotten a raise, and Franni and Tom's girlfriend, Lucy, drove east from California with our belongings because we were confident that we had a long-term job.

On October 2, 1975, nine days before the first *Saturday Night Live* ever, Franni and I eloped and were married at City Hall in lower Manhattan.*

Of course, I had been correct as a brash, overconfident twenty-four-year-old. The show was pretty much an instant hit. Over the decades, *SNL* has gone through periods of sustained brilliance and a few rough patches, but after forty-two years, the show has been a touchstone for generations of overentertained, underinformed Americans.

Lorne started putting Franken and Davis in front of the camera every once in a while. We'd be part of the dress rehearsal, and if enough stuff in dress tanked,

---

* Five years later, when Franni became pregnant, Fran insisted that Franni produce the marriage certificate.

he'd put us on the air. Our first appearance was on a show hosted by Elliott Gould. We did a bit from our act called "The Bureau of White Man Affairs." The premise was simple: "What if the Indians had won?"

I played the host of *Pow Wow with the Press*, Howard K. Screaming Eagle, and Tom played the chief of the Bureau of White Man Affairs, both wearing suits and fedoras with a feather sticking out. The topic: recent complaints over racially insensitive team nicknames in Major League Lacrosse, such as the Milwaukee Dagos.

> TOM: We had a big uproar about a week ago over an insignia on a bubblegum card for the Cleveland Kikes. They objected to the little screaming rabbi.
>
> AL: Well, can't these names be offensive to white people?
>
> TOM: Ahh, no. No. These are white man names that the white man uses himself to ridicule each other's tribe.
>
> AL: I didn't know that.
>
> TOM: Well, the Dago is an Italian, whom we know are a stupid, violent, greasy people. They wear black, pointy moccasins. And Kike is a Jew...Jew white man, and he's the most shrewd of all white men, as you probably know.

AL: Yes, as I understand it, the Jew white man really knows the value of a buffalo chip.

It was Bob and Ray—with an edge.*

* * *

When people come up to me to talk about *Saturday Night Live*, they almost always mention my on-camera work, whether it was our Franken and Davis show-within-the-show, the Al Franken Decade, my One-Man Mobile Uplink Unit, or Stuart Smalley.

But at the end of the day, Tom and I were writers. And because we were part of a great writing staff with a cast that included gifted writers, like Chevy and Danny, and performers who could create hilarious characters for themselves, like Billy Murray's lounge singer or Gilda's Roseanne Roseannadanna and Emily Litella, Tom and I collaborated together and separately with others on the show.

Of the original cast, Danny was the one we teamed up with the most. He and Tom created the Coneheads after taking a trip together to Easter Island. Tom and I wrote Danny as Julia Child bleeding to death after cutting herself deboning a chicken. We collaborated

---

* Forty years later, as a U.S. senator, I would join forty-nine other senators on a letter to the NFL, demanding that the Washington Redskins change their name.

with him on sleazy characters like Irwin Mainway, purveyor of dangerous toys for kids, like Bag o' Glass. Danny played two presidents with his mustache: a hypercompetent Jimmy Carter early in his term, taking phone calls with Bill Murray's Walter Cronkite and masterfully talking down a young man on a bad acid trip (played by Tom, of course), and an inebriated Nixon talking to White House portraits during those stormy Final Days.

I worked with so many talented men and women going through exhilarating but also sometimes very difficult periods of their lives. Putting on a live ninety-minute comedy show week after week can be thrilling, and it can be painfully stressful. And of course, we were all of a very tender age. People had sex and fell in love. But mostly had sex. I personally had 227 sexual encounters during my fifteen years at *SNL*. All of them with Franni.

*   *   *

A show week at *SNL* was kind of crazy. On Monday, around 5 p.m., the cast and writing staff would crowd into Lorne's office, where we'd meet the host. Lorne would introduce him or her: "This week our host is Burt Reynolds." We'd applaud politely. Then I'd yell excitedly, "And next week, Steve Martin!!!" We'd all cheer and go nuts. Welcome to the show, Burt!

During the meeting, writers and cast would pitch

ideas. Most of them were half-baked at best. Sometimes they were fake ideas, just to cover for the fact that you had nothing. You could see the terror growing in the host's eyes as he/she heard lame idea after lame idea.

But the meeting served a purpose. Often, someone's idea would spark one of your own. After the meeting, things would start percolating. "I liked that VD Caseworker idea. What if you did this with it...?" During *SNL*'s life span, the show has been at its best when there's been an equilibrium between the writing staff and the cast. When the cast dominates, we see popular recurring characters beaten into the ground. When the writers dominate, there's a lot of interesting stuff that the audience doesn't find all that interesting or all that funny.

Read-through was on Wednesday afternoon. So Tuesday night was writing night. As the season wore on, we'd start later and later, and soon Tuesday night became an all-nighter.

Woody Allen once said that writing comedy is either easy or it's impossible. When it's easy, there is nothing more fun. Conversely, when it's impossible, there is nothing quite as anxiety-provoking. To this day, I still have nightmares that it's a Tuesday night at *SNL* and I cannot think of a thing.

After read-through, Lorne would huddle with the host and production staff to decide what sketches were going to be put into rehearsal. This was a complex calculus: What works? What does the host like? What sketches bump with each other? You can't have two Oval Office pieces. What combination of sets will fit into the studio? How many cast members are being served by the material?

Lorne put the writers in charge of guiding their own piece through the week. Essentially, writers were the producers of their own sketches. That meant hanging around after read-through to answer any questions Lorne or the production staff might have. Can we recast this? Can you put it in a smaller set? Talk to Eugene or Leo, the set designers.

Thursday was for promos and camera blocking. You'd work with graphics, makeup, and hair, maybe props. The "satellite dish" mounted on the helmet for my One-Man Mobile Uplink Unit was a "flying saucer" sled with a basketball pump sticking out.

Thursday night was a late night as well. Writers would sit around the read-through table rewriting. Usually, sketches were improved, often with the most memorable jokes coming from the table. Rob Schneider wrote a piece called "Massive Headwound Harry" about a cheery guy (Dana Carvey) with a massive head wound who bums out everyone at a party because of his massive head wound. During the Thursday late-night rewrite session, Tom came up with the idea of rubbing Dana's bandage with cooked shrimp and having a blind guy with a guide dog enter at the end. Sure enough, the dog found Dana sitting on the couch and tugged the bandage. As the dog kept tugging, the audience howled with laughter, Dana finally cheerily saying, "He must smell my dog."

Sometimes everyone knew a sketch was shaky at best, but we'd do our best to make it work. That was known as "turd polishing." It could be a tough room. In the wee hours, things could get pretty dark and raunchy. Around the time that the term "hostile work environment" came into the lexicon, Christine Zander, a one-of-a-kind writer with the world's best Gatling-gun laugh who worked at the show for seven seasons, developed a running joke for just these occasions: "Dear Lawsuit Diary."

Friday was a very long day of rehearsal. And it often included writing something new for the cold opening—the sketch at the beginning that ends with "Live from New York, it's Saturday night!" The benefit of doing a live comedy show is that you can react to breaking news. The drawback is that you *have* to react to breaking news. If the country learns on a Friday that the surgeon general said that teaching masturbation to kids is a good idea, you better have a take on Saturday.

On Saturday morning some of us would come in to write jokes for "Weekend Update." Then a full day of rehearsals, hopefully (but almost never) running through every sketch of the show. Then dinner, while the music guest did a sound check and a run-through for cameras. Then dress rehearsal at eight, ending at 9:50, meaning we're twenty minutes over. A quick turnaround. Lorne decides what's in, what's out. You want your sketch in? Lose two minutes!

Quick meeting in Lorne's ninth-floor office, where everyone sees the new running order. Some cast and writers are elated, some devastated. Lorne gives notes in shorthand. The writers call out cuts and rewrites. Cast absorbs them. Have a good show, everybody! Cue cards make the changes. Cast gets into wardrobe and wigs. The band is playing warm-up for the studio audience. It's 11:30!

Maybe the studio audience is hot and laughing at everything. We need more cuts. Or maybe the audience isn't laughing. Maybe that's because we have a hot band and their fans got tickets because they all know someone who has an uncle who works in ad sales at NBC. Put that sequence back in this sketch. No? Doesn't make sense with the other cuts? Okay, let's run a commercial parody after "Massive Headwound Harry."

The show ends at 1 a.m. The cast get out of their costumes and makeup and roll around to the after-party at some restaurant around 1:45. It's hard to come down from the adrenaline of performing live for ten million Americans. Two or three hours of discussing what worked and what didn't. Introducing your friends from back home to George Harrison. At some point, the sun comes up.

You stumble home, sleep till two in the afternoon, read the Sunday *Times*, catch some football, and have dinner with your boyfriend or girlfriend, or in my case, your wife.* Your clock is all screwed up, so around midnight Sunday night, you start thinking of new ideas for next week.

And then it all starts again Monday morning. Okay, Monday afternoon. Okay, Monday evening. But Monday.

---

* And later, kids. That, of course, radically changed things for me. When he was six, my son, Joe, decided to play hockey, and as you can imagine, ice time in NYC is pretty hard to come by. So I'd take him to an indoor rink in lower Manhattan at six on Sunday mornings. Mercifully, he switched to basketball the next year.

Chapter 4

Saturday Night Live
(The Drug Part)

Actually, now that I look at the show schedule, it was certainly no busier than being in the Senate. As at *SNL*, we senators get recesses, but Senate recesses aren't really breaks. They're just periods of time where we're doing different kinds of work, like traveling around our states meeting with people, or raising money, or going overseas on the jam-packed congressional trips known as CODELs (congressional delegations).*

---

* Example: Franni and I went on a CODEL to Africa in 2015 led by Delaware senator Chris Coons, who as a young man had been a relief worker in Kenya and as a senator has been very active on the Foreign Relations Subcommittee on Africa. The bastard had us fly all night, land in Senegal in the morning, then do a full day there, inspecting a water project and other programs. The next morning we flew to Ethiopia, did a full day there. Next day to Rwanda. Next day to Gabon. Then on the way back, a half day in Cape Verde.

Either way, senators certainly do a lot less drugs than we did at *SNL*. Unless I'm just completely clueless.

As *SNL* became a cultural sensation, it began to leak out that some of the cast and writers at the show were smoking dope and snorting cocaine. At first, there was some official denial. "You can't do a ninety-minute live comedy show week after week and do cocaine," we'd say, and it sounded convincing, at least for a while.

The truth is that many on the show thought that you can't do a ninety-minute live comedy show week after week *without* doing cocaine. Which, of course, is folderol.[USS]

Until John Belushi's death, we at *SNL* didn't really understand that drugs can kill you. But by the time Chris Farley got in trouble, we at the show understood all too well.

* * *

A couple years after John was found dead of an over-dose at the Chateau Marmont Hotel in Hollywood, Bob Woodward of the *Washington Post* (and Woodward and Bernstein fame) wrote a book called *Wired: The Short Life and Fast Times of John Belushi*. During his research phase, I had agreed to be interviewed by Woodward, but I didn't like the tone of his questions, which seemed to be only about drug use. So I told

NO POSTAGE
NECESSARY
IF MAILED
IN THE
UNITED STATES

CNSJD992A

BUSINESS REPLY MAIL
FIRST-CLASS MAIL   PERMIT NO 304   HARLAN IA

POSTAGE WILL BE PAID BY ADDRESSEE

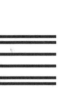
CR ConsumerReports®

PO BOX 2100
HARLAN IA 51593-2289

Buying smart is just the start

✓ YES! Send me one full year of Consumer Reports for only $30.

Here's what you get:

12 Monthly Issues $83.88
Buying Guide 2019 ...$10.99
Buying Guide 2020 ...$10.99

Total Retail Value.. $105.86

Your Cost: Only $30!

You Save $75.86

Name _____
(please print)

Address _____ Apt. # _____

City _____ State _____ Zip _____

☐ **Check enclosed** (payable to Consumer Reports)   ☐ **Bill me later**

Please allow 4 to 6 weeks for delivery. Rate is for the U.S. only.
Double issues may be published, which count as two issues. Plus
applicable sales tax. Savings off cover price. If the Post Office alerts
us that your magazine is undeliverable, we have no further obligation
unless we receive a corrected address within two years.
To view our privacy policy go to cr.org/privacy

JD992A

him that the only time I had seen John snort coke was with Carl Bernstein. Which wasn't true, but it cut the interview short.

When *Wired* came out, we all hated it. Not because it chronicled John's drug abuse, but because that was more or less *all* it covered. Tom said it was like if someone titled your college yearbook *Puked*, and all it talked about was who puked, and when they puked, and what they puked: No one read Dickens for the first time, no one learned chemistry, no one fell in love. Everybody just puked.

The book made no attempt to capture why John was so funny, what his influence was as an improvisational comedian, and how magnetic he was as a person and a performer. Woodward, who has of course written authoritatively about Washington, seemed obstinately tone-deaf to the world he was writing about. Lorne said it was as if he wrote a book about rock and roll and referred to "the Beatles, a popular British band of the '60s."

There was no one who knew Chris Farley who didn't love him. In no small part that was because Chris was not just an extraordinarily committed, explosively hilarious performer, but also such a genuine fan of everyone else's work.

Chris struggled mightily with his addiction—he must have gone to a dozen rehabs—but ultimately couldn't beat it.

After Chris returned to the show from yet another stint at rehab, I created a character for him called "The Relapse Guy." The sketch starts with the exit session at the rehab before a patient goes home. Tim Meadows, the counselor, assures the family (Phil Hartman, Julia Sweeney, Mike Myers, and guest host Shannen Doherty) that *this time* Chris has finally gotten it, which they clearly are not buying. Tim tells them that the rehab has gotten Chris a job—as an organ courier. CUT TO: the operating room, where the doctor and his transplant team are waiting impatiently for the liver, which is hours late. Enter Chris, drunk out of his mind. He opens the cooler, pulling out a prepackaged calf's liver from a supermarket meat case, and hands it to the doctor before he passes out, collapsing on the patient on the operating table. Chris loved it. Every few weeks, he would ask me, "How about another 'Relapse Guy'?"

That was Chris. And, really, that's dark comedy: a guy who couldn't get clean doing a sketch about a guy who couldn't get clean. And we probably all found it funnier precisely because so many of us had seen the damage addiction can do, not just when it costs people their lives, but as it destroys their careers and hurts the ones they care about most.

For my part, I never really got into trouble with drugs. I used to say, "I only did cocaine so I could stay up late enough to make sure nobody else did too much cocaine," which was a joke, but not too far from the truth. For whatever reason, I never became addicted. There but for the grace of God go I.

But the thing about addiction is, you don't have to *be* the addict to be affected. And my life has been profoundly affected by substance abuse because two of the most important people *in* my life struggled with addiction. But it took me a long time to realize that.

* * *

I grew up in a household that consumed very little alcohol. My first drink came during my freshman year in college, when my roommate Dave Griffin and I split a fifth of scotch and got stupid drunk and threw up a great deal.

So I was pretty clueless about what was going on when Franken and Davis would go on the road and Tom would always want to go to a bar before the gig. I'd sit with him, going over our act, thinking, "I wonder what Tom sees in this place? It's so boring. Why in the world does Tom like going to bars?"

We had a lot more time to spend on the road after 1980, when we followed Lorne out the door at *SNL*. We went back to doing our act, including a Franken and Davis special for Showtime, writing some TV and some screenplays, and playing baggage handlers in *Trading Places.* Tom got high more and more. But he was still my partner. And my best friend. When

Franni and I had a daughter, we named her Thomasin Davis Franken.

Then, in 1985, Lorne came back to the show. He brought me and Tom back, along with a few other "Lorne Again" writers. Lorne asked the two of us to produce the show, and we jumped at the opportunity. But Lorne, on a youth kick, hired a group of talented but very young cast members, like the twenty-year-old Robert Downey Jr. and seventeen-year-old Anthony Michael Hall, who were not suited to the kinds of sketches *SNL* had done before—you know, sketches where cast members play *adults*.

The reviews were scathing. Since 1976, year two of *SNL*, we had all lived with "Saturday Night Dead" reviews, but that season we deserved it. With Tom routinely disappearing and me presiding over endless rewrite sessions and trying to hold the show together, I felt overwhelmed.

Meanwhile, at home, after more than a decade of happy marriage, Franni and I were having trouble. After our second child, Joe, was born, Franni fell into a postpartum depression, which she secretly medicated with alcohol. Something was wrong, but I didn't know what.

After the disastrous 1985–86 season, Tom and I decided to leave the show again. We'd go back to doing our act and working on screenplays. But in September 1986, Franni's drinking came to be just too much. She had been going through her own kind of hell, trying as hard as she could to both be a good mother and keep her drinking problem a secret. And, thank God, she went to rehab.

Taking care of a five-year-old Thomasin and an almost-two-year-old Joe, I needed a steady job in New York. I asked Lorne if I could come back to the show. He said, "Of course."

After getting Thomasin off to school and Joe off to day care, I'd arrive at 30 Rock about ten hours before the other writers, with the exception of Bonnie and Terry Turner, a husband-and-wife team from Atlanta who had a daughter Thomasin's age. Tom had decided to take a break from the show, so when he'd find time, we'd get together to work on our screenplay. I'd write during the day, pick the kids up, make them dinner, tuck them into bed, and, leaving them with a sitter, go back to *SNL*.

That's when I started going to Al-Anon, a twelve-step program for family members and friends of alcoholics based on the principles of AA. Like AA, Al-Anon isn't for everybody. But once I started, it didn't take long for me to realize a few important things.

For one thing, I finally realized that Franni wasn't the only addict in my life. My best friend since high school and writing partner for nearly twenty years was addicted—to alcohol, to cocaine, to pretty much anything that came his way.

But I also realized something about myself: that my reaction to Franni's and Tom's addictive behavior had made me a much less pleasant person to be around.

As in AA, the fourth step in Al-Anon is to make a searching and fearless moral inventory of yourself. The fifth step is to admit to (your concept of) God, to yourself, and to another human being the exact nature of your wrongs.

That's to "another human being," and not to everyone who reads this book. But I will say that I had developed a tendency to lose my temper, be judgmental, and roll my eyes when I thought someone said something stupid. In other words, at times I could be a bit of a jerk.[USS]

I also discovered how much I could learn from listening to other people's stories—even people who at first blush didn't seem like the kind of people you could learn much of anything from.

Thus the birth of Stuart Smalley, the healing nurturer and member of several twelve-step programs who hosted "Daily Affirmations" on *SNL*. Stuart became my most popular character on the show.

Guess who hated Stuart? Tom. We still wrote together sometimes, but he was becoming less and less of a presence on the show. One late Friday night, Tom came into the office and strolled past the big rewrite table, where Jim Downey and I and a couple other writers were trying to come up with a cold opening for the next night's show. "What are you working on?" asked Tom.

Downey said, "*Saturday Night Live.*"

By 1991, Tom and I were still Franken and Davis, at least in theory. But while Franni was doing great in recovery, Tom was screwing up and in big trouble. So I organized an intervention.

In an intervention, you usually present the alcoholic/addict with some consequences if he/she refuses to go for treatment. It was hard to do—Tom had been my best friend since high school, I had named my daughter after him, and despite the tension between us, I still thought he was the funniest guy I knew (certainly, in my mind, the funnier half of Franken and Davis). But I told him during the intervention that if he didn't go to rehab, we'd no longer be a team. It didn't work.

It was a sad day. It was the end of our partnership and, at least for a few years, our friendship. And as is the case so often with addiction, things got weird. After the intervention, Tom found a guy who threatened to sue me if I didn't split the income I'd made from projects I'd done without him. I tried to reason with Tom, but he refused even to speak with me.

But Tom and I had forgotten that, well before the intervention, we had agreed to be the Alumni of the Year for Blake. For a host of reasons, it was something we couldn't not do.

So Tom and I found ourselves at our old campus, arguing in the wings of the auditorium about the threatened lawsuit, as Mr. Fecht explained to the K– 6th graders, "Al and Tom were two boys who went to school here. And they had a dream. That dream was to be on TV. And they worked very, very hard, and the dream came true!"

* * *

Addiction can take an unimaginable toll on the people who love addicts. And that's true even when the addicts in question find recovery. When Franni came back from rehab, things were still difficult. It turns out that early recovery can be hard on everyone. That experience became the basis for the 1994 movie *When a Man Loves a Woman*, which I wrote with my friend (and Oscar winner) Ron Bass. The movie, which starred Andy Garcia and Meg Ryan, has a happy and, I like to think, moving ending.

And of course, Franni and I had a happy ending, too. We're still married. We never argue about anything ever. And the Higher Power removed all of my character defects, making me the most well-adjusted senator in the history of the body.

Oh, and the movie made money for the studio. Ron and I each got a fruit basket after the opening weekend.

The next summer, I shot a Stuart Smalley movie I

had written and was starring in, with Harold Ramis directing. Harold, who died in 2014, had been a friend since 1974, and was one of the comedy giants of our generation.

Stuart Saves His Family, however, was by far Harold's least successful film, dying a terrible death at the box office. No fruit basket.

* * *

In the end, Tom never actually sued me. We reconciled a few years later and he asked me to be the best man at his wedding. We remained extremely close, reuniting for special performances and for frequent appearances on my radio show and sharing our devotion to the Grateful Dead and the inevitable disappointments from our beloved Minnesota Vikings.

In 2009, he was diagnosed with cancer, and given six months to a year. He lived three years with courage, grace, and humor—a gift to me and all who knew and loved him.

I visited Tom a few days before he died at the house we once shared in upstate New York. Dan Aykroyd and his wife, Donna, came that day as well, and we laughed about how Tom had lain behind the counter during the Julia Child sketch, controlling the pressure on the spurting blood by working an insecticide sprayer that sent the dark red liquid through plastic tubing that ran up Danny's leg and through his sleeve, ending at his wrist. It was a special effect, which, technically, is supposed to be performed by a union guy on the crew. But the crew loved Tom, and besides, he knew the bit, and he and Danny worked it to perfection live on air.

Tom's humor was always sardonic. As you can imagine, it was even more sardonic that day. He was ready to go. The last few months hadn't been a lot of fun, but he told me he did enjoy crushing up the Dilaudid pills he'd been prescribed and snorting them.

I told Tom that the way he was making his exit was an inspiration to me. He said, "I hope you go a little faster."

When Tom died, I called his mom, Jean, who recalled how much she loved hearing us laugh from their basement.

A tremendous outpouring of love and affection for Tom flowed in from all over the country. It was wonderful to read people's memories of their favorite lines or sketches. Clearly, Tom had touched people's lives, or at least made them laugh.

I spoke on the Senate floor about Tom a couple days later. I'm a crier, so I practiced the speech aloud about forty times so I could make it through. I held it together until "Rest in peace."

The next day, I was sitting in a Judiciary Committee hearing when a staffer slipped me a note: "Leader

Reid is on the phone for you." It was unusual for the majority leader to call me in the middle of a hearing. I got up and went to the anteroom and picked up the phone.

"Harry?"

"Al, I read your eulogy to your friend. He was quite a guy."

"Yes, sir. He was."

"I loved this part. 'The Dark Side of Death.'"

I smiled. Then Harry read a passage from a piece Tom had written about dying: "In the foreseeable future, I will be a dead person. I want to remind you that dead people are people too. There are good dead people and bad dead people. Some of my best friends are dead people. Dead people have fought in every war."

Then Harry said, "It's perfect."

"Yes," I said. "Perfect."

Chapter 5

Saturday Night Live
(The Part Where I Leave)

Over the fifteen years I spent at *SNL*, I worked on hundreds of sketches, many of them just big, dumb, silly stuff, like Belushi as Elizabeth Taylor choking on a chicken bone. But the body of work I'm proudest of is the political satire the show produced. It's important to emphasize that that work reflects the contributions of many writers and cast members. But more than anyone else, the credit for the sustained quality of *SNL*'s political satire belongs to Jim Downey, the show's longtime head writer, producer, and occasional performer.*

Jim had a hand in virtually every *SNL* debate sketch during the nearly thirty-five seasons he spent

---

* This past season, the rise of Trump has brought the show back to its glory days of political satire.

at the show, including the genius "Strategery/Lockbox" debate he wrote between George W. Bush and Al Gore, played brilliantly by Will Ferrell and Darrell Hammond. (Bush never said "strategery" until Jim put it in Will's mouth.)

There's a good argument to be made that Jim's 2000 debate sketch was the most important piece of writing in that election cycle. Americans knew that Bush had trouble with the English language—Bush made fun of that himself. But Jim caught a certain superciliousness with Darrell's Gore that Americans hadn't quite put their finger on. Jim and Darrell nailed it so specifically that anyone who watched the sketch couldn't help but associate the real Gore with the fake Gore's repeated sighs and constant invoking of the Social Security "lockbox." With that election decided by some five hundred votes in Florida (and a 5–4 Supreme Court decision), it's easy to argue that Jim Downey changed the course of history, I would say tragically. I think Gore would have been a great president, may well have prevented 9/11, and would not have sent us to war in Iraq based on manufactured evidence. And he'd have addressed climate change, which to me is the greatest existential threat facing mankind.

So, thanks, Jim.

During the George H. W. Bush administration, Jim and I wrote any number of cold openings, knowing that Dana Carvey's "Nah gah dah"* Bush could get laughs pretty much at will. Jim and I would craft a piece that had a progression: "This vial of crack was found in Lafayette Park just across the street from the White House. This hypodermic needle was found on the White House lawn. And this bag of cocaine was found right here in the Oval Office just two feet from this desk! It's bad! It's bad!! It's gettin' *baaad*!!!" Dana could get so many laughs along the way just with his hands that the audience would sometimes lose the through line, and between dress rehearsal and air Jim and I would actually have to tell him not to get so many laughs. Dana, of course, to his enormous credit, understood and delivered every time.

Jim is an open-minded political conservative. I like to think I'm an open-minded liberal. We, like Lorne and everyone else on the show, felt it wasn't our job on *SNL* to have a political bias and advocate for one side or the other. That was fine for a show like *Murphy Brown*, a sitcom created by one person, Diane English, and starring Candice Bergen as a feminist TV journalist. *SNL* was a comedy-variety show, with many writers and performers, each with distinct voices and views. Sure, the preponderance of the cast and staff had your garden-variety Hollywood liberal views, but we tried to do well-observed political satire that made

---

* "I'm not going to do it." As in "Nah gah dah. Wouldn't be prudent."

the audience laugh and had the virtue of not being stupid. Jim's rule was to reward viewers for knowing stuff about politics without punishing them for not.

So *SNL* wasn't the place to push my own personal political agenda. I saved that for my son's Little League practices. At the show, I was part of a team of dozens of writers and performers, and for our team, funny was the only thing that mattered.

* * *

I did, however, start taking advantage of more and more opportunities to do political satire outside the show, where I could be a little more pointed about making fun of people who really deserved it.

In the summer of 1992, I anchored a series of specials on Comedy Central covering every night of both the Democratic National Convention in New York City and the Republican National Convention in Houston. We called the show *Indecision '92*.

We broadcast out of a small studio in lower Manhattan. Our pledge was that viewers of our coverage wouldn't miss anything that happened. To accomplish this, I sat at an anchor desk with a screen behind me carrying the live "feed" from the convention floor that the networks shared. Writer and humorist Roy Blount Jr. sat nearby in a Barcalounger watching four TVs tuned to the coverage on ABC, NBC, CBS, and PBS.

That way, if anything important and/or interesting

happened, we could bring it to you within ten seconds. For instance, if Dan Rather said, "If a frog had
side pockets, he'd carry a handgun," Roy would let us
know right away.

Modern political conventions tend to be tightly
scripted, which is why the broadcast networks devoted
only two hours a night to covering them. We did
four hours a night, giving us plenty of time for com-
mentary and comedy from a slate of special guests
designed for political junkies—Norm Ornstein, Chris-
topher Hitchens, Calvin Trillin, Ben Stein, Lawrence
O'Donnell Jr., and Roger Ailes. Yes, Roger Ailes, who
actually was very funny and who, as far as I know, did
not sexually harass anyone during the two hours he
was with us. Between the two conventions, my favorite letter came from a viewer who wrote, "The guy you
had play Norm Ornstein was perfect."

During the first night of the Republican National
Convention in Houston, Ben Stein and I did com-
mentary live during Pat Buchanan's "religious war"
speech, the one that Molly Ivins said "probably sounded
better in the original German." Watching the speech, I
made the comment that Buchanan's angry tone would
hurt the Bush campaign. And, of course, it did—which
traditional pundits wouldn't pick up on for weeks. In
their 1992 year-in-review, *Rolling Stone* said, "It was
disorienting to watch a comedy broadcast that almost
incidentally told more truth and offered more insight

than most networks and newspapers and at the same time was so much more comfortable to watch."

Today, of course, the idea of "comedy that tells the truth in a way that serious political analysis misses" isn't strange. Jon Stewart and Stephen Colbert became not just successful comedians, but respected political figures, because night after night, year after year, they offered more truth and insight than most real TV news.

But they didn't invent meaningful political satire. They just brought it to a level of unprecedented popularity and influence. Before *The Daily Show* and *The Colbert Report*, there was *Politically Incorrect* with Bill Maher. And before *Politically Incorrect*, there was *Indecision '92*. And before that there was something Jonathan Swift wrote about the Potato Famine.

After the eight nights of coverage of the conventions, we added a ninth show on election night 1992. The evening began with a balloon drop as we called the election for Bill Clinton, several hours before the networks did—based on exit poll data we had obtained from sources inside one of the networks.*

By disregarding the notorious unreliability of exit polling, Comedy Central became the first source to break the news that Bill Clinton had been elected the forty-second president of the United States. And I'm

---

* Norm Ornstein.

afraid that maybe I was just a little too visibly happy about it.

* * *

You see, in 1994, I was vying for a job I had wanted for years at *SNL*: anchoring "Weekend Update." But because I'd been wearing my bleeding liberal heart on my sleeve more and more, it was next to impossible for me to be an unbiased voice on the show's signature segment commenting on the week's news.

That year, I headlined the White House Correspondents' Dinner, which Beltway nerds nerdily refer to as the "Nerd Prom" because it allows the Washington elite to mingle with the *significantly* more attractive Hollywood elite. Shortly after my performance, I was in Lorne's office with Steve Martin and Lorne. "Al, I saw that White House Correspondents' Dinner," Steve said, grinning. "You were great! *That's* what you should do!"

When Lorne didn't say, "Well, Steve, that's *exactly* what Al's going to be doing! As the new anchor of 'Weekend Update'!" I kind of knew where things were headed. Lorne and Don Ohlmeyer, then the head of NBC, went with Norm MacDonald, who in retrospect was a much better choice.

Losing out on "Update" was a big part of the reason I decided it was time to move on after fifteen seasons at *SNL*. It was a difficult decision. I loved the show. Lorne had created a safe haven for writers and performers, and there was nothing quite like writing something on a Tuesday night and seeing it *kill* on Saturday. But as we learn in Ecclesiastes, there is a time for all things. A time to kill. A time to heal. A time to leave the show. A time to stay much too long at the show.

* * *

After the Correspondents' Dinner, the whip-smart Leslie Schnur, who had edited the Stuart Smalley book that eventually turned into the Stuart Smalley movie, suggested I try my hand at a political book. The title came to me in a flash: *Rush Limbaugh Is a Big Fat Idiot and Other Observations.*

The title, you see, was an ironic comment on the loss of civility in our public discourse. Limbaugh, with an audience of twenty million listeners a week, had been the bombastic cheerleader for the Gingrich Revolution, which culminated in the 1994 midterm elections when Republicans took the majority in the House for the first time in forty years.

The distinctly antigovernment Limbaugh/Gingrich agenda swept in a significant number of radical Republicans and with them a partisan enmity that has just grown even worse over the past two decades. In addition to the nastiness, there seemed to be a new willingness to lie about basic facts. According to

Limbaugh, there is no conclusive proof that nicotine is addictive, and there are more American Indians alive today than when Columbus landed in 1492, and if all the polar ice caps melted, sea level would not rise. (Rush explained that if an ice cube melts in a glass of water, the water level remains the same. Unfortunately, Greenland is a landmass, not an ice cube.)

Leaving *SNL* seemed like a good opportunity to use my comedic chops to influence the national political conversation instead of using my political knowledge to inform the comedy on the show. In *RLIABFIAOO*, I not only focused on Limbaugh and Gingrich, but also took on the whole cast of characters from the whack-job right: from elected officials to conservative activists to columnists and TV pundits. When I finished the book, I had the publisher send Rush a copy with a note saying, "Al thinks it would help sales if you mentioned the book on the show." Well, one thing Rush Limbaugh isn't is an idiot. (He was, however, very fat.) So he kept his mouth shut. Nevertheless, *Rush Limbaugh Is a Big Fat Idiot and Other Observations* shot to number one on the *New York Times* bestseller list and stayed there for twenty-three weeks.

Even better was the reaction I was getting from readers. When I traveled around the country on the book tour, progressives would come up to me and say things like, "Thank you," or "It's about time somebody took these guys on," or "Thank you—it's about time somebody took these guys on."

This was new. I'd always thought there was nothing better than hearing people laugh. But hearing people tell me that they were not only entertained, but also energized to go out and take these guys on themselves, was thrilling.

It felt good to land on my feet. And made it a lot easier to laugh along with Norm on "Update." Hey, I'm human.

Chapter 6

Paul

After the success of the Rush book, I started getting gigs on the lucrative lecture circuit. It turns out there aren't that many speakers who know a whole lot about politics and are also funny. Usually, this meant being flown first class to Scottsdale or Palm Springs or Vail to speak to a corporate conference on real estate investment trusts or reinsurance or how to get kids in third world countries to drink more Sprite.

But I also became a popular speaker on the significantly less lucrative (as in, I didn't get paid) national progressive circuit. And my favorite Democrat to speak for was Paul Wellstone.

My parents introduced me to Paul back in 1990, when he first ran for the Senate. By then, Dad had made the transition from Jacob Javits Republican to George

McGovern Democrat.* In 1990, he was eighty-two and part of a senior citizens' theater troupe for Wellstone that toured nursing homes. I never saw their show. But Dad had Paget's disease, a softening of the bones, so I imagine the choreography was somewhat limited.

Paul was a little guy. And he was a fighter. Like me, Paul was a high school wrestler. Unlike me, he was a very good high school wrestler, and at the University of North Carolina was the Atlantic Coast Conference champion at the 126-pound level in 1964 and was subsequently inducted into the College Wrestling Hall of Fame, located in Wrestlingville, USA, and very much worth a visit if you're in the area.

Wellstone brought his wrestler's energy and intensity to his activism. While teaching political science at Carleton College in Northfield, Minnesota, in the early '70s, he organized poor single parents to fight for a publicly funded day care center, public housing, and free school lunches.

Paul kept getting arrested: for protesting the Vietnam War, for protesting farm foreclosures, for selling

---

* For those who got the Grindr joke back in chapter 1, Jacob Javits was a liberal Republican who represented the state of New York in the Senate from 1957 until 1981. For those who got the Jacob Javits reference without any help, Grindr is a popular gay dating app—and "app" is short for "application," which for some reason is what you call a computer program now.

uppers to other wrestlers.* After he picketed with strikers at the Hormel meatpacking plant in Austin, Minnesota, Carleton College fired him. But after Carleton students staged a protest, the college reinstated him and gave him tenure. Paul Wellstone remains the youngest tenured professor in the school's history.

In 1990, Paul won a long-shot race against sitting senator Rudy Boschwitz, even though Paul was outspent by a seven-to-one margin. Boschwitz was the only incumbent U.S. senator to lose that year, in large part because Paul ran an energetic grassroots campaign. He even had a senior citizens' troupe perform at nursing homes!

As a senator, Paul fought for the poor and dispossessed, for homeless vets, for people suffering from mental illness. "Politics," he would say, "is not about power. Politics is not about money. Politics is not about winning for the sake of winning. Politics is about the improvement of people's lives." And that's what he tried to do every day he served in the United States Senate.

* * *

The last time I campaigned for Paul Wellstone was at the University Club in St. Paul, about eight weeks

---

* No, of course Paul never sold uppers to other wrestlers. But there's a rule in comedy called the Rule of Three, and he was only arrested twice. See, this is the kind of footnote you're just not going to get in Condoleezza Rice's memoir.

before the 2002 midterm election. Paul was in the middle of a very tight, very bitter race with former St. Paul mayor Norm Coleman, who had been hand-picked by the Bush team to run against him.

As you may recall, at the time, the White House was pushing Congress to grant President Bush authority to go to war against Iraq. On October 2, 2002, just a little over a month before the election, Paul Wellstone became the only incumbent senator up for reelection to come out against the war. At the time, with war fever running high and pretextual lies coming fast and furious, this was pretty close to political suicide. That day Paul told friends in the Senate and in Minnesota that he understood the vote would probably cost him his seat. As it turns out, even though a majority of Minnesotans supported going to war in Iraq, they respected Paul's principled vote, and he moved ahead of Coleman in the polls.

The people of Minnesota value a politician who believes what he says and says what he believes and votes that way. Paul never prevaricated. And Minnesotans always knew where Paul Wellstone stood.

Minnesotans also knew Paul's heart. Many of them had a personal story about how his warmth, his humility, or his wit had touched their lives on a level that had nothing to do with politics. Here's mine.

That evening at the University Club—the last time I saw my friend—the first thing he said to me, in the thick of a battle for his political life, was, "How's your mom?" As it so happened, I had just come from her nursing home in Minneapolis, where in her room Mom kept a photo of Paul signed by him to her: "Phoebe, Keep fighting! Paul."

"Well, there are good days and bad days," I told Paul. As he knew, she was suffering from sporadic dementia. "And today was a bad day. It was tough. I couldn't even have a conversation with her."

Paul nodded, put his hand on my shoulder, and said, "You know, touch means so much."

That was Paul. "Touch means so much."

Two weeks after the vote on the war, Paul and his wife, Sheila, and their daughter, Marcia, died in an airplane crash in northern Minnesota along with three staffers, Tom Lapic, Mary McEvoy, and Will McLaughlin, and pilots Richard Conry and Michael Guess.

I didn't realize it at the time, but Paul's death would end up being part of the story of how I came to be a senator, serving in the same seat he held for twelve years.

But while I certainly would never have run for the Senate if Paul hadn't died, I also don't think I would have run had I not known him in life. Paul's greatest contribution to the progressive cause wasn't what he accomplished in the Senate (although he accomplished a lot). It's the way he inspired others to take action, and taught them to be effective, and gave them the confidence to stand up and shout about what they believed in.

The more time you spent around Paul, the more his energy, and his passion, and his courage infected you and made you think you could make a difference, too.

And to this day, if you travel around Minnesota and meet people who work in progressive politics, you'll hear many of them explain that they do it because of Paul.

Some of them were part of his campaign and never stopped working for change even after he was gone, as a way to keep their hero's memory alive.

Some of them trained with Wellstone Action, the nonprofit that became one of Paul's legacies, teaching people how to organize for progress.

And some are too young to have ever really known him—but they're still inspired by his courage and his energy, the way this happy warrior never forgot that "politics is about the improvement of people's lives."

I can't think of a better tribute to Paul's life than the fact that more than a decade after his death, the passion he brought to politics is still alive. There are a lot of people who are more politically active than they ever thought they'd be because they love who Paul was and what he stood for, and felt called to do their part to carry forward the fights he led.

I'm one of them.

Chapter 7

A 99 Percent Improvement

In April 2003, I was scanning political stories on my laptop when I noticed a profile of Minnesota senator Norm Coleman in *Roll Call*, one of the Capitol Hill dailies. It was the first profile of Coleman, who had been in office just a little over three months. According to *Roll Call*, Norm had already become "an emerging star on the GOP's rubber-chicken circuit."

I read on: "'Most of it is because of beating Mondale,' said Coleman as he gesticulated his points with an unlit cigar in his new Hart office."

Huh. As someone who had only ever gesticulated with an unlit cigar to make fun of people who gesticulate with unlit cigars, I got the impression that maybe Norm's ascent to the world's greatest deliberative body had gone to his head a bit.

Then I read it: the sentence that would change my life.

"To be very blunt, and God watch over Paul's soul, I am a 99 percent improvement over Paul Wellstone."

"I am a 99 percent improvement over Paul Wellstone." I'm sorry, but you don't say that about *anyone* who died within the last six months. And, my God, you don't say it about a guy who *everyone* agreed was a compassionate, tireless champion of the little guy, a loving husband and father, and a colleague whom every senator recognized for his passion and decency.

Until that exact moment, I had never considered running for political office.* But when I read that quote on the *Roll Call* website, my immediate thought was this: "Somebody's got to beat this guy."

Except I didn't think exactly that. Instead of "guy," I thought "jerk."

Except I didn't think that, either. It was something else. I can't write it in this book. But it's not as bad as you might think. Okay, it was "bastard." No, it wasn't. It was worse than that.

---

* As evidenced by the fact that I spent thirty-five years writing things like "Placenta Helper," an unproduced *Saturday Night Live* commercial parody for a product that "lets you stretch your placenta into a tasty casserole. For example, Placenta Romanoff—a zesty blend of cheeses that makes for a zingy sauce that Russian czars commanded at palace feasts." The censors cut it, depriving America of a good hearty laugh.

Fine, it was "dingus."[USS] "Somebody's got to beat this dingus."[USS] That's what I thought.*

* * *

Now, that's a really bad reason to run for office. And over time it would become less and less about beating Norm Coleman, and more and more about the people of Minnesota. By the time I clobbered him on election day (in the narrowest clobbering in political history), I had almost forgotten that the germ of the idea to run had come from such a petty place.

And anyway, at the time, I didn't think that the "somebody" who was going to beat this guy would end up being me. True, for a brief moment, I did find myself considering the fact that Franni and I were about to be empty nesters—our son, Joe, was about to head off to college the next year. It would be easy for us to move back to Minnesota and explore the idea. Then again, being an empty nester is not a good reason to run for the Senate, either. It is, however, a great

---

* Important note: That's how I felt *at the time*. It doesn't mean I currently think that Norm Coleman is a dingus.[USS] Norm is a loving father who dotes on his kids. And he did some really good things as mayor of St. Paul. He was, however, in my opinion, a cruddy[USS] senator. When Norm apologized for calling himself a 99 percent improvement over Paul Wellstone (after a couple of days of outrage from Minnesotans), he said that what he meant was that he was a 99 percent improvement over Paul *in terms of supporting the Bush White House*. Which was all too true.

reason to take up a new hobby, such as gardening or paddle tennis, which can help ward off depression.

In any event, I quickly set the thought aside. "After all," I reminded myself, "first I have to finish this book, and then I've committed to doing a three-hour radio show five days a week."

How's that for exposition?

See, I was reading the article while sitting in my office at the Shorenstein Center on Media, Politics and Public Policy at the Kennedy School of Government at Harvard, where I was a fellow.

When I accepted the position, I thought I was going to be a teaching fellow. But I wasn't. I was just a fellow. They told me, however, that I could lead a study group on any subject I wanted. I asked if it was okay if I taught students how to research a satirical book on politics. They said sure. As it turns out, a lot of professors at Harvard teach students how to research their books.*

The book, which became *Lies and the Lying Liars Who Tell Them: A Fair and Balanced Look at the Right*, would argue that the right-wing media had created a

---

* In the interest of full disclosure, I should tell you that Harvard did turn down my first proposed topic for my study group, which was "How can you build a nuclear weapon in your garage with just $100 worth of supplies from Home Depot?" Harvard felt that this would be more appropriate for the graduate school of applied science, or maybe its acclaimed business school.

right-wing echo chamber that often intimidates the mainstream media into reporting its distortions and outright lies.

The centerpiece of the book would be a chapter detailing how the right had exploited the Wellstone memorial, a long and boisterous event held shortly after his death—and shortly before the 2002 election—that reflected the deep passion that had animated Paul throughout his life, as well as the strong emotional connection so many people felt they had had with him.

Republicans had promptly seized the opportunity to paint the memorial as an inappropriately partisan event. The Coleman campaign and its allies lied about everything from the content of the eulogies to the audience's reaction, effectively hijacking Paul's memorial for their own selfish partisan purposes by falsely accusing Democrats of hijacking it for our own selfish partisan purposes.*

I still feel strongly about this. And so do lots and lots of other Minnesota Democrats. Losing Paul was a crushing blow. Losing Paul and then watching Republicans lie about his memorial service for political

---

* If you haven't read *Lies*, go find a bookstore near you, grab a copy off the shelf, and just read that chapter. Tell 'em Al sent you, and that I said it would be fine if you hung out in the aisle for half an hour reading without buying anything. Or, hell, get a coffee or an app or whatever it is they're selling to stay in business these days.

purposes was adding a despicable insult to a still-fresh injury, and watching their scheme succeed was dispiriting beyond words.

To then see Norm Coleman immediately start bragging, not just about how he had ended Walter Mondale's political career, but about how he was a better senator than Paul because he was so loyal to the Bush administration? It was almost too much.

That's why I had such a strong reaction to Coleman's "99 percent improvement" line—and it's a big part of the reason why, for me and for so many other Minnesota Democrats, my 2008 campaign would end up feeling like it was about more than just a Senate seat.

As emotional and difficult as that Wellstone chapter was, the rest of the book was just fun. Team-Franken did a lot of fact-checking on well-known conservatives like Ann Coulter, Dick Cheney, and Bill O'Reilly, who up until then had merely been *suspected* of being congenital liars. The book put to rest forever any doubt that they and many other prominent right-wingers were very much indeed lying liars.

But even before the book came out, something interesting happened. Bill O'Reilly and Fox News sued me. It was really just a simple misunderstanding. O'Reilly and the Fox legal team apparently didn't understand that in America satire is protected by the First Amendment, even if the object of the satire doesn't get it.

In any event, Fox was literally laughed out of court. Literally. The *New York Times* headline read, "In Courtroom, Laughter at Fox and a Victory for Al Franken." Aided by the free publicity generated by O'Reilly, *Lies* skyrocketed to the top of the bestseller list for months, selling over a million copies. (Arianna Huffington told me, "It's as if Bill O'Reilly walked up to you and handed you a check for a million dollars.")

Readers responded to my thesis that the right's complaint about a liberal bias in the mainstream media was disingenuous right-wing fiddle-faddle.[USS] They also liked the way I took on Bush's policies, and his poppycock[USS] claims, like, "The vast majority of my tax cuts go to those at the bottom."

On the book tour that fall, once again, I kept hearing things like, "Finally, someone's taking it to these guys!" It felt good, even when they were visibly intoxicated. And every so often, someone would come up to me and say, "Why don't you run for office?" Especially in Minnesota, where people were already thinking ahead to 2008, when Norm Coleman would have to run for reelection.

But I had other things on my mind.

While researching *Lies*, I learned that 22 percent of Americans were getting their news from talk radio, which meant right-wing talk radio. Liberals had ceded the airwaves to Rush Limbaugh and the Rush Limbaugh wannabes and also, in those days, the band Linkin Park, which was getting a lot of airplay. So in March 2003, while I was still researching and writing the book, I had taken the plunge and committed to hosting a daily three-hour progressive radio show.

I quickly learned a few things about radio. Radio stations have "formats." "Classic Rock" is a format. "Country" is a format. "Hot Adult Contemporary," whatever that means, is a format.*

"Talk Radio" is not a format. "Conservative Talk" is a format.

Placing my show between Rush Limbaugh and Sean Hannity (or between Mark Levin and Michael Savage) would have been like putting three hours of hip-hop on a station that otherwise carried a day of its polar opposite: hop-hip.

So we had to invent a new format, "Progressive Radio." And that meant creating an entire day of programming. And while we were at it, an entire national radio network, called Air America.

The concept for my show was simple: We would not try to be the mirror image of right-wing radio, but its opposite.

My executive producer, Billy Kimball, put together a staff of researchers, writers, and producers. Katherine

---

* I think it's Rihanna and Justin Bieber and stuff like that?

Lanpher, a seasoned journalist and a fixture at Minnesota Public Radio, came aboard as my cohost. And on March 31, 2004, *The Al Franken Show* (then called *The O'Franken Factor* in an effort to further irritate Bill O'Reilly) went live:

> This is Al Franken speaking to you from thirty thousand feet under Dick Cheney's bunker and *this* is Air America Radio...We have watched the right wing take over the Congress, White House, and courts and, as insidiously, the airwaves. We need a great watchdog to track them, and until one comes along, I'll have to do.

We laid down some basic rules right off the bat. No call-ins. No actors talking about politics (we called that "the Tim Robbins Rule").

And while we did some stuff that was just funny for the sake of funny, like when I played Strom Thurmond bragging about his sexual conquests ("Katherine, I screwed 'em *allll!*"), or when my old partner Tom Davis would come on as the CEO of a sketchy outfit called "Accountants Without Borders," I also wanted ours to be a show that was serious about public policy. After all, as long as I would be committing to preparing for and doing a daily three-hour show, I might as well learn something.

So we decided that our guests would be people who knew stuff.

For example: You often hear people say that Elizabeth Warren was talking about income inequality before almost anyone else. Well, one of the places she was talking about it before almost anyone else was on our show. We'd have her on to discuss the 2005 bankruptcy bill (an outrageous handout to the credit card industry), conservative attacks on pensions and Social Security, and the general deterioration of the middle class.

But the thing we talked about more than anything else was Iraq.

* * *

Lies and the Lying Liars was already on bookshelves by the time it became clear that the Bush administration's biggest lie wasn't about tax cuts.

"There is no doubt," Dick Cheney had declared in the lead-up to the invasion, "that Saddam Hussein now has weapons of mass destruction. There is no doubt he is amassing them to use against our friends, against our allies, and against us."

He was lying. And it's still crazy to think that he, and the president, and so many others (including, for God's sake, Colin Powell) just flat-out lied us into a war. Heck, I was in the process of finishing a scholarly masterwork about how they lied *all the time*, and even I didn't think they would lie us into a war.

But by the end of 2003, it was obvious that anyone who had maintained even the barest shred of faith in the administration's integrity and basic decency had made a mistake. There were no weapons of mass destruction. Worse, it turned out that Bush et al. hadn't just lied us into a war. They'd lied us into a disaster.

That Christmas, I went to Iraq for the first time, on a USO tour. USO tours are the best thing I've ever done—I've done seven now, four of them to Kuwait, Iraq, and Afghanistan. I would spend two weeks doing shows with an eclectic group of entertainers, including NFL cheerleaders and extremely right-wing country stars like Darryl Worley. Franni knew I loved these tours, but one year she said to me in frustration, "You don't see Bill O'Reilly going on USO tours."

"That's not fair, honey," I said. "He has no talent."

Between shows, we'd hit DFACs (dining facilities) three, four, five times a day. Walking with your tray, looking for a place to sit down, you could see who wanted to talk.

I learned a tremendous amount on these USO tours. Later, as a senator, I'd go on to visit Afghanistan on a CODEL where we'd meet with top officials, most of whom would tell us exactly what they were supposed to tell us. Traveling with the USO, you could learn a lot more from the privates, lieutenants, command sergeant majors, and one-stars shooting the breeze in the DFACs in between shows.

Everyone had different points of view. Back then, truck drivers were beginning to get blasted with IEDs. Guys fighting outside the wire were a lot more on edge than guys inside the wire.

On my first Middle East tour in '03, while we were at our first stop in Kuwait, troops found Saddam Hussein in a spider hole near his hometown in Tikrit. But even in the flush of capturing Saddam, the message we got was that Operation Iraqi Freedom was not going quite as planned.

Adding to the cost, both in blood and treasure, was the waste, fraud, and abuse by military contractors during Iraq's reconstruction. Billions were being ripped off by shady contractors. Work was not completed, or on some projects never started. And the inability to replace the loss of key infrastructure—roads, electricity, water, and sewage—sent the country spiraling further into chaos. Everyone in Iraq was paying the price. So were American taxpayers. And so were our troops, often with their lives.

Oh, and by the way: Guess who was officially in charge of exposing and reining in the waste, fraud, and abuse in Iraq? It's someone you may remember from earlier in this chapter. No, not Katherine Lanpher. It was Norm Coleman! The newly elected Coleman had been given the plum chairmanship of the hallowed Permanent Subcommittee on Investigations, known as PSI. The chairman of PSI is the only United States senator with sole subpoena power. He can investigate anything he wants.

Originally, PSI had been the Truman Committee in the lead-up to and during World War II. Before the war, Harry Truman—then a senator from Missouri—personally drove around the country in his car to inspect training camps and found widespread mismanagement and downright theft. Because the committee saved millions and so strengthened our war effort, Truman made the cover of *Time*, and in 1944, FDR chose him as his running mate.

Truman's committee did 432 separate hearings on fraud, waste, and abuse in war contracting. While Coleman was chairman of PSI, his committee did exactly 432 fewer hearings on contracting in Iraq.

I went back to Iraq with the USO each of the next three winters. And every time I went, it seemed like things were getting worse. But even on that first visit, it was clear that some basic problems were not being taken care of.

In Kuwait, they divided us up to go to different bases around the country. I volunteered to go to Tikrit—Saddam's hometown and, they thought, a potentially dangerous place.

As we boarded our plane in Kuwait, a soldier took

me aside and suggested that I should make sure I got a flak jacket equipped with modern Kevlar plates. The Vietnam-era flak jacket I was wearing, he said, wouldn't really stop a bullet. So when I got to Iraq, I should insist on upgrading to the Kevlar. He emphasized the word "insist."

I nodded. *Insist.* Got it.

When our plane landed in Baghdad, we were transferred quickly to a waiting helicopter for the flight to Tikrit. As I was climbing in, I turned to an airman and said, "Um, I've been told to ask for the Kevlar plates for my flak jacket?"

The airman said, "We don't have any."

"Uh-huh. But I was told to insist."

"Well, that's fine. But we just don't have them."

There was an uncomfortable moment before I tried one last time. "Okay. I'm *insisting.*"

"I understand. We don't have any."

So off I went to Tikrit, supposedly the most dangerous place in Iraq, where, fortunately, I was not shot. And neither were the cheerleaders.

This failure to properly equip and protect our troops would become an ongoing scandal. Right before I went on my third trip in 2005, it came out that troops in Kuwait were going to dumps in search of metal they could use to up-armor their own Humvees. In response to the outcry, Donald Rumsfeld famously said, "You go to war with the army you have, not the army you want." This was particularly galling since the date he said this was further from 9/11 than V-J Day was from Pearl Harbor.

In preparation for that year's USO tour, I asked *SNL* to make a flak jacket out of a garbage can and wore it during my opening monologue at our shows, saying, "We've got some good news and some bad news. The bad news is that there aren't any cheerleaders this year. The good news is"—pointing to my garbage can flak jacket—"I've got a hundred more of these."

* * *

The radio show had started with an explicit goal of defeating President Bush in his 2004 reelection campaign. We all worked really hard to take down a guy whom we already were pretty sure was one of the worst presidents in history—and we failed. So 2005 was a pretty dark time for progressives. Just as in 2016, a Republican had won a presidential election despite things that to many of us seemed obviously disqualifying (in Bush's case it was Iraq and not his entire life story and personality), and now conservatives had a lock on all three branches of government, plus a lie-amplifying propaganda machine.

But the political infrastructure we'd started to build during the campaign—David Brock's media watchdog group Media Matters, the Center for American

Progress think tank, and even Air America itself—was working to help the progressive movement regroup, get reenergized, and find a new direction.

Right after he got reelected, President Bush promised to privatize Social Security. We stopped him. And despite Karl Rove's predictions of a "permanent Republican majority," we were slowly figuring out how to fight back. We were getting better at debunking Fox News, and learning how to counter the kind of smear campaign that Republicans had run to perfection in 2004, as well as generating powerful ideas of our own.

When I first started writing about politics, I just wanted to prove that the right-wing figures who got under my skin were liars and frauds. I was in what I now think of as the "get it off my chest" phase of my political development. But now it felt like I was part of something bigger—a real movement to change the direction of the country.

By the summer of 2005, I was working on the follow-up to *Lies: The Truth (with Jokes)*. Except this time, instead of just making fun of the Bush administration's mouthpieces, I found myself focusing more on making the case against the Bush administration itself and its terrible policies.

The last chapter of *The Truth*, "A Letter to My Grandchildren" (named Hillary, Barack, and Joe

III),* flashed forward ten years to October 2015, and told what I hoped would be the story of the intervening decade, one in which Democrats would take back Congress in the 2006 midterms, changing the political landscape by offering a slew of great ideas and setting the stage for a Democratic president to be elected in 2008. Then we would pass all sorts of legislation, beginning with universal health care and an "Apollo" Project for renewable energy, and continuing on to tackle tax fairness, public education, and increasing youth turnout by legalizing voting by AOL Instant Messenger.†

Oh, and in this scenario, I would be elected to the Senate in 2008.

I hadn't forgotten about the whole "99 percent improvement" thing. And as Iraq fell apart, Norm Coleman's failure to perform his oversight responsibilities was only making me more sure that somebody, indeed, had to beat this guy.

But by now I was beginning to think that maybe— just maybe—that somebody should be me after all.

---

* My daughter, Thomasin, had our first grandson, whom she named Joe, in 2013. Two years later, my son, Joe, and his wife, Stephanie, had a son, whom they refused to name Barack. I'm still hoping that a future grandchild might be named after the great mountaineer Sir Edmund Hillary, one of my personal heroes.

† Which, I am told, nobody uses anymore.

Chapter 8

Year of the Bean Feed

In late 2005, I told a friend that I was very seriously considering running for the Senate.

"Why would you do that?" he asked incredulously.

"Well," I said, "I think I could accomplish a lot. And what do I really have to risk?"

My friend looked dubious. "Um, public opprobrium?"

The truth is, no one debating whether or not to run for office is worried about the upside. The problem is the downside. Sure, as an empty nester who had already had a successful career, I was playing with house money. But while the stuff in the "pro" column was pretty compelling—I was confident I could do a lot of good, it would feel great to beat Coleman, and also, like a lot of people, I kind of really wanted to be a senator—there were a lot of what Donald Rumsfeld charmingly referred to as "known unknowns."

For example: Would I be a good candidate? Did I know enough about the issues? Could I deal with the long hours and the tough questions and the personal attacks and the groveling for money?

What if I sucked at it? What if I hated it? What if voters hated *me*? What if I lost a race that someone else could have won? What if I was humiliated? What if I had to give a concession speech where I graciously congratulated Norm Coleman on his victory? And what *was* "opprobrium," anyway?

Most of all: Was the risk of things going wrong worth the potential good I could do (and fun I could have) if things went right?

There were a lot of questions. And I didn't know the answers. But I told Franni, "I don't want to not do the things I'll want to have done if I decide to run."

"What?" replied Franni.

"Never mind. You know how we've been talking about moving back to Minnesota and maybe running for the Senate?"

"Yeah."

"Let's do it."

"Oh. Okay. Sure. If that's what you want to do, honey."

* * *

As in most marriages, my wife and I have a division of labor when it comes to the day-to-day operations of our household. Basically, it's this: Franni's in charge.

I had a vision: I wanted to buy a house near where I grew up, in the western suburbs of Minneapolis. Something a little bigger, of course, with a nice big yard. Franni said no. Absolutely not. She told me that a house requires constant upkeep and that she'd end up having to do it, because I'd be doing the radio show and going all around the state of Minnesota while she had to deal with every plumbing problem or beetle infestation.

So instead of a big house with a big yard and bad plumbing and a beetle problem, Franni found us a town house very near downtown Minneapolis. Less upkeep, less hassle, and, best of all, I could walk to work.

We broadcast the show from atop the historic Foshay Tower, which when I was a boy was the city's tallest building, smugly thrusting its antennae into the innocent Minneapolis sky. But modern skyscrapers now tower above the once proud Foshay, which cowers meekly among the indifferent glass and steel.*

In my free time, I started laying the foundation for a potential campaign. That meant learning as much as I could about Minnesota issues and getting as much advice as I could from key political players. And it meant showing up everywhere I could to rally

---

* I've submitted this paragraph to a middle school writing contest.

DFLers* across the state for the critical 2006 midterm elections—a sort of dry run for what my own campaign might be like.

I also set up a political action committee (PAC), which would allow me to meet big-shot donors, gauge my fund-raising appeal, and build some goodwill by supporting deserving candidates in Minnesota and around the country.

Setting up a PAC is a lot easier than it might sound. Basically, you just appoint a treasurer (I picked my high school buddy Tom Borman), fill out a four-page form available on the Federal Election Commission's website, and, voilà, you have a PAC.

I named mine Midwest Values PAC, drawn to the clever acronym MVP. Unfortunately, MVP.com already directed to the online store for CBS Sports. Bastards! I thought about just giving up on the whole Senate thing. But no. We would overcome this first hurdle and just buy midwestvaluespac.org. Not as good. But as I would learn, politics is the art of the possible.

Things got easier, mostly because I hired some people who knew what they were doing. Dinah Dale, a soft-spoken Arkansan who had overseen Paul Wellstone's fund-raising operation, was in charge of

---

* In Minnesota, the Democratic Party is known as the Democratic-Farmer-Labor Party, or DFL Party, for reasons that are detailed authoritatively on Wikipedia.

connecting me with wealthy progressives who might be interested in contributing to my PAC.

Dinah brought in another Wellstone alum, A. J. Goodman—a lawyer who had defended murderers and drug dealers in Miami before she turned to the more high-stakes, cutthroat world of political fund-raising—to set up MVP events around the country.

We also started a direct mail fund-raising program. Turns out, the number one determinant of whether someone gives money in response to a mail solicitation is whether or not they open the envelope. And because I had something of a following from my books and radio show, instead of just tossing my envelopes into their trash cans—or, if they were environmentally conscious, their recycling bins—people tended to open them.

Inside, they'd a find a letter that didn't sound exactly like every other fund-raising letter they were getting. Mine began, "Dear Person I'm Asking for Money." Moderately amused liberals from coast to coast sent in contributions.

Midwest Values PAC was off and running. The money we raised wasn't for me. The point was to give it away to progressive candidates and causes in Minnesota and around the country. And for me to get credit for it. Smart, huh?

* * *

Next step: coffee. A lot of politics gets done over coffee. That's true all over the country, but especially in Minnesota. Minnesotans just *love* coffee.

My first coffee was with my friend Jeff Blodgett. Jeff had been the campaign manager for all of Paul Wellstone's Senate campaigns. As fiery and passionate as Paul was, Jeff is calm and measured.

Jeff kind of looks like a prototypical Minnesota guy. Trim, clean-cut, the kind of man who spends thirty years of his life looking like he's forty-five years old. Jeff is reserved but intense. Also, not funny.

He gave me lots of sound advice about where I should go and who I should meet. But the one piece of advice that I remember most vividly was Jeff's suggestion that, as an exercise, I write a five-minute speech without *any* jokes in it. "Why," I thought, "would anyone want to do that?"

I was a comedian. All the validation I had received in my career had been for making people laugh, even if I was talking about something serious. Clearly, I had a lot of learning to do.

*   *   *

I was insanely busy. There was the three-hour daily radio broadcast, for which I stubbornly insisted on actually preparing every night. There was national travel, where I'd take the show on the road in conjunction with book signings and promotional appearances for our local affiliates. There was fund-raising for MVP. There was a lot of coffee. And of course, there was traveling around Minnesota. Which brings me to bean feeds.

Bean feeds are essentially the organizing medium of DFL politics. They are exactly what they sound like. People show up, maybe make a small donation to the local chapter of the party, they eat, and there's a speaking program.

To be clear, not every bean feed is literally a bean feed. There are burger bashes, spaghetti dinners, corn feeds, and walleye frys. But the classic bean feed—for example, the one in Kandiyohi County—is the best. It's basically a potluck, with tables filled with assorted bean dishes. Baked beans. Bean salads. Chili (with beans). And other bean dishes.*

Why go to all these bean feeds? Not just for the food. Minnesota has a caucus system, through which the DFL and Republican parties "endorse" candidates

---

* A few words about farting. Thanks to Lord Byron's famous "musical fruit" poem, when you bring up beans, most people think of flatulence. And if you've never been to a bean feed, you probably imagine that the speaking program that follows the meal would be punctuated by loud, outboard-motor-ish farts, as well as a pungent aroma. Well, you're wrong. While a skeptical senior might occasionally fart loudly to indicate disapproval of something specific that was said or a speaker in general, in my experience this is always done deliberately and sparingly. And because bean gas is largely produced by cellulose and not by decayed animal matter, the odor of bean feed farts is generally inoffensive to the point of being virtually undetectable.

for office. The folks at the bean feeds are the people who participate in the caucuses, get elected as delegates to the state convention, and decide who gets their party's endorsement.

The upshot of all that is that if you want to serve Minnesota in the United States Senate, you start by going to a lot of bean feeds.

Of course, I wasn't running for the Senate in 2006. Amy Klobuchar, now our senior senator, was. And thank goodness, because I learned a lot about how to run for the Senate by watching Amy.

No human being works harder than Amy Klobuchar. If Amy wasn't at a bean feed I went to, then her husband, John Bessler, and their daughter, Abigail, were there. If John and Abigail weren't there, Amy's father, Jim Klobuchar, the beloved *Star Tribune* columnist, was there. If none of them were there, I wondered, "Why am *I* here?"

Following Amy's example, I tried to show up everywhere I was invited. Fortunately, I had plenty of invitations. And because I wasn't actually running, I felt free to ignore Jeff Blodgett's advice and mix in a healthy dose of The Funny.

I was having fun. Eating a lot of beans. Drinking a lot of coffee. And discovering something about myself, which is that while I may not have been blessed with a lot of natural political talent, one thing I did have going for me is that I really like people.

Now, I was fifty-five years old, so I kind of knew that about myself already.* But I didn't realize that being an extrovert actually counted as a skill when it came to politics.

For a lot of people who run for office, constantly having to talk to people is exhausting. For me, it was energizing. I really liked learning about people's lives. I really liked hearing their stories. I really liked meeting their kids.

And because it was clear that I was really enjoying getting to know these folks, they really enjoyed getting to know me. And they were maybe just a little bit pleasantly surprised about that.

You see, Minnesotans are skeptical of people in show business—as well they should be. And because I had been on TV, some folks made weird assumptions about me. For example, that I had a trophy wife who was twenty years younger than me. Well, I did have a trophy wife: Franni, who is almost a full five months younger than me.

If the fact that I was friendly and approachable challenged people's assumptions, meeting Franni blew them away.

---

* Back at *SNL*, Jim Downey used to call me Dog Man. Partly because I was kind of a sloppy eater, I liked to roll around on the floor, and I would run after any ball. All of which are still true. Also, one time I bit Don Pardo.

Early on, we went to a bean feed in Minneapolis, and Franni decided to bake and bring an apple pie. When we arrived, the organizer looked at this gorgeous, massive pie, and said, "Oh, my! Let's make this an item for the silent auction!" The pie got seventy-five bucks.

Word got around about Franni's pies. Lori Sellner, the DFL chair for southern Minnesota, bought one for a hundred bucks at a bean feed at the Jackpot Junction casino near Redwood Falls. The next time I saw Lori, she raved and raved about Franni's pie. Having once been in show business, I decided to make a thing out of it. At every event in Lori's district, I'd auction the pie immediately following a short bit of shtick with Lori.

"So, Lori, you bought this pie at the bean feed at Jackpot Junction?"

"Yes."

"And how was it?"

"Unbelievably good! The most delicious apple pie I've ever had."

"Uh-huh. And this is a big pie, right?"

"Oh yeah."

"How many people did this pie feed?"

"Eighteen."

"Eighteen people. And those were big pieces?"

"Yes."

"Now, Lori, I understand you are not a crust person."

"No, I'm not. I normally don't like the crust that much."

"But tell me about *this* crust."

"Well, it was light and flaky. And delicious. I couldn't get enough of this crust."

Then I'd auction the pie. It was not unusual to raise two, three hundred dollars. Which could help get a lot of voters out to the polls in local races where a few votes can make all the difference.

Franni baked well over a hundred apple pies over the next couple years—for volunteers, for state legislators, even for Walter Mondale.

During a crowded bean feed in Princeton, I watched a guy in his sixties pointing to Franni and asking a friend, "Who's that?"

"That's the pie lady."

"Oh! The pie lady!"*

* * *

If 2006 was a test run for a potential campaign, the results couldn't have been more encouraging.

We raised more than a million dollars for Midwest

---

* At one point during the campaign, a reporter from the *Economist* came out to spend a day on the trail. Later, our press team got an email from the *Economist*'s dogged fact-checker seeking to confirm a quote from a campaign spokesman, who had said, "You think the crust is going to collapse, but the apples go all the way to the top." Was this right? We were happy to confirm: The apples did indeed go all the way to the top.

Values PAC and helped elect dozens of candidates in Minnesota and around the country. DFLers across the state kept telling me they hoped I would run, and the crowds that showed up at bean feeds made me feel like I'd have plenty of support if I did.

So not only did running feel like it might be a lot of fun, it felt like I might just have a good chance at pulling it off. And more important, the more time I spent talking with Minnesotans, the more I wanted to be their senator.

All year, as I met with teachers and nurses and farmers and folks from all walks of life, I appreciated how decent, hardworking, loving, innovative, and compassionate they were. And as I did, I couldn't help but get excited at the prospect of working for them in Washington. The idea of running had become less and less about beating Norm Coleman, and more and more about improving people's lives.

As Democrats celebrated their big win in November 2006, it was time for me to make a final decision about running. If I was going to beat an incumbent, I'd have to start early.

Franni was all in. But, of course, we wanted the kids to have a say.

"Everyone has a veto," I announced at Thanksgiving dinner. We discussed the pros and cons. Joe expressed some qualms about the time I'd be away from the family, especially if I won. "What do you want me to do?" I asked. "Give speeches for a lot of money and write a book now and then?"

"That sounds pretty good," Joe said, only half kidding. But both kids were on board. I think they could see how badly I wanted to do it.

"Okay," Thomasin said. "But if you have something to tell us, tell us now." Essentially, my daughter was saying, "I'm all for this, unless you've done something horrible that we don't want to know about." But aside from the chainsaw massacre Franni and I had participated in years ago on the way to a Satanist orgy, we were clean.

So I had everyone's blessing. Now it was just up to me. Did I really want to do this? Did I really want to spend every minute of my life making phone calls to raise money, running around the country to raise money, and running around the state to raise money? And what about that public opprobrium thing my friend in New York had mentioned?

The time had come to look up "opprobrium" in the dictionary. Trembling with anxiety, I went to the family dictionary on our dictionary stand and thumbed to the O's. "Opprobrium," I read: "harsh criticism or censure."

Oh, was that all? I could handle that! After all, I had written *Stuart Saves His Family* and produced *SNL* during the Anthony Michael Hall season. I had nothing to fear from public scorn.

I gave myself till the new year to make the final call. In the meantime, as I had done the previous three Christmases, I went with the sergeant major of the Army's USO tour to Kuwait, Iraq, and Afghanistan for two weeks. It seemed like as good a place as any to do a gut check.

Many of the troops we met that year were on their third, fourth, or fifth tour of duty and had served in both Iraq and Afghanistan. Confirming the reports we'd heard back home, many told us that neither war was going well.

The toll on our troops was mounting. More than three thousand of our men and women had been killed in action in Iraq and Afghanistan. Of those who came home, many were returning with limbs missing and suffering from traumatic brain injury, the signature wound of the post-9/11 wars.

The emotional wounds were mounting, too. The chances of post-traumatic stress rose exponentially with each deployment.

But we learned that more than explosive devices, more than bullets, more than anything else, what our troops feared was a "Dear John" letter. Something they probably had in common with military men from previous wars, though now a "Dear Jane" letter was also a possibility. On some bases, soldiers taped their letters up on a wall of heartache.

This was our fourth year of shows with the sergeant

major of the Army. The first year our show was two and a half hours, which we worried was too long. It wasn't. The second year it was three hours. The third year, three and a half hours. That fourth year, we did a four-hour show. And they loved every minute of it, even if, like at the show at Camp Phoenix in Kabul, it meant standing in 29-degree cold for four long hours.

At the end of each show, the Army band played a number of tunes that we all sang along to: "God Bless America"; "Stand by Me"; and a Toby Keith song, "American Soldier."

> Oh, and I don't want to die for you, but if
>   dyin's asked of me
> I'll bear that cross with honor, 'cause freedom
>   don't come free

I will never, ever forget the feeling I had singing that song, watching our servicemen and -women swaying back and forth, arm in arm, belting out those words, and meaning them with every fiber of their being.

It made me feel a little silly for being so worried about the long days, or the nights not spent sleeping in my own bed, or the nasty attacks on my character, that would come with running for Senate. If you replace the word "die" in the song with "be insulted personally," you'll note that it loses much of its power.

From that day forth, I resolved, I would never

complain about any of the inconveniences or indignities that might come with running for office.

No, that's not true. I complained a lot. I still complain a lot. A lot of this book is in fact me complaining.

But, hell, I felt like I could do some good. And spending two weeks with all these men and women who were risking far more than I would ever have to risk made me even more motivated to do as much good as I could, even if it would never compare to the sacrifices they were making for me and my fellow Americans.

As it turned out, it was actually a pretty easy decision. I was going to run.

Chapter 9

The DeHumorizer™

In the rare cases where running for the Senate is some-one's first foray into politics, the candidate has gener-ally had some notable success in another field, most often business or the Spanish-American War. These first-time Senate candidates generally fall into one of two categories.

Category 1: "I've been successful because I'm incredibly smart, I've always followed my own instincts even when people said I was wrong, and I know what the hell I'm doing. I don't need to listen to any-one's advice!" This apparently only works when you're running for president. And get help from the Rus-sians.

Category 2: "I've been successful in my field, and one reason I've been successful is that I know what I don't know and when I should rely on expert advice. One thing I *definitely* know is that I have *no idea* how to run for office. I better get some advice from experienced people!"

I fell squarely into Category 2. As I would have ample opportunity to prove throughout the campaign, my own political instincts were not foolproof. But at least they were good enough to indicate from the jump that I'd need a lot of help to pull this off.

This worried many of my friends who knew that I was thinking of running. "Please, Al!" they'd beg me. "Whatever you do, don't listen to those political consultants! They'll just make you sound like every other candidate!" Or: "Please, puh-leeeeeze don't hire a bunch of political consultants! Political consultants are just Beltway whores!"

One friend who didn't feel that way was political consultant Mandy Grunwald. I first met Mandy in 1993, when she was working for President Bill Clinton. Since then, she had made ads for both Paul Wellstone and Amy Klobuchar, so she knew Minnesota.

When I floated the idea of running for the Senate to Mandy, she said, "Don't. It's a horrible life." So my friends needn't have worried: I was perfectly capable of rejecting advice from a political consultant.

Mandy agreed to help me with my campaign, but she cautioned that she'd be very busy with her work for Hillary Clinton's 2008 presidential race. In fact, as I discovered in trying to find a campaign manager, a lot of the political talent in the country had already signed up for a presidential campaign, be it for Hillary, for Barack Obama (who landed Jeff Blodgett), or for John Edwards, who at the time seemed like a fine fellow.

Heading into 2007, the closest thing I had to a campaign manager was Andy Barr, a whip-smart[*] baby-faced twenty-three-year-old who had been working for me since he was a sophomore at Harvard. Andy had been a key member of TeamFranken, the ragtag gang of goofballs who'd helped research *Lies and the Lying Liars Who Tell Them.*

After graduating, Andy joined the radio show, and at 2 p.m. central he would shift from soundboard engineer and radio sidekick to political director of Midwest Values PAC, which meant he fielded requests for appearances and donations and acted as my body man at bean feeds.[†]

---

[*] I noticed that in *Double Down*, their narrative of the 2012 presidential campaign, Mark Halperin and John Heilemann promiscuously use the adjective "whip-smart" to describe individual staffers in both the Obama and Romney campaigns. Let's see how many times I can use it as a crutch before it wears out its welcome.

[†] A "body man" on a campaign is the person (male or female) who makes sure you stay on schedule, briefs you about the people you're about to meet and any issues you should know about, and collects business cards from supporters who want to donate money or invite you to another bean feed or give you their screenplay that's just perfect for Eddie Murphy.

MVP's other staffer was the whip-smart* David Benson, twenty-six, who had some actual campaign experience—about eighteen months' worth, some of it working for South Dakota senator Tom Daschle.

David proved extremely capable when it came to the nuts and bolts of campaign management: things like budgets, campaign finance regulations, and human resources. For example, he was the one who realized that we needed a frank and somewhat grim employee handbook, covering things like how to report expenses or bomb threats. And how to act outside the office:

> You work for a political campaign, which means that, whether you're on the clock or not, your actions leave an impression and ultimately affect people's perception of Al and of our organization. Sucks for you, but this is the life you chose.

Traveling around the state with me in 2006, Andy had gotten to know the young organizers who worked for the state party or for other campaigns. Several soon joined our team—like the burly, bald, resourceful Dusty Trice, who always knew a terrifying amount of Minnesota political gossip and couldn't be stumped by any logistical request. Need three hundred red, white, and

---

* Wow, that was fast.

blue kazoos by midnight? Looking for a DFL-friendly coffee shop for an event in Beltrami County? Want a couple donkeys to march in your July Fourth parade? Dusty's answer was always the same: "I got a guy."

The next iteration of TeamFranken was coming together. What they lacked in experience, they made up for in youthful enthusiasm and general whip-smartness. Campaign manager or no campaign manager, I was ready to get started.

* * *

You cannot be a candidate for public office and have a radio show on the air. At least not according to the Federal Election Commission and the Federal Communications Commission. And so in a nod to my commitment to adhere to federal law, I announced that I was running for the United States Senate on February 14, 2007—Valentine's Day—as I signed off the air for the last time.

Then Franni and I went home and spent a romantic evening calling friends for money.

Meanwhile, we released a seven-minute web video featuring me talking directly to the camera—telling Minnesotans my story and Franni's, assuring them that I was ready to take seriously the responsibility I was asking for, and explaining that I was running to restore the middle class.

Not for the first or last time, I invoked Paul Wellstone's

words: "The future belongs to those who are passionate and work hard."

That afternoon, the chairman of the Minnesota GOP, Ron Carey, held a press conference. "In the spirit of Minnesota Nice, and in the spirit of Valentine's Day, I'd like to welcome Al Franken into the race, and offer a gift basket to Al on behalf of the Republican Party of Minnesota."

I know what you're thinking: "That was awfully sporting of him. I guess people *are* nice in Minnesota!" But hold on. See, the basket was filled with stuff like a map of the state, because "for over the last thirty years, Al has largely lived in Los Angeles and New York City." Which was true, except for the Los Angeles part.

To "help Al with his anger," there was also a DVD copy of *Anger Management*, starring "his sidekick, Adam Sandler,"* and to "help Al keep up with what is happening in Hollywood," there was an issue of *Entertainment Weekly*.

There were a bunch of other things that he had picked up at CVS, but you get the idea.

In addition to painting me as a short-tempered carpetbagger, Carey also released to the press the first of what would be hundreds of research documents

---

* Adam, of course, played my sidekick in our very popular *Wayne's World* movies.

detailing examples of stuff I'd said or written over thirty-five years in comedy that Republicans said proved I was profane, rude, and just plain out of touch with Minnesota values.

This was my first brush with the DeHumorizer™, a $15 million machine Republicans built using state-of-the-art Russian technology. The DeHumorizer™'s function was to take a joke and strip away everything that made it, well, a joke.

When you do satire, you make use of things like irony: saying one thing while clearly meaning its opposite. And I'm pretty sure Republicans know what irony is, because Ron Carey made extensive use of it in his press conference.

But with the DeHumorizer™ stripping away anything that made it clear I was engaging in irony (or hyperbole, or ambiguity, or any number of other comic devices), Republicans could simply present my words to Minnesotans at face value. Without their comedic context, those words often weren't funny anymore. And in fact, they could appear downright offensive.

Here's an example. In *Rush Limbaugh Is a Big Fat Idiot*, I was satirizing Republicans' willingness to balance the budget on the backs of the elderly (as well as their chronic underfunding of NASA), and I jokingly suggested that we kill two birds with one stone: Just start sending the elderly into space and don't worry about whether we actually get them back. Continuing to riff on this modest proposal, I added another idea:

> Every Sunday, we put an elderly (or terminally ill) person in a rocket, fire it over the Snake River, and put it on pay-per-view. The revenues go straight into reducing the debt.

Did you laugh at that? No? Hmm. Well, did you at least understand that I wasn't actually proposing to murder elderly Americans? Okay. Good.

But the DeHumorizer™ removed the setup that made it clear that I was engaging in irony to further a satirical argument that was actually making a serious point. And in the Republicans' research document, it just read:

> FRANKEN PLAN TO REDUCE DEBT: BLAST THE ELDERLY IN ROCKETS OVER SNAKE RIVER AND PUT IT ON PAY-PER-VIEW.
>
> "Every Sunday, we put an elderly (or terminally-ill person) in a rocket, fire it over the Snake River, and put it on pay-per-view. The revenues go straight into reducing the debt."

The DeHumorizer™ was up and running.

* * *

Fortunately, so was the Franken campaign. The day after the announcement, I visited a health clinic in Minneapolis where my friend Dr. Margie Hogan worked. I spent time meeting with health care providers and patients and listening to some of the horror stories that were commonplace before the passage of the Affordable Care Act.

One of the stories Margie told me became a mainstay of my stump speech. It involved an incredibly promising seventeen-year-old girl from a Hmong family* who was doing college-level work as a junior in high school. But she had lupus. And her family earned just enough money to no longer qualify for MinnesotaCare, a program that covered low-income families in the state. The girl lost her health insurance.

Lupus is a chronic disease, and the medication that controls it is extremely expensive. The girl told her parents to stop buying it so they could afford to take care of the other kids in the family. It broke their hearts, but she was right: They couldn't afford the medicine,

---

* During the Vietnam War, there was a secret war in Laos. The Hmong, a mountain people in Laos, fought on our side during that war. Because of the Hmong, there are thousands fewer American names on the Vietnam War Memorial wall in D.C. After the war, hundreds of thousands of Hmong fled from the Communist Laotian regime, and over one hundred thousand came to the United States. Today, the thriving Minnesota Hmong community numbers over sixty thousand, the second-largest in the country after California.

not with everything else weighing on the family budget. So they stopped buying it.

The next time Margie saw the girl was six weeks later, back in the hospital. But this time, she was in the emergency room, suffering from renal failure. She had to be put on dialysis, and doctors thought she might have to be on dialysis for the rest of her life.

"Now, that's wrong," I would tell crowds that had invariably gone quiet by this point in the story. "But it's not just wrong—it's stupid! How much is it going to cost our system to give her dialysis throughout her life? And how much is this going to cost *her*, in terms of her potential and her quality of life?"

According to the most recent data when my campaign began, there were 46.6 million Americans living without health insurance, including 21.5 million who worked full-time and, worst of all, 8.3 million children. And on my radio show, I talked about this issue all the time with guests like Elizabeth Warren, who told me that half of all bankruptcies in America were tied to a medical problem.

But at bean feeds, I met people who had lived it. Or who would tell me about their sister or their cousin who had lived it. And traveling around Minnesota, stopping in cafés and coffee shops and VFW halls, I couldn't help but notice the flyers up on bulletin boards announcing barbecues or potlucks or spaghetti dinners to benefit families that had gone broke because someone had gotten very sick or been in a terrible accident.

Getting to universal health care was always going to be a central focus of my campaign. But now, instead of talking about it just as a policy issue, I was also talking about it as a personal issue—because that's what it was for so many Minnesotans.

* * *

After that first event, we hit the road, holding two jam-packed labor rallies in northeastern Minnesota—one at the Labor Temple in Duluth, and another at a union hall in the tiny town of Nashwauk on the Iron Range.

The Range sits on the richest deposits of iron ore in the country. "Rangers" have been providing the iron ore for America's blast furnaces for well over a hundred years. You may never have wondered where the ore for your blast furnace comes from, but if you have, the answer is that almost certainly it comes from the Iron Range.

The Range is largely Democratic because Rangers are heavily unionized. But they like their guns, they're socially conservative (though they have a lot more bars than churches), and even though Rangers live in and care for one of the most beautiful parts of the country, they're not terribly fond of environmentalists. I know what you're thinking: These sound like the kind of Democrats who wound up voting for Donald Trump. And you know what? You're right. A lot of them did.

I got along well with Rangers in part because I was a member of four unions myself: the Writers Guild, the Screen Actors Guild, the American Federation of Television and Radio Artists, and the Directors Guild.

Labor in Minnesota didn't really care that my unions were in jobs where you don't get your hands dirty, or lift stuff, or fix anything except a script. What they cared about was that I paid my dues—literally, that I was a member in good standing. And that I understood what labor has done for this country. Unions gave us the forty-hour workweek, the weekend, and the middle class.

As we kept traveling the state, I met countless people at informal coffee-shop get-togethers, or while I grabbed a bite at restaurants, or just waiting in line to pee at a SuperAmerica. The stories people told me began to inform what I said on the stump—and they still inform what I do as a senator.

For example, at one point early on in the campaign, we started doing roundtables on college campuses— small events where I'd try to do more listening than talking. The skyrocketing cost of college was always the first thing that would come up: Back when kids like Franni had used them to go to college, a full Pell Grant paid for 80 percent of a college education, but now it was down to 35 percent.

Students I met were working twenty, thirty, even a full forty hours a week just to pay tuition—and that's in addition to going to school full-time. Then, at a roundtable at MSU-Mankato, I met a student named Casey Carmody, who told me that despite working forty hours a week, he still couldn't afford his tuition—so he'd resorted to selling his blood plasma.

In the car between events, I'd look out the window at the beautiful Minnesota landscape and think about how these issues I'd spent so many years talking about really affected people, resolving to do something to improve their lives.

Okay, that's not true. Mostly, I made fund-raising calls, because that's what you have to do in the car. But sometimes, while I waited for people's outgoing voicemail messages to finish so I could leave a message inviting them to a fund-raiser, I thought about Margie's lupus patient. Or Casey Carmody, selling his blood to get an education. Or the miner in Hibbing who asked me, "What are you gonna do to protect my pension?" Or the parents of soldiers serving in Iraq who asked me whether I could do anything to bring their son or daughter home.

* * *

We finished our kickoff tour with a big Saturday afternoon rally at my junior high school in St. Louis Park, just a couple blocks from where I grew up. Twelve hundred enthusiastic supporters ignored a driving snowstorm and packed into the gym, with hundreds donating and signing up to volunteer.

When I got home from the St. Louis Park rally, I decided to check out the prestigious Internet to see if anyone had had any reaction to our incredible display of grassroots energy. I quickly found a website called "Minnesota Democrats Exposed," where I read a headline saying something to the effect of, "Disastrous Turnout at Franken Rally." Underneath was a picture of a nearly empty gym with our campaign signs hanging forlornly on the walls. Apparently whoever had taken the photo had gotten in early and shot it before the crowd was let in.

I showed this to Andy, who said, "Yeah. That's Michael Brodkorb. He's a right-wing blogger."

"Oh," I said. "Well. He doesn't seem very ethical." I was more confused than angry. Why would anyone do that?

You may be thinking, "Aren't you the guy who wrote several books about how Republicans love to lie?" I know. I guess it's just a little different when it happens to you.

But I have to say, it was hard to resist the impulse to set the record straight when Republicans and their mouthpieces would lie about me, even when it was something small like how many people had shown up for a rally.

And it was even harder when they would lie about

my career in comedy. Every time I was attacked (very often unfairly) for something I'd said or written, I'd say that I understood the difference between what a satirist does and what a senator does, and assure Minnesotans that I wouldn't embarrass them in Washington. Which was true. But it always felt a little wrong. What I really *wanted* to do was put these words back through a ReHumorizer and turn them back into jokes again.

Unfortunately, there's a saying in politics: "When you're explaining, you're losing." As I would eventually learn (if not necessarily accept), in a campaign, you can't correct every intentional or accidental misinterpretation of your words, or your record, or your ideas. And you especially can't litigate comedy.

Chapter 10

I Attempt to Litigate Comedy

Shortly after the campaign began, Eric Black, a political writer for the *Minneapolis Star Tribune*, asked to interview me on the topic of how my comedy past was relevant to my run for office.

I was thrilled: Eric seemed to me to be an incredibly sharp journalist and I was confident that he would understand, and relay to his readers, how my career as a comedy writer and satirist had prepared me for politics by training me to pick out absurdities and inconsistencies and speak truth to power.

My team was horrified. But I was very committed to winning this unwinnable argument. So Andy called in reinforcements.

Jess McIntosh, 25, was the communications director

for the state DFL Party, and had a well-earned reputation for talking candidates out of doing stupid things
that they wanted to do. Andy set up a phone call to
have Jess talk me out of doing the interview with
Eric.

It went very well. Jess explained a few things. First
and foremost, the campaign was trying to get the
media to focus *less* on my career in comedy and *more*
on my public policy positions.

Oh. Right. I remembered that.

Also, she continued, even though she was sure I
could explain the relevance of my previous career in
a very clear and convincing way, no matter how persuasive I was, there was no guarantee that Eric's story
would end up being helpful.

Eric shared a blog with a conservative columnist
named Doug Tice, who also happened to be the *Star
Tribune*'s political editor. Both were obsessed with
what Tice referred to as my "outbursts," which, he
opined, were "too crude" to print.

As a work-around, Tice referred readers directly
to "the estimable Michael Brodkorb of Minnesota Democrats Exposed." Yup, the same not-very-
ethical guy who had lied about our rally in St. Louis
Park.

For example, Tice linked to a Brodkorb post about
a line in *Lies and the Lying Liars* in which I joked that

I wanted to title my next book *I Fucking Hate Those Right-Wing Motherfuckers!**

Now, remember a few chapters ago, when I mentioned that my next book after this one will be called *The Sorrow and the Gavel: The Sad Inner Lives of U.S. Senators*? Did you laugh at that? No? Not even a little? Wow. You're a tough nut to crack. Okay, but you got that I am not *actually* planning to write a book with that title, right? You picked up on the irony? It would be ridiculous for a United States senator to write that book. And that's why it's a joke.

Well, this was another example of the same comic trope. In *Lies*, I had been refuting Republican attacks on the Clinton administration's counterterrorism strategy, and examining the shortcomings in approaches to fighting terrorism under Presidents Reagan, H. W. Bush, and W. Then I wrote:

> But you know what, I don't want to get into a whole partisan politics thing here. Not in this book, anyway. We'll leave that for my next book, *I Fucking Hate Those Right-Wing Motherfuckers!*, due out in October 2004. I'm hoping

---

* I know I promised I wouldn't swear in this book, but I'm just quoting from a blog endorsed by the largest paper in Minnesota, so I hope this exception is okay.

it will "fire up the troops" for the final weeks of the campaign season.

The joke, of course, was that I was already *being* partisan in my very partisan book entitled *Lies and the Lying Liars Who Tell Them: A Fair and Balanced Look at the Right*. But I was doing it in an austere, civil tone, which contrasted with the vulgarity in the fake title— I'm sorry. I know this is pedantic. But it's also kind of obvious, right?

After the phone call in which Jess talked me out of helping Eric Black with his blog post, we hired her as press secretary. And on her first day, she staffed me at an event at the Hubert Humphrey Institute of Public Affairs in Minneapolis. It was a panel of important political people, and the audience was made up of important political people who weren't on the panel.

After the program, we spotted Gwen Walz, a friend and the wife of Congressman Tim Walz, in the crowd. Jess suggested I go say hi.

As she tells it, "Until that day, I never understood when mothers of missing children would say, 'I only had my back turned for a second.' I only had my back turned for a second. When I looked back, there was Gwen, walking toward the door, Al-less."

Where was Al? I was standing in an aisle, surrounded by important Minnesota politicos, picking a fight with Eric Black. Now, going at it in public with a widely respected political journalist is a bad idea for a candidate under any circumstances. What made it worse was the substance of the argument. I believed that Eric understood that *I Fucking Hate Those Right-Wing Motherfuckers!* was a *joke.* And I wasn't going to back down until he admitted it.

"C'mon, you know I wasn't going to write a book with that title! No one could possibly think I was going to write a book with that title!! YOU COULDN'T EVEN SELL THAT BOOK IN A BARNES AND NOBLE, FOR GODSAKES!!!"

Jess sprinted over, making her way through the gathering circle of rubberneckers, and put her hand on my back, our team's signal to me that it was time to go (a signal that I never once successfully interpreted during the entire campaign). "Hey Eric," she said, "if you'd like to continue this off-the-record chat, just shoot me an email. We have to go now!"

* * *

It was a long and quiet drive back to headquarters. When we arrived, Jess told Andy what had happened, expecting to be fired on the spot. Andy just sighed. "Yeah, well. He'll do that."

Later, Jess and Andy explained to me that sometimes reporters will pretend not to understand something, or play devil's advocate, just to see how you'll react.

They want to know what puts you on the defensive, what makes you angry, what gets a rise out of you. Eric wasn't being purposefully obtuse.

"How do you know that?" I asked. "I mean, isn't pretending not to understand something, isn't that being purposefully obtuse?"

Andy and Jess could see they had to concede that point to get to the real point. Which was that there is no percentage in arguing with the press. If I wanted to win this election, I was going to have to let go of things.

"Let go and let God," I nodded.

Now Jess and Andy were confused. "It's an Al-Anon expression," I explained.

"Fine," said Jess. "Let go and let God. Great. Whatever. Just don't argue with reporters, okay?"

I nodded again. "I get it. So treat the press like they're alcoholics."

"What?!" said Jess, visibly regretting taking her new job. "No. That's…no. Just…just don't argue with reporters."

I felt like we had all learned some valuable lessons. I learned that in politics, unlike in show business, being right doesn't *give* you the right to be a jerk. I learned that even though aggressively challenging every misstatement and contesting every minor argument had helped me write three *New York Times* number one bestsellers, it wouldn't help me win this race. I learned that campaigns have their own rules, their own laws of physics, and that if I wasn't willing to accept that, I would never get to be a senator.

I would have many more opportunities to learn these lessons over the course of the campaign, because, frankly, they never really sank in.

And for their part, Andy and Jess had learned never to let me out of their sight again, not even for one second.

Chapter 11

Hermann the German and the Pull-Out Couch

That night I went home and told Franni that I had messed up.

Franni said, "Okay, listen. You've spent most of your life as a comedian. When you said something, all that mattered was, 'Is it funny?' Now you're in a totally different situation. Before you open your mouth, you have to ask yourself three questions."

"Okay," I said. "I'm listening."

"First: Is it true?"

"Of course," I insisted. "That's my thing. That's what I do."

Franni nodded. "I know, honey. Okay. Second: Is it necessary?"

"Uh-huh. Like what I did today with Eric Black wasn't necessary?"

"Nope."

"Okay," I asked, "what's the third thing?"

"Is it strategic?"

"And the thing today was not strategic."

"Doesn't sound like it."

I knew, of course, that Franni was right. I had always thought that I could make a seamless transition from comedian to satirist to activist to candidate to senator and then someday, at long last, host of "Weekend Update." And some things *did* come easily. For instance, I'd always been something of a wonk and had followed politics and public policy all my life. So learning about the issues—countercyclical payments on agricultural commodities, workforce training programs, the importance of the 148th Fighter Wing to Duluth's economy—was something I enjoyed.

But I would also have to learn a set of weird and occasionally sociopathic Politician Skills.

For example, you may be familiar with the phenomenon of "trackers." A tracker is someone who works for your opponent's campaign and follows you around with a video camera waiting for you to do or say something incredibly damaging—like telling a baby you're going to raise its taxes or pushing an elderly constituent to the ground.

Republicans had started tracking me early, before I had even announced. And right away, my driver/body man—a tall, self-effacing twenty-three-year-old from

Moorhead, Minnesota, named Kris Dahl—had come up with a plan.

Every time we got out of the car, we'd pretend we were in mid-conversation. Kris would emerge from the driver's side first. Stepping out of the passenger side, I'd say, "Kris, I don't know why you don't just buy the pull-out couch."

"They're uncomfortable," he'd explain.

"They *used* to be. But new technology has changed everything. The pull-out couch people have made some *huge* advances in recent years. Go to a show-room," I'd tell Kris, pretending I didn't notice the college kid walking backward four feet in front of me holding up a video camera.

"I don't know," Kris would say, clearly racked with indecisiveness.

"Kris, you don't need a two-bedroom apartment!" I would yell as the tracker stumbled on the curb, barely maintaining both his balance and his grip on the camera. "I'm telling you, man, the pull-out couch will pay for itself in six months!"

Kris and I would have this exact conversation or a slight variation ("Have you even *gone* to a showroom yet?!") *every time* the tracker taped us getting out of the car. My fervent hope is that some Republican staffer had to spend two years of his or her precious life transcribing hundreds of hours of me trying to persuade Kris Dahl to get a pull-out couch, and that he or she is still wondering whether Kris ever ended up getting one.

Well, good news: He did.

No, he didn't. There was never any pull-out couch.

*   *   *

I figured out that one. What I didn't get much better at was remembering people's names.

Some politicians, like Bill Clinton, are famously good at meeting someone once and then magically recalling their name when they meet three years later in an entirely different context, even if the other guy has lost* 150 pounds. Hubert Humphrey was like that. And so was Bernie Madoff. But most of us aren't. Here's a tip. If you want to get an officeholder to dislike you, go up to him or her and say, "I bet you don't remember my name."

This is why the most important items at fundraisers are name tags. I've gotten very good at turning to speak to someone, my eyes sweeping diagonally over their chest on the way up to their face, and saying, "Hey, Dennis, it's great to see you!"

Trouble remembering names is a wonderful bonding subject for U.S. senators and their spouses. In our first term, Franni and I had a semiregular dinner with three other couples: Diana and Mike Enzi, Republican

---

* Or gained.

of Wyoming; Jill and Tom Udall, Democrat of New Mexico; and Stephanie and Mike Johanns, Republican of Nebraska. It took me five dinners just to remember all of *their* names. And Mike Enzi still calls me "Arnie" now and then.

I happen to love Stephanie Johanns, because she has the best laugh and, even better, laughs at almost anything I say. But one evening, Stephanie made all of us howl with laughter. We were discussing our most awkward moments blanking on the names of constituents. Stephanie painted a picture of a typical political event back in rural Nebraska with folks milling about, chatting and having a great time. Stephanie said she was talking to a small group and then turned around and saw a woman whom she knew, but couldn't place. Stephanie said, "I knew I knew this woman, and I panicked. Then I figured out who she was and said, 'Oh—hi, Mom!'"

* * *

Probably the most ridiculous Politician Skill I had to learn, though, was how to "pivot," a term which basically means "not answer questions."

For example, say a reporter asked me, "In the latest polls, you trail Norm Coleman by twenty points. How can you get DFLers to support you for the endorsement if you're so far behind?"

My instinct would be to answer the question.

But that's not what you're supposed to do. You're supposed to say, "When I go around our state, Minnesotans don't talk about polls. They talk about their kids' education, and how they're worried that they'll go bankrupt if someone in their family gets sick." And so on.

I understood the concept. For some reason, I was unable to use it. I had always been taught by my parents and my teachers to answer questions directly and completely. Which I did for the first ten months of my race, driving my team nuts. But of course, my team was right. Reporters would just use the most interesting (and, usually, unhelpful) sound bites in my lengthy responses to their questions, instead of writing about the message that we wanted to get out that particular day.

Take for example, the "Hermann the German" incident.

New Ulm, a beautiful small city in south-central Minnesota, was founded by German immigrants in the mid-nineteenth century. It boasts an enormous monument to Arminius, the Germanic warrior who led the slaughter of twelve to fifteen thousand Roman soldiers in the Battle of the Teutoburg Forest in 9 A.D., when Jesus was just a kid. Locals call the twenty-seven-foot statue "Hermann the German."

Hermann stands upon a seventy-foot base, so I was literally speaking in Hermann's shadow while addressing a small crowd one fall afternoon in 2007. Now, you should understand that I grew up in St. Louis Park, known statewide as *the* Jewish suburb of Minneapolis.

So here's the situation. I'm a Jew. I grew up in St. Louis Park. I'm in New Ulm standing in the shadow of a massive monument to Hermann the German. *And* I had been in comedy for thirty-five years. So what immediately occurred to me was: "Now, I grew up in St. Louis Park, and we had a much smaller statue than Hermann the German here. Ours was called 'Stu the Jew.'"*

But I didn't! I didn't say it! There was a tracker there—and in the nanosecond that I made the decision *not* to go with "Stu the Jew," I imagined that, put through the DeHumorizer™, Republicans could use the video to intimate that somehow I was blaming the good people of New Ulm for the Holocaust. And then it would get written up not as "Coleman Takes Hilarious Franken Joke Way, Way, Ridiculously out of Context," but as "Republicans Slam Franken for Blaming Holocaust on New Ulm."

So instead I bit the inside of my cheek and talked about universal health care, climate change, and Norm

---

* Okay, in the campaign, the story was known as the "Stu the Jew" incident, not as the "Hermann the German" incident. But I didn't want to spoil it for you.

Coleman's dismal record in the Senate. I was on message! And as we walked back to the car that day, Kris resuming the conversation about his pull-out couch ("Plus, I'd have to drag it up all those stairs…"), I knew that what he was really saying was that he, and the rest of the team, were proud of me.

But a few weeks later, a writer from *New York* magazine came to Minnesota to follow me around and do a story on my campaign. At one point the writer asked me, "Do you ever think of something funny and decide not to say it?"

"Sure," I answered.

"For example?" she asked.

And then I recounted the Stu the Jew story. Because, you see, she had asked me for an example. And of course, Stu the Jew appeared prominently in the article.

Reading the Stu the Jew story in *New York* was a turning point. "Why did I do that?" I thought to myself (immediately after Jess and Andy asked me, "Why did you do that?").

My team pointed out that a perfectly good response to "For example?" would have been, "Gee, I can't think of one offhand." And then *pivot*, by saying, "But you know what isn't a joke? The fact that so many health crises lead to bankruptcies."

It was a learning moment. Unlike the many previous potential learning moments from which I could have learned, but didn't. So I sat down with Jess and did yet another practice session on pivoting. And this time, I was determined to get it right.

A couple of days later I had a sit-down interview with a Minnesota print reporter who had interviewed me a number of times before. I have no recollection of the actual content of the interview, but I distinctly remember the thrill of using a new skill.

Right out of the box, I pivoted to avoid answering a perfectly valid question so I could instead talk about whatever it was I was supposed to talk about that day. And the reporter seemed just fine with it!

So I did it again on the second question. Again, the reporter seemed to have absolutely no problem. On the next question, just for the hell of it, I really overdid it, pivoting gratuitously. Again, I completely got away with it. The rest of the interview involved a string of egregious pivots followed by my hammering home some point or other.

When the interview ended, the veteran reporter turned to Jess and Andy. "Hey, he's getting a lot better!" he said with a smile. "I think he's got a real shot!"

Chapter 12

No Joke

Because I was in comedy for thirty-five years, it was (and sometimes remains) hard to get the national political press to focus on the substance of my message as a candidate. The day after I announced, newspapers nationwide featured some version of what our team would come to call the "No Joke" headline. Stuff like:

No Joke: Franken Announces Senate Bid

No Joke: Franken Running for Senate

Franken Announces Run for Senate:
No Joke

And so on. I imagine that the writers of all these headlines were very pleased with themselves. And to be fair, sometimes you shouldn't overlook the obvious. But it just never stopped.

No Joke: Franken Wins DFL Nomination

No Joke: Franken Wins Recount

Franken Takes Oath of Office
Mondale and Klobuchar Escort New Senator
to Well of Senate for Oath—No Joke

No Joke: Franken Passes Bill to Fund Vaccine for Zika Virus

They're a dog with a bone. They can't help it. And they'll never stop. I know when I shuffle off this mortal coil, some future media outlet will run an item entitled:

No Joke: Former Three-Term Senator Dead at 93

Hell, let's make that "Dead at 106." Seriously.

Chapter 13

Harry and Chuck

My growth as a candidate notwithstanding, I had a big political problem on my hands in those early days. I was running more or less against the wishes of the D.C. Democratic establishment, personified by Senate Majority Leader Harry Reid and Senator Chuck Schumer, chairman of the Democratic Senatorial Campaign Committee (DSCC).

The DSCC can make or break a Democratic Senate candidate's campaign. They make a judgment about whether you're a good candidate, whether you're running a smart campaign—basically, whether you have a shot at winning. And that judgment matters, because even though they won't generally put out a press release declaring you a loser, they make their opinion known to influential politicos.

So if the DSCC doesn't like you, analysts might reflect their pessimism in the horse-race-obsessed coverage that dominates the news. You might have a hard time getting your calls returned by major donors, who may have heard that your race might not be a great investment. You might even have trouble getting senior staff to sign on, because the world of Democratic operatives is small and nobody wants to spend months on a campaign only to lose.

And then, of course, when the general election heats up and it's time for the DSCC to start running ads and investing in field operations, they spend their money strategically. The last thing you want is to find yourself being pummeled with negative ads in October and have the DSCC shrug its shoulders because they think they'd be throwing their money away.

Obviously, the DSCC doesn't want to throw away a seat, either. So they don't usually settle for just being disappointed in the candidate they end up with. Instead, they tend to intervene below the radar to make sure they get a candidate they like. And if you're not a candidate they've specifically recruited to run, trying to earn their support can feel a lot like a hostile job interview.

* * *

First, I met with Harry Reid. I had never met the soft-spoken majority leader before, and didn't quite know what to expect.

The first thing Harry asked me was, "How do you

make a living?" The question didn't completely surprise me. A lot of people don't know that the comedy
they see on television is actually *written*, especially on
a talk show or even a sketch comedy show like *SNL*.
So I explained my career as quickly as possible.

It occurred to me a few years later that Harry might
have been pulling my leg. So I asked him if he had
been joking. Harry said, "No. It's a good first question.
Some guys have no way to make money while they're
running and do funny things with campaign funds."

He meant "funny—illegal," not "funny—haha."

Anyway, after I had explained the comedy business
to Harry, he passed me off to Chuck.

I had known Chuck Schumer since college, where
he had seen me in a one-act play in which I'd played
a character named Bernard, who became transformed
whenever he called himself "Spike." Since I lived in New
York for quite some time and traveled in Democratic
circles all my adult life, I'd run into Chuck many times
over the previous three and a half decades, and he'd
always started each interaction by calling me "Spike"
to remind me that he remembered the play. I found this
slightly irritating, but also kind of adorable.

The day I went to see him in the Senate, he greeted
me with a grin and a hearty "Spike!" And then things
took a turn.

Chuck was very candid, telling me he and the
DSCC were not excited about the idea of my running.

"We should have a 60 percent chance of winning this seat," he explained. "You have about a 40 percent chance."

I made my case: I told him about all the groundwork we had laid, the size and enthusiasm of our rallies, all the money coming in.

But Chuck was looking for someone else, and even asked my opinion of a couple of state legislators he was thinking of recruiting. Both were friends of mine, which I explained to Chuck, not sure what else to say.

Chuck nodded, and apologized for being so frank. I told him I appreciated his honesty. Which was absolutely true. At least I knew where he stood.

And Chuck never called me "Spike" after that.

* * *

While I would need help from the Democratic establishment to win in November, I had my own plan for becoming the DFL nominee. With or without Harry and Chuck on board, it was full speed ahead.

Minnesota's primary was scheduled for September 2008, but traditionally the nomination is won when a candidate is endorsed at the DFL state convention, which was scheduled for June 2008 in Rochester.

The endorsement process was set to begin on February 5, 2008, at local precinct caucuses, where DFLers would meet in their neighborhoods and choose delegates to move on to their senate district or county conventions. At those regional conventions, delegates to the state convention would be elected. And in Rochester, those state convention delegates would join superdelegates (mostly state legislators and party officials) in voting on which candidate to endorse. If you got 60 percent of the state convention delegates, you got the party's endorsement—effectively becoming the nominee.

Because I announced so early—February 14, 2007— we had nearly a full year before caucus night to get ready. What was our plan? Simple: Do everything we could to appeal to the people who were likely to show up on caucus night and participate in the complicated multistep delegate selection process—the bean feed regulars I'd been getting to know since returning to the state. Meanwhile, develop relationships with superdelegates, and compete for the support of unions, environmental organizations, progressive advocacy groups, and other groups whose endorsement carried a lot of weight for party members who were likely to be politically active.

Now, if all this seems a little dry to you, imagine instead the training montage from a *Rocky* movie, with a driving soundtrack and energetic editing. But instead of jumping rope, I'm eating hotdish at an assisted living facility that traditionally has high caucus turnout. Instead of guzzling a dozen raw eggs, I'm being driven five hours to speak for five minutes at the Otter Tail County convention. Instead of hitting a

speed bag, I'm playing phone tag with a state representative who's on the fence.

The grizzled veteran in charge of our field and outreach operation (my Burgess Meredith, if you will) was
twenty-five-year-old James Haggar. James had worked
on Paul Wellstone's last race in 2002, and like many
young (and not-so-young) people who had poured
their hearts and souls into that tragic campaign, he
was initially hesitant about joining mine.

I mentioned earlier that Paul's life, and the tragic
circumstances of his death, and the ugly political
aftermath, made every step in my political journey
feel a little heavier. And I was just Paul's *friend*. The
entire Minnesota DFL community was full of people
who had been at headquarters that October day when
the call came in, who had worked side by side with
Mary McEvoy and Tom Lapic and Will McLaughlin
(the staffers who had died in the crash), whose entire
political consciousness had been shaped by the work
they did for and with Paul and Sheila Wellstone. And
for them it's impossible to overstate just how much
Paul's memory hung over the 2008 campaign.

So when you tried to hire those people, you weren't
just asking them to help you. You were asking them
to *trust* you—to live up to Paul's legacy, and to carry
on his work, and, frankly, to avenge him a little bit.
And that's a lot of trust to ask for. Especially if you are
the kind of candidate who is prone to, say, yelling at a

prominent political reporter about the use of the word "motherfuckers."

It took a few weeks to convince James to come aboard. But when he did, he worked like a guy who had a lot more at stake than just his win-loss record. He put in eighteen- or twenty-hour days, seven days a week, plowing through the pile of cheap candy that was always on his desk and staring up at a whiteboard that listed which way all the key players in the state were leaning—key players like Tom Rukavina, the hilarious, irascible curmudgeon who represented a big slice of the Iron Range in the state legislature.

(A story about Tom: He was once in a parade and a guy he knew called out, "Hey, Tommy! Why do you only care about the poor?" Without missing a beat, Rukavina responded, "You *are* poor, dummy.")

*   *   *

I may have been focused on the kind of patient grass-roots organizing and relationship building I would need to win the DFL endorsement, but I wasn't ignorant of the extremely valid concerns that Chuck had raised about my chances in a general election.

Early on, we hired a pollster, Diane Feldman, another Wellstone veteran whose job it was to help me figure out the right way to talk to the broader audience of Minnesotans about who I was and what I wanted to do as their senator.

We also needed another media consultant, since Mandy was still tied up with Hillary, who was still battling Obama for the presidential nomination. After a few meetings, we hired Saul Shorr, a garrulous bulldog of an adman from Philadelphia who was almost more excited than I was about going after Norm Coleman.

With the team in place, it was time to get some data. The first internal polls we took roughly matched the public polling at the time: I was down by double digits against Coleman.

As we convened our first focus groups in the summer of 2007, our goal was to figure out how to get around the fact that I had an awful lot of edgy, dark, or off-color jokes on the record. Republicans had continued to process joke after joke through the DeHumorizer™, blasting each one out in one irritating press release after another. The question was: How could we fix this?

At the focus groups, Diane handed people a packet of information about me and asked them to underline the stuff that stood out to them. At one session in suburban Edina, she prodded a bit at the part about my using foul language to attack Republicans, rereading that section aloud: "Franken has a history of using inappropriate language, including the 'F' word, and launching personal attacks against public figures including many sitting members of the U.S. Senate. For example, he once said that Republican politicians are shameless dicks."

At that, a woman sat up in her chair. "Oh!"

Diane pounced. "Is it the 'F' word, or..."

There were a few uncomfortable laughs. "I just... I read what was here," said the woman, turning red. "But I thought it was 'shameless ducks.'"

The focus groups were helpful in determining a strategy for handling what from then on was inevitably referred to around our office as the "shameless ducks dossier."

The results were actually pretty surprising. A few of the folks understood that I had been using the language for satiric effect. But in general they were not terribly impressed that I'd spent my entire adult life writing stuff like that.

They didn't think the fact that I had been a successful comedian meant that I was intelligent. So it turned out that telling people I went to Harvard was a good thing, because it reassured them that despite having no experience in politics and having called some people some bad names, I was probably at least smart enough to handle government work. It was the first recorded instance of it being a good idea to tell people you went to Harvard.

The books, it turned out, were also a good thing. People liked that I had written books, because it showed that I had several books' worth of serious thoughts about public policy in my brain, or at least that I had the work ethic to finish writing several books. Basically, the results we got from the focus groups were: Harvard and books—good. Comedy—bad.

This called for a slight change in strategy. For example, Dusty had tracked down a pallet of kazoos somewhere, and when TeamFranken did parades around the state, we had our supporters march playing "Ring of Fire" and other hits on kazoos. We had fun, but after the focus groups, the consultants made it clear: Get rid of the kazoos. Unless we could find some kazoos with the Harvard logo on them. Dusty said he'd look into it.

* * *

As summer turned to fall, I had company on the campaign trail.

Back in April, Mike Ciresi had announced his candidacy. Mike was a successful trial lawyer who had represented the state of Minnesota in the big lawsuit against the tobacco industry, famously pressing the case until the tobacco companies released damaging internal documents, and in the end securing a $6 billion settlement. So Mike was well-known, and also rich, and a serious candidate—my main rival for the DFL endorsement.

But not my only rival. Jack Nelson-Pallmeyer was a professor of peace studies at the University of St. Thomas in St. Paul, tall, white-haired, and distinguished in that "cardigan sweater, corduroy sport coat" kind of way. Jack's campaign was built upon three clear issues: peace, the moral urgency of addressing climate change, and single-payer health care.

I was for all those things in principle, but felt that some of his specific proposals (for example, a 50 percent cut in the Defense Department budget) were not just unrealistic, but irresponsible.

Then there was Jim Cohen, an effusively friendly gadfly who had once run unsuccessfully for the U.S. House in Connecticut. We'd show up at events and he would proclaim, "You don't have to be rich [talking about Mike] or famous [talking about me] to run for the Senate." The crowd agreed, but were also a bit confused about what, having stated what he *wasn't*, Jim *did* bring to the race.

The four of us found ourselves all showing up at the same events, my blue-and-yellow signs competing for space with Mike's yellow-and-red gear, Jack's green, and Jim's none.

*   *   *

Meanwhile, I continued to update Chuck Schumer on our campaign's momentum: We were raising a ton of money, we were rolling up endorsements left and right, and we were taking it to Coleman as best we could. Chuck was happy to hear that things were going well, but still not particularly interested in getting behind me. But over the summer, we'd followed some "advice" (really, a command) from the DSCC and conducted another poll to test our theory that the "shameless ducks" dossier was survivable. The results came in. And when we saw them, we breathed a sigh of relief.

Armed with our poll, we scheduled another trip to Washington to sit down with Reid and Schumer and make our case. At the meeting, we carefully explained that while Minnesotans did have some concerns about my history of "questionable" humor, we had found a response that worked.

Reid interrupted. "What kind of jokes are we talking about?"

We all looked at each other, not sure what to say. Reid tried again, looking at his notes. "It says here, 'Franken made jokes about the Holocaust.' What does that mean?"

Diane handed our poll to Harry and pointed to the joke we had tested: "I think a bad Hanukkah gift for Anne Frank would have been a drum set."*

I watched Harry closely as he read the joke and then... burst out laughing. In fact, he started *shaking* with laughter. It was a surreal moment, sitting nervously with my consultants, watching Harry Reid convulse in hysterics over the idea of Anne Frank playing drums in the attic. Finally, he turned to me.

I just shrugged.

---

* Oddly, it wasn't even my joke. It came from original *SNL* writer Rosie Schuster and found its way into a piece that I got credit for.

Chapter 14

Icarus Soars

That fall, I got a letter from my fourth-grade teacher, Mrs. Molin. It started this way:

> *Dear Mr. Franken,*
>   *If you're the Alan Franken who I taught in the fourth grade at Cedar Manor, then it doesn't surprise me that you are running for the Senate, because you were a very good student.*

This isn't my way of telling you I was a very good student in the fourth grade, though I was. It's my way of telling you about my first campaign commercial. But, seriously, I was a very, very good student in fourth grade.

Anyway, I looked Mrs. Molin up in the phone book* and gave her a call. "You remember me!?" she asked.

---

* A phone book, for those of you born after 1990, is just what it sounds like: a book shaped like a phone.

"Yes, Mrs. Molin. Of course! I remember all my teachers at Cedar Manor." Then I went through my elementary school teachers, working backward. I loved Mr. Knutson, my sixth-grade teacher. And Mrs. Long-abaugh, my fifth-grade teacher. I told Mrs. Molin that she was my favorite, because she was. Then I told her that I didn't much like my third-grade teacher, whom I will not name here.

"Well, she wasn't very nurturing," Mrs. Molin conceded in her adorable seventy-four-year-old Minnesota accent.

I invited Mrs. Molin to a campaign event at a house not far from hers. She came, and I instantly remembered why she had been my favorite. Mrs. Molin, still a small package, is a fireball of positive energy. I did the math and realized that she had been twenty-seven when she taught me to do the math. When I told her that in the fourth grade I thought she was kind of middle-aged, she laughed and gave me a little tweak on the cheek.

When you're a kid, you don't usually learn very much about your teachers. Mrs. Molin was one of seventeen children. Seventeen! She and her husband, Dean, didn't have kids themselves. But over thirty-four years of teaching, she poured her energy and love into her students.

I ran the idea of Mrs. Molin doing my first ad by my media consultants, Mandy and Saul. I sometimes joked that between me and Norm Coleman (who grew up in Brooklyn and sounded like it), I was the only New York Jew in the race who had actually grown up in Minnesota. What better way to establish my roots than to feature my lovable spitfire of a fourth-grade teacher?

Mrs. Molin said, "Okay, Alan!" and we were all set to go. Mandy was with Hillary working on ads for the battle with Obama that would last almost all the way to the convention. So Saul, whose best work generally involved ripping some deserving Republican a new belly button[USS] produced an adorable ad featuring Mrs. Molin.

It was a back-and-forth—Mrs. Molin in a classroom, me at campaign headquarters.

"So, I read about this man running for U.S. Senate and I thought, 'That's the Alan Franken I taught in St. Louis Park.'"

"I got this letter from Mrs. Molin. She wanted to help with the campaign. So I asked her to be in a TV ad."

"A TV ad?" Mrs. Molin offered the camera a perfect look of surprise. But she was immediately game, saying with a swing of her arm, "Okay! Here we go!"

Then Mrs. Molin gave my bio, accompanied by photos from my life. A nerdy, gap-toothed fourth-grader. Getting my diploma at—that's right, she dropped the H-bomb—Harvard.

"He was funny, too," she said, as we cut to a photo of me with the *SNL* cast. "I guess that's why he became a comedian."

"I was really more of a satirist," I protested, still at headquarters.

"Okay, Alan," she said, as if to a nine-year-old. Mrs. Molin went on to say I had written six books. Over a stunning shot of the six books piled on top of each other.

Then to video of me and Franni cooking in our kitchen. "He's been married to Franni for thirty-two years, and they have two grown kids." A photo of Thomasin and Joe looking like two nice, clean-cut human beings who share Franni's and my gene pool.

"And you know he's visited our troops in Iraq and Afghanistan four times." Over pictures of me entertaining the troops.

Then, the reasons I was running. "In the Senate, he'll work to make college affordable, fight for universal health care, and end the war in Iraq." Over pictures of students on a campus, a patient being treated by a friendly, super-competent health care provider, and troops getting off a plane.

Then a shot of me alongside Mrs. Molin in the classroom. "Thanks, Mrs. Molin."

"You're welcome, Alan."

I turned to camera with a delighted smile. "I'm Al...*an* Franken, and I approve this message, because I'm *serious* about fighting for Minnesota families."

We ran the ad for a couple of weeks right before the caucuses, and it was a huge hit. We started getting emails at the campaign from Mrs. Molin's former students and forwarded them on to her. Mrs. Molin would share some of them with me. I will never forget one in particular. I read it to teachers all the time.

Dear Mrs. Molin,

You were my favorite teacher. I wasn't a very good student. I had a hard time with math, and your spelling tests were hard! But you saw that I liked art, and I remember you staying after school one day to paint a window with me. You made me feel special (loved). Now I'm a teacher too. I teach special ed kids. And I try every day to make them feel the way you made me feel. And I just wanted to say thank you.

* * *

On February 5, 2008, Minnesotans gathered for their local caucuses. I spent the night running from caucus site to caucus site, giving the quickest stump speech I could to fire up the crowds. But they were pretty fired up even without my help. Barack Obama had brought new energy to the Democratic primary, and new people to the process. Minnesota's previous record for caucus attendance was around 80,000. That year, we had 214,000.

Best of all, the overwhelming majority of them were supporting me.

The people who had been selected as delegates on caucus night would now go on to their county and senate district conventions, where they would elect the delegates who would get to confer the party's endorsement for U.S. Senate at the state convention on June 7 in Rochester. And since all four DFL candidates had committed to abiding by the convention's endorsement, that was the ticket to taking on Coleman in the general.

Everything was falling into place! We had passed our first test with flying colors. But as Minnesota journalist Doug Grow wrote on caucus night, I still had work to do.

Interestingly, Franken was the most cautious in assessing the situation: "It sounds like we sent a lot of people to the district conventions."

That's not exactly a snappy response, Franken was told.

"Many a slip twixt cup and lip," he said.

A reporter and a couple of Franken supporters looked at the candidate, blankly.

"What did you say?"

"You guys never heard that?" said Franken.

He went slower for the reporter.

"Many a slip twixt..."

"Twixt?" the reporter asked.

"Yes," said Franken. "Many a slip TWIXT cup and lip."

"What does that mean?"

"I don't know who said it," said Franken. "Google it. But it means a lot can go wrong between the start and finish."

Chapter 15

Twixt Cup and Lip

On March 10, 2008, the *New York Times* broke the news that the governor of New York, Eliot Spitzer, had been a client of a high-end escort service, spending thousands of dollars on prostitutes while serving as New York's attorney general and in his current position as chief executive of the Empire State.

Watching the news in my tiny office at campaign headquarters in St. Paul, I was shocked. And more than a little bummed out. I had really admired Spitzer, who had been a crusader for progressive reforms, taking on Wall Street banks and powerful corporations with an incomparable fearlessness, almost a swagger. I had even thought of him as a potential vice presidential candidate in 2008, or maybe someday the first Jewish president. Now all that was out the window.

The more I thought about it, the more depressed I got. I thought about how hard he must have worked to win his first election, and how many people had helped, and how important it must have been to all of them that he get the chance to make a difference. I thought about all the important work he had done as attorney general and was now doing as governor, and what would happen to his mission of reining in corporate abuse. I thought about other politicians who had made similar mistakes, like Gary Hart, who, confronted with rumors that he was cheating on his wife, dared reporters to follow him. When some reporters actually followed him they discovered that he was in fact cheating on his wife. Hart's behavior wasn't just self-destructive—it was batcrap[USS] crazy. How could these guys risk everything that they'd worked for like that? How could they live with themselves after letting so many people down?

While I was staring off into the middle distance, musing about the fallibility of man, a great cheer erupted out in the bullpen. Still lost in thought, I opened the door to my office. By now, our campaign had expanded: We had dozens of staff and interns, most of them frighteningly young, doing—well, at some point I lost track of what everyone was doing, or, indeed, who everyone was. And now they were all running around excitedly, high-fiving and fist-bumping and doing weird young-people hugs, toasting each other with these horrible little 5-Hour Energy shots that everyone seemed to be hooked on. It was like V-E Day.

"What's going on?" I asked, to no one in particular.

Someone interrupted the revelry long enough to fill the candidate in: "Ciresi dropped out!"

"Oh," I said.

It's not that this wasn't good news. I was now the presumptive nominee!

But I was still stuck in my funk, distracted by the tragic fall of Eliot Spitzer. And I couldn't help but feel a strange sense of foreboding. No, I wasn't worried about getting caught patronizing high-end escorts, or, for that matter, escorts at any price point.

The truth, however, was that Ciresi dropping out was kind of a mixed blessing. We'd been laser-focused on the convention in June, but now the general election was effectively under way, three months ahead of schedule. We were the dog that caught the car. And in retrospect, it's clear that we weren't ready for what was coming next.

* * *

It started with a post on Michael Brodkorb's blog, "Minnesota Democrats Exposed." Apparently the company I had set up to handle the business side of my writing and public speaking work (called Alan Franken, Inc., or AFI for short), had had a $25,000 judgment filed against it in New York State for failing to carry workers' compensation and disability insurance from June 2002 to March 2005.

This was news to me. And that was exactly the problem.

When you run for office, you generally commission what's known as a "self-research book" long before you launch your campaign. It's basically an investigation of yourself that reveals stuff like old workers' comp judgments so you can take care of them before they're sprung on you by hostile bloggers.

We had hired a firm to do that—but we should have hired them earlier. As it happened, they had recently discovered the workers' comp judgment during a public records search, but were waiting to tell us about it until they had finished looking into it, which I guess would have been a thoughtful gesture had it turned out to be nothing worth worrying about.

In any event, it was embarrassing not to be able to explain how the screwup had occurred. But it wasn't a fatal blow. We continued slowly gaining on Coleman in the polls, and even Harry and Chuck were gradually thawing.

Meanwhile, however, Republicans were digging into AFI's activities in the state of California, where we had briefly registered the company while I was working on *Lateline*, a short-lived sitcom I had done for NBC.

Soon, Michael Brodkorb had another scoop: AFI hadn't terminated the registration correctly, and when it had stopped paying the small annual "franchise fee," the registration was "forfeited." Which sounds bad. And it was embarrassing to get caught off guard again. But it was easy enough to explain: My accountant had simply sent in the wrong form to notify the state that I was no longer doing business there.

Republicans, however, had something else up their sleeve. They pointed to news reports about speeches I had given in California and suggested that since I hadn't been paying the franchise fee, perhaps I'd dodged paying taxes on the income I'd earned there as well.

Franni and I knew that was ridiculous—we pay our taxes every year. But we realized that we had paid taxes on the income from those speeches to the state we were living in (until 2006, New York), and not to the states where I had done the speeches.

In other words, the good news was that I hadn't committed the unpardonable sin of evading taxes. The bad news was that I had committed the relatively understandable but harder-to-explain mistake of paying those taxes to the wrong place.

And the worst news was that we were on defense yet again—it took us a long, horrible weekend to reconstruct years of back taxes. We sent $70,000 in checks to seventeen very confused states that didn't generally get sent money they hadn't asked for (and requested corresponding refunds from New York, where we had overpaid our taxes by almost exactly the same amount). And I spent an entire day explaining what had happened in a series of agonizing interviews.

It was not my favorite day of the campaign. But it felt good to be able to lay it all out there. And after a week of brutal press, the stories were less awful than we'd feared. It was an honest mistake, and when we learned about it, we fixed it. People could understand that.

Especially people who were suddenly realizing they'd made the same mistake themselves. For example, presented with an opportunity to beat up on me on the Fox News morning show *Fox and Friends*, Newt Gingrich gave me a pass. Watching it, I realized, "I bet *Newt* doesn't pay taxes to the right states for *his* speeches, either!"

We lived to fight another day. And I was proud of how I'd handled the crisis. I'd always known that sometimes people are judged more by how they deal with a mistake than by the mistake itself. At the beginning of the campaign, I'd even considered deliberately making a mistake so I could be seen as handling it well. And as it turned out, I didn't need to!

* * *

Still, Coleman was now up by seven points in the polls, and as we'd gotten sidetracked by workers' comp and taxes, Jack Nelson-Pallmeyer, the peace candidate, had begun to gain some traction in an endorsement race that most people assumed was over.

But we felt like we were okay—in large part because we finally managed to land a campaign manager.

I'd known Stephanie Schriock for a few years, since she was the finance director for Howard Dean's 2004 presidential campaign, where she had revolutionized grassroots small-dollar fund-raising.

I had actually tried to hire her to do the same job for Midwest Values PAC back in 2005. She'd passed, choosing instead to manage Jon Tester's successful 2006 Senate campaign in her home state of Montana.

But she and I had really hit it off, and we knew she had ties to Minnesota (her grandmother lived here and she'd gone to college in Mankato). As we'd gained momentum in the early spring, Chuck Schumer had grown more willing to help us out. And as we'd lost momentum in the late spring, he realized that the best way to help us out was to convince Stephanie to come back to Minnesota to manage my race.

She finally agreed to come on board, promising that she'd arrive in Minnesota the week before the June 7 convention. And despite everything, we still felt like things were more or less on track, with the endorsement still mine to lose and Coleman within reach.

And then.

Chapter 16

Public Opprobrium

The January 2000 issue of *Playboy* magazine was its Millennial Issue, and they had asked important writers like William F. Buckley, father of American conservatism, and prolific science-fiction author Isaac Asimov to pen thoughtful articles pegged to the turning of the millennium.

They also asked me to write something funny.

Since it was *Playboy*, I thought I'd write a parody of a *Playboy* article—specifically, the kind of feature they always used to have about some hip new technology that every hip guy should be hip to. You know, hi-fis, Jet Skis, or, in this case, since we were talking about the future, virtual sex. Funny idea, right?

So I wrote about my visit to a citadel of higher learning, the Minnesota Institute of Titology. As you may have guessed from its name, the institute was fictitious,* as were all of the activities depicted in the piece, which devolved into a lengthy and vivid description of my participation in various "virtual sex" acts. I had given the piece the unfortunate title of "Porn-O-Rama," proving that, as of late 1999, I hadn't been planning a run for political office.

CUT TO: May 19, 2008, three weeks before the DFL convention. Republicans were trying to make hay over a fund-raiser I'd held in Chicago with Christie Hefner, the progressive activist and daughter of *Playboy* founder Hugh Hefner. And to call further attention to my unsavory association with the Hefner dynasty, Michael Brodkorb published the text of "Porn-O-Rama" on "Minnesota Democrats Exposed."†

Once again, it came as a surprise to our team. Although this time it was because the research firm we'd hired had only looked for articles listed as being written by "Al Franken," and this one was listed in the Nexis database under the byline "Franken, Al."‡

---

* In a later focus group, a number of women expressed relief when Diane clarified that the Minnesota Institute of Titology was not, in fact, a real thing.

† You gotta hand it to the guy! And, actually, that's exactly how it worked. Republican researchers did the actual legwork on all this fantastic "oppo" and just handed it to Brodkorb, who would dutifully write it up on his blog.

‡ Not kidding.

A stricken Jess McIntosh walked into my office, where Kris Dahl was cracking the whip on another endless call time session. "Al, do you remember writing an article for *Playboy* where you talked about having sex with robots?"

"Oh, yeah. It was kinda funny! Have you read it?"

"Um, yes."

"Uh-huh. Did *you* think it was funny?"

Jess turned to Kris. "Can we have the room?"

*   *   *

Republicans, as you might expect, did their best to turn "Porn-O-Rama" into a big story. A group of GOP women legislators wrote an open letter attacking me for "demeaning and degrading women."[*]

Meanwhile, we got a stern email from an "Eric White" of a company called VR Innovations.

SUBJ: Trademark Use

Please advise Al, the term "Virtual Sex Machine" is a trademark of VR Innovations/Eric J. White, and was in 2000 when he wrote the article for Playboy (reference USPTO.Gov). We chose not to pursue the matter then, but will not tolerate confusion with our

---

[*] I know this seems quaint, but back in 2008, Republicans did not consider "demeaning and degrading women" to be senatorial, let alone presidential.

trademark today as some sort of "political attention getter."

If he chooses to use that term in his upcoming speeches, please be sure it is in reference to our products and services.

Thank you.

But a trademark infringement lawsuit was the least of my concerns.

As Hurricane Porn-O-Rama gained momentum, I began to feel slightly beleaguered and a little sorry for myself. So I emailed my friend Al Gore asking for a little advice:

I would love to discuss with you sometime personal coping mechanisms for being a politician who is being unfairly attacked. I'm doing well, but I'm finding there are aspects of running for office that are unpleasant.

Gore wrote back:

Suck it up.

"Suck it up" became a mantra of sorts. I wrote it on a sheet of paper and tacked it up to the wall in my office at headquarters, where I would spend hours calling delegates and other politicos, trying to explain myself, asking them not to bail on me.

Truly, there would be much for me to suck up in the days that followed.

Hurricane Porn-O-Rama made landfall on May 29, nine days before the convention, when Representative Betty McCollum, a DFLer who represents St. Paul, finally broke the dam by telling the Associated Press that my "pornographic writings" were "indefensible."

Republicans attacking me for something I'd written was one thing. A prominent DFLer doing it made the story exponentially more damaging.

That afternoon, *Politico* reported that all five members of the DFL congressional delegation had met to share their concerns about what my baggage might mean for their chances down the ballot. Even Tim Walz, the freshman congressman for whom I had campaigned tirelessly in 2006 and who was one of my best friends in Minnesota politics, couldn't help but speak up, telling the AP that the piece was "pretty inappropriate" and suggesting that he might not want to share a ticket with me:

> I'm concerned that from the top of the party all the way on down, people make a simple assumption that there are commonalities if we're all in the same party. I don't want to get associations made that I can't control.

This was officially a crisis. I felt terrible. On the one hand, I felt like if I could just sit down with everyone who read, "Franken writes sex article for *Playboy*," I could rescue the piece from the gears of the DeHumorizer™ and explain why I'd written it. On the other hand, it seemed like people didn't really care whether there was a good explanation. There was no ReHumorizing this one. Even in context, the fact that I had written it at all freaked some people out.

Still, when I talked to Chuck Schumer the next day and he suggested that I consider apologizing for writing the piece, I balked. What would I even be apologizing for? For writing a silly humor piece? That was my job for thirty-five years! It felt wrong—no, worse, it felt like a betrayal of myself—to renounce one particular piece just because people felt it crossed the line. Once you even acknowledge that there is a line, that there are things you shouldn't be allowed to joke about, that there are words that can't be said no matter the context, you're selling out the very idea of comedy.

* * *

Stephanie Schriock's first day in the office was June 2, and she walked into a building on fire. Frankly, we were relieved she showed up at all. When the *Playboy* article surfaced, Stephanie had been in Washington. She'd read it and taken it to Jim Messina, a Montana buddy of hers and the man who would manage President Obama's 2012 campaign. "Is this a campaign killer?" she asked him.

Messina scanned it. "No," he said. "He can survive this." But Schriock noticed he was blushing.

And then that day, Republicans had held another press conference to denounce a whole new list of old jokes that fit under the umbrella of "offensive to women."

Twenty-two-year-old Natalie Volin had the unenviable job of managing our outreach to a progressive feminist community that was deeply divided about all this. When she would tell me that I needed to call one of her people right away, I'd jump to do it. Though sometimes she would decide that the call should come from someone, anyone, other than me.

Natalie did heroic work building and maintaining and in some cases rehabilitating those relationships. But if I was going to get past this, I myself was going to have to find a way to address and allay people's fears and concerns, whether they were judgmental ("Anyone who writes something like that has no business being a senator") or strategic ("Republicans are going to eat him alive").

Because with the convention just days away, our numbers were beginning to drop. James's nightly reports on delegate calls grew less confident and more troubling. And some of the superdelegates who had been on his whiteboard for months as supporters were starting to waver.

On Tuesday, June 3—four days out—a field organizer from the 8th Congressional District (Duluth and the Iron Range) reported in with an S.O.S.:

Subject: HELP

    Bleeding dels*...the top loser is
Mary B 9 percent last night in the first.†
I am losing them in the 8th I think my
strongs‡ are below 50 percent now...
the 7th Congressional§ is the same. The
phones are saturated, they aren't answering its impossible to connect with these
people...emails most are older Women
who don't use email...its 3 days out we
cannot mail them something...If you get
them you spend first ten minutes getting
chewed out for harassing them too much.
    WE NEED to reach them...
    Al and his 'child porn'¶ stuff is kill-
ing me!

---

* Delegates.

† Southern Minnesota—Tim Walz's district.

‡ People reporting that they were "strong Franken" supporters.

§ Rural western Minnesota.

¶ No, I'm proud to say that I have never written any "child porn," but I wasn't going to quibble.

> This is bigger than Tax Issue, I don't
> want to seem sensational—sorry.

What could I do? What could I say to these folks that would restore their rapidly dwindling faith in me? The team and I were spending hours on the phone calling delegates, James divvying up the names and numbers based on his calculation of what they needed to hear and who they needed to hear it from.

And as we all—me, Franni, Thomasin, the staff, everyone—hit the phones that night, more and more Strong Frankens were turning to Lean Frankens, more and more Lean Frankens were turning to Undecideds, and more and more Undecideds weren't returning our calls.

Forget about winning in November—it began to seem possible, very possible, that my campaign wouldn't even survive the DFL convention.

Then, improbably, things got worse.

* * *

The next day—June 5, the Thursday before the Saturday convention—Republicans accused me of joking about rape.

During the 1994–95 season of *SNL*, a *New York* magazine writer spent a week at the show. Lorne had given the writer full access to everything, and the resulting article, entitled "Comedy Isn't Funny," was kind of a hit piece on the show, and on Lorne himself. That happens. My "joke about rape" came during a 2 a.m. rewrite session, where we were working on an Andy Rooney piece that Norm MacDonald had written for himself.

Norm's take on Andy Rooney, the extremely popular long-standing humorist for *60 Minutes*, was that his humor could be a little on the banal side. In his sketch, Norm played Rooney cleaning out his desk:

Here's a letter from California. Here's one from Illinois. Here's another one from California. Here's one from Maryland. This one's from California, too. Here's another one from California. There must be a lot of people who live in California.

All of us around the table were looking for a turn in the piece, and I suggested that we suddenly transform Rooney into a monster after he finds an empty bottle of sedatives in another drawer: "I give the pills to Lesley Stahl. Then, when Lesley's passed out, I take her to the closet and rape her."

Understand that I was not intending for this extremely dark joke to be aired on American television. It was a joke "for the room" suggesting a direction for the turn. I was like a NASA engineer who designed a hydraulic pump for the Mars rover that provided the breakthrough that led to the final hydraulic pump on the Mars rover. We eventually settled on Rooney saying he had spiked Mike Wallace's drink and photographed him nude in a variety of positions.

There was a reason Republicans saved this one for last. It had the feel of a knockout blow. Joking about rape? What the hell?

The thing of it was, I could answer that question. Here's what the hell: *SNL* had developed a culture which prized—no, celebrated—dark humor. The best example I can think of took place at a party at Laraine Newman's house in L.A. Billy Murray carried Gilda Radner around the room after her second series of chemotherapy, saying, "Say your goodbyes now, everyone—she's a goner!" Gilda was laughing hysterically.

That isn't an excuse, necessarily, but it is an explanation. When I discussed the situation with Conan O'Brien, who had been an *SNL* writer with me from 1989 to 1990, he wondered how I could ever explain the culture of a comedy rewrite table at two in the morning. "If I was on the stand at a trial," Conan said, "and the prosecutor asked me, 'Mr. O'Brien, have you ever joked at a rewrite table about defiling Lincoln's body immediately after he was shot?' I'd have to throw myself on the mercy of the court."

I knew exactly how a person who wasn't completely ignorant of the horror of sexual assault could end up saying something in a writers' room that made it sound like he was. But I didn't know how to explain it to Minnesotans. Frankly, I didn't know if they'd even let me.

* * *

So that was my day on Thursday, the day before delegates would start arriving in Rochester for Saturday morning's convention. Late that afternoon, with the newspapers asking for what felt like a really important comment from me on the Lesley Stahl story, my staff and consultants were in crisis mode on a long and unpleasant email thread that, fortunately for my own sanity, did not include me. If you've ever wondered how campaigns make decisions in crisis situations, perhaps you'll enjoy reading it as much as I don't enjoy reading it.

One of my consultants* offered this pitch at 5:40 p.m.:

> I understand that some people have seen my satiric writings as representing my views about women in real life. That is not true. I respect

---

* I'm not telling you which consultant said what, because this was basically the same kind of thing as the writers' room that produced the Lesley Stahl joke: people workshopping ideas with no expectation that they'd be made public.

women—I have been married for 32 years, and
Franni and I are proud of our children, including our daughter Thomasin, who is a teacher.
I respect women in the home and in the workplace.

Jess piped up: Could we hit Norm at the end? She
added "...and I will work to represent them in the
U.S. Senate—something that Norm Coleman has
been doing a very bad job of."

Another consultant: "The line about their kids
sounds very odd." She pitched:

I understand that some people have seen my
writings as representing my views in real life.
They don't. They are satire. Some of it not very
funny. In real life, I've been married for 32
years, have two wonderful children, and respect
women in the home and the workplace.

Wait, replied Jess. What about the pivot to Norm?

By now it was 7:20, and the DSCC's guy on the
email chain was concerned: "I don't think the pivot is
as important, but we could wordsmith this to death
over the next hour. You gotta get something to the AP
so they can move a rewrite."

Schriock chimed in: "This seems to have gotten

weaker. And read it out loud and it sounds arrogant or at least defensive."

At 7:26, a new draft:

> I understand that some people have seen my writings as representing my views in real life. They don't. In real life, I have been married for 32 years, and Franni and I are proud of our children. I respect women in the home and in the workplace and I will work to represent them in the U.S. Senate—something that Norm Coleman hasn't been doing for the last six years.

7:30. The DSCC: "Go."

7:31. Yet *another* consultant: "I suggest adding the kids' names so that it is at least obvious one is a daughter."

A few minutes later, the team decided to come to me for final approval of this quote:

> I understand that some people have seen my satirical writings as representing my views in real life. They don't. In real life, I've been married to my wife Franni for 32 years, and have two wonderful children, a daughter and a son. I have always respected women in the home and the workplace and I will work to represent them

in the U.S. Senate—something that Norm Coleman hasn't been doing for the last six years.

At 7:39, Andy returned to the email thread with bad news: "Al hates it." He relayed a suggestion from me:

> I'm proud of my career as a satirist, which doesn't mean every joke I've ever told was funny or, indeed, appropriate. In real life, though, I've been married for 32 years. Franni and I are proud of our son and daughter. I respect women—both at home and in the workplace. And I will work incredibly hard to represent them in the Senate—something Norm Coleman hasn't been doing for the last six years.

A minute later, one of the consultants: "I understand why he wants to say he's proud of his career as a satirist, but keep in mind, there is a large segment of the electorate for whom the only aspects of that career they will know about are the 'rape' and 'Playboy' aspects. That introductory language strikes me as satisfying for Al, but dangerous with older women—voters who know the least about Al's career, and those most likely to be offended."

And another consultant, getting directly to the point: "Andy, does he hate it strategically or personally?

I think we are in real trouble here and need to say something that affirms Al's respect for women. We are about to miss the opportunity to do so pre-convention."

Fifteen minutes passed. We heard from the consultants, and from the DSCC, and eventually I signed off on this, with the word "regret" as suggested by Chuck Schumer himself:

> I'm proud of my career as a satirist, which doesn't mean every joke I've ever told was funny—and I regret that some of them have caused offense. In real life, though, I've been married for 32 years. Franni and I are proud of our son and daughter. I respect women—both at home and in the workplace. And I will work incredibly hard to represent them in the Senate—something Norm Coleman hasn't been doing for the last six years.

At 7:56, two consultants weighed in simultaneously. One said, "Almost all of them have caused offense...and he really doesn't regret it (except now). This is a dangerous half apology. If we do it it's because we need to save ourselves now...but we will be dealing with which writings caused 'regret' for a very long time."

The other: "Send it!"

Finally, after several more phone calls, and with

reporters' deadlines approaching (or perhaps past, as it was well after 8 p.m.), we settled on this:

> I'm proud of my career as a satirist, which doesn't mean every joke I've ever told was funny, or, indeed, appropriate. I understand and regret that people have been legitimately offended by some of the things I've written. In real life, though, I've been married for 32 years. Franni and I are proud of our son and daughter. I respect women—in both my personal and professional life. And I will work incredibly hard to represent them in the Senate—something Norm Coleman hasn't been doing for the last six years.

Jess sent it around, writing, "Floor's open for 5 minutes. Call if you think this will end the campaign."

*　*　*

"DFL convention begins with Franken fending off criticism," read the *Star Tribune* headline the morning of Friday, June 6, as delegates began to arrive in Rochester. The story included our heavily workshopped statement, and also a quote from Norm Coleman, who was clearly enjoying the whole situation:

> While Al Franken was joking about raping women and a host of other degrading and

humiliating jokes throughout his career, I was in the Minnesota attorney general's office working to throw rapists behind bars. I was in the mayor's office working with advocates for battered women.

But I didn't have time to worry about him. I had my hands full with the convention. Everyone wanted me to do something to reassure delegates. But it wasn't clear what that something was.

I felt worse than ever. I felt like people whose respect meant a lot to me had begun to feel like I was a terrible person. I thought about Eliot Spitzer again, and about all the people he had let down because he couldn't stop his own flaws from sabotaging his desire to do good. I thought about Paul Wellstone and wondered if I was letting him down, not to mention all the people who had trusted me to carry on his legacy (or at least win back his seat).

On the way down to Rochester, I got a call. Schriock.

"Forget about whatever anybody has told you," she said. "What do *you* think about this?"

I sighed miserably. "I feel bad that people feel bad about this, and I want to apologize for that."

"Then that's what we're going to do."

I spent the afternoon and evening working delegates. And that night, Schriock, Andy, and I stayed up late working on the "closing argument" speech I'd give immediately before the delegates voted. It felt like the whole campaign was coming down to what I'd say on that stage.

I felt inadequate, guilty, confused, unworthy. But I didn't have time for a dark night of the soul. I had about an hour. Maybe two if I had one of those energy drinks. I had to suck it up. I had to stop feeling sorry for myself. I had to pull myself out of the shame spiral and confront this head-on.

All campaign long, I'd avoided apologizing for things I'd said or written, because it felt like doing so would mean apologizing for everything I'd done over forty years in comedy, ever since Tom and I were performing at chapel back at Blake. To say I was sorry for writing a joke was to sell out my career, to sell out who I'd been my entire life.

And I *wasn't* sorry that I had written "Porn-O-Rama" or pitched that stupid Lesley Stahl joke at two in the morning. I was just doing my job. But running for office is a different job. When you run for office, you're asking people to stand with you and work for you and believe in you. And you're making a promise that it'll be worth it. People had to know I understood that.

It was nearly two in the morning when Andy hit "send" on the final draft, after which he had to *start* writing two more speeches: a victory speech that I would deliver after I had won the endorsement—and a concession that I would deliver if I lost it.

* * *

Saturday. Endorsement day.

I took the stage to what I can only describe as nervously enthusiastic applause.

"I'm Al Franken," I began. "And I'm going to beat Norm Coleman."

I talked about a few of the people I had met along the way who were there in the room as delegates. Sitting with the Blue Earth County delegation was Casey Carmody, the MSU-Mankato student who had told me he sold his blood plasma to pay for tuition. Among the tiny delegation from Kanabec County was Kathy Kawalek, a nurse who had told me she saw elderly patients rushed into her intensive care unit because they couldn't afford their medications. And there from Anoka County was Sergeant Sam Scott, whom I'd met on a USO tour in Iraq in 2006. "Many of the men and women he served with are still there," I told the crowd. "Some aren't coming home."

I took a deep breath.

"That's why I'm doin' this. For Casey. For Kathy. For Sam. For the people of Minnesota. That's who I wanna work for. And that's what this election is about."

Another deep breath.

"That's not exactly what this past week has been about," I continued. "I've had some tough conversations this week."

The tension in the room was incredible. The delegates didn't know what was coming, but they knew that whatever it was, whatever they'd been waiting for, whatever they'd staked their hopes on, it was coming right now.

"It kills me that things I said and wrote sent a message to some of my friends in this room and people in this state that they can't count on me to be a champion for women, a champion for *all* Minnesotans, in this campaign and in the Senate."

And then: "I'm sorry for that."

Sitting up in the rafters where she could observe the crowd, Stephanie Schriock said there was the briefest moment of absolute silence, and then she heard—*heard*—the collective exhale of some thirteen hundred delegates. And then they stood and cheered. It was the first time I'd ever gotten a standing ovation based entirely on a crowd's overwhelming sense of relief. The applause drowned out the next line, but I kept going:

Because that's not who I am.
I'm a husband—married to my favorite person on earth, Franni, for thirty-two years. I'm a father of a son and a daughter who we taught

to respect everyone and who we're incredibly proud of.

And for thirty-five years I was a writer. I wrote a lot of jokes. Some of them weren't funny. Some of them were inappropriate. Some of them were downright offensive.

I understand that.

And I understand that the people of Minnesota deserve a senator who won't say things that make them uncomfortable.

But I'm in this race because there are some people in Washington who could afford to feel a little less comfortable.

And that's what I'm gonna do.

Now I had the audience behind me. Now I could have some fun. I lit into the oil companies, and the drug companies, and the insurance companies. I declared that it was time to stop waiting for health care reform and get it done.

And I promised that the first person I was going to make a little uncomfortable was Norm Coleman.

It was in the delegates' hands now. But we could sense that something had changed for the better. A weight had been lifted.

As the first ballots were being counted, it was clear that I had surpassed the 60 percent I needed to win (although not by much). Jack Nelson-Pallmeyer graciously offered to have the convention endorse me by acclamation (so that no one would need to know how close it had been). I never had to look at Andy's draft of a concession speech, which is good, because, exhausted and bitter, he had larded it with profanity.

But it wasn't just that I had survived the convention (although "survived" was almost certainly the correct verb). As Schriock later told me, "It wasn't just what you said, it was the way you said it. I think the delegates realized, 'We get the candidate we want.'" They understood how badly I wanted to win, how passionate I was about doing good—as Paul would say, about improving people's lives. Having won them over in the most excruciating manner imaginable, they were with me for good. Schriock says we never had a base problem after that, never had to worry about finding people to volunteer, to knock on doors, to make phone calls.

That night I went to bed early. Schriock took the team out to get steaks and cocktails. Everyone was exhausted, barely coherent, their kidneys damaged irreparably by energy drinks. "Oh my God," Jess moaned. "Food! Actual food! On plates!" Meanwhile, Andy was falling asleep in a bowl of mashed potatoes.

And then, the next morning, we all went back to the Twin Cities and got back to work.

Election day was 149 days away.

Chapter 17

My First Powwow

When I first started running, I was almost completely ignorant about Indian country.

But we have eleven reservations in Minnesota, and I knew enough to know that tribes in our state and all around the country face enormous problems. These problems can seem so big and so numerous that people in a position to do something about them often give up. Not Paul Wellstone. Paul had been the last Minnesota senator to serve on the Indian Affairs Committee. In that tradition, I wanted our tribes to be well represented in the Senate.

Two days after I announced my candidacy, I visited the Fond du Lac Band of Lake Superior Chippewa (or Ojibwe) in northeastern Minnesota. Karen Diver, Fond du Lac's no-nonsense but affable chairwoman, was puzzled that I had come up to meet them so early in the campaign, instead of waiting to check that box in the last couple weeks before the election, as almost every candidate does. I said I wanted to learn about Indians.

Karen began by talking about sovereignty. The Constitution recognizes Indian tribes as sovereign nations. Now, you'll be shocked to hear this, but there's no way to sugarcoat it: Historically, the United States has not always respected tribal sovereignty.

Karen told me about a recent study on sovereignty by Harvard's Kennedy School of Government, which concluded that tribes who govern themselves do better than those dictated to by the federal government.

I found the study online and called Karen a few days later to discuss it. She was surprised I'd actually gone home and read it. So one of the first things I learned about Indians is that they don't expect much from politicians.

* * *

During the campaign, I visited most of our reservations and attended roundtables with native leaders. But it wasn't until August 2008 that I was invited to a powwow by the Red Lake Band of Chippewa. The Red Lake Reservation is a good 250 miles north of the Twin Cities and is the poorest twelve hundred square miles in our state, with tremendously high rates of unemployment. Its population of around fifty-one hundred has seen more than its share of tragedy. In

2005, a fifteen-year-old boy shot and killed his grand-father and his grandfather's girlfriend, then went to his old school and killed seven others before committing suicide.

But a powwow is a happy occasion, a celebration of cultural heritage. Excited, I sat down with Peggy Flanagan, a half-Ojibwe twenty-something Minneapolis school board member who was advising me on Indian issues (and who is now a Minnesota state legislator). Peggy had about half an hour to prepare me for my first powwow.

"Okay, don't call them 'costumes.' They're wearing 'regalia.'"

"I wasn't planning on calling them anything," I said. "But okay. 'Regalia.'"

"And don't dance," Peggy told me definitively.

"Don't dance?"

"Don't dance."

"Why shouldn't I dance?"

"Governor Pawlenty danced a couple years ago, and they haven't stopped making fun of him," she said with half a grin.

"Okay. Don't dance."

"Don't dance. Now, Indians volunteer for military service at a higher rate than any other group in the country."

"I didn't know that."

"And they respect their warriors. So, the drums

will start, and then the warriors will lead in their traditional regalia."

"Regalia. I got it." I nodded.

"But they'll also be wearing their veterans' caps and carrying flags."

"Right. Sure."

"And after the veterans, the others will come out in their regalia, and everyone dances around the circle to the drums, and they'll dance a number of dances."

"And should I dance?"

Peggy knew me well enough to ignore this. "Now, after the dances, the drums will stop, and everyone will go sit in the bleachers, and Chairman Jourdain will introduce you."

"Okay."

"So, what do you plan to say?" she asked.

I realized that I hadn't given that a lot of thought, but tried out some of what I had learned. "Well, I guess I'd say to them that because of the cultural trauma that your people went through, you've experienced a lot of pathologies, like chemical dependency and domestic violence."

"Yeah. They've heard that," Peggy said matter-of-factly. "They're going to expect you to be funny."

That took me a little by surprise. Peggy wasn't with the campaign full-time, but she'd been involved enough to know our key strategic objective. "We're trying to get away from The Funny," I reminded her.

Peggy nodded. "I know. But they're going to expect you to be funny. And after you speak, there'll be more dancing. Don't dance."

* * *

Peggy couldn't come on the six-hour drive to Red Lake the next day, and while I felt I had internalized her instructions, I was frankly pretty nervous about my remarks. I had never spoken to a large Indian audience before, and I wanted to let them know I had given some serious thought to their issues.

But I trusted Peggy. On the drive up, I told Kris that I decided I'd just have to read the crowd and go with my gut.

Kris and I arrived at Red Lake just in time and drove right to the powwow grounds. The arena was a set of concentric circles. In the middle was a circular gazebo, and around it a wide dirt circle for dancing. All around the outside of the dance circle were drums, which provided the rhythm for the dancing. The drummers would sing traditional Ojibwe songs as well.

The outside circle was comprised of bleachers, where a good crowd of spectators had gathered for the festivities. The drums started, and, just as Peggy said, the veterans led in their regalia and caps from the Gulf Wars, from Vietnam and Korea. There was even one member of the Greatest Generation wearing his World War II cap. They were followed by others in their regalia—men, women, and children, dancing around the outdoor arena.

I stood on the outside of the dancing circle, enjoying myself. At least until a middle-aged man danced up to me and said, "Why don't you come in and dance?"

He danced in place, motioning with his arm that I should come in and join everyone.

"Um," I said uncomfortably. "I, uh . . ."

"We'll respect you more if you dance," he said with great seriousness.

"Okay. Maybe later. Maybe later," I said with great lameness.

One nod and he moved on. "Hmmm," I thought as I backed away from the circle, "maybe I should have had Peggy come with me." Or maybe I should have at least asked her what I should say if someone asked me to dance.

After about thirty or forty minutes of drumming and dancing, the sun had set. The emcee announced the speaking portion of the powwow and the dancers took their seats in the bleachers with the others.

Buck Jourdain, the long-standing chairman of Red Lake, took a hand mic out to the arena under the lights. It was turning dark and the heat of the afternoon had dissipated. The stars were out. The air was soft. It was an exquisitely beautiful northern Minnesota night.

And I was very nervous.

Buck started his introduction. We had met a few times before, and in the intro he called me a friend. That meant a lot to me, because I had been really impressed with Buck. He was in his forties, tall and handsome with a beautiful braided ponytail, and he carried himself with strength and dignity. My friends with ponytails were mostly people in show business: aging, paunchy, bespectacled Jews whose ponytails always seemed like a desperate affectation signaling unsuccessfully that the wearer is still young and cool despite their recent hip replacement. But on Buck, the ponytail looked good.

Buck gave me a small man-hug and passed me the mic to polite applause. I took in the crowd for a moment, trying to get a read from the faces. Not much of anything. I thanked Buck and told the crowd they had a great chairman.

I started in on how the federal government was failing to meet its treaty obligations in terms of fully funding Indian education and health care and how, if I won, I hoped to be on the Indian Affairs Committee and fight to change that. No reaction. Peggy was right. They'd heard this before. *They're going to expect you to be funny.* I decided to call an audible.

"So I guess if we don't fulfill our treaty obligations, we should just give you all your land back and call it even."

That got something of a laugh, and a few nods. "And as far as education, I guess other Americans need to know that Indians are a contemporary people who like to celebrate their culture. Just like every other group. For example, I'm Jewish."

This got exactly the reaction I had hoped for: nothing.

"Let me try that again," I said, feigning offense. "I'm Jewish." Laughter, applause, and cheering! "My God," I thought. "Peggy's a genius!"

"And Jews like to celebrate our own heritage, just like you're doing today." The crowd was nodding and smiling. And in that very instant, I figured out the whole dancing thing.

"Now, earlier a gentleman asked me to dance. Well, I'll make a deal with you. I will dance. But only if all of you agree not to make fun of me after I leave."

More laughter.

"So, I need a show of hands. How many agree not to make fun of me after I leave if I dance?"

Everyone looked around at each other, and about two-thirds of the crowd raised their hands. "That's not enough," I said. "I need *everyone* to raise their hands." More laughs. And sure enough, every single person there raised a hand.

All right! I grinned, thinking how silly it was that I had been so nervous. *Why, I've got them in the palm of my hand! I* will *dance!*

That's when one of the drummers hit his drum. Joined on the second beat by another, then another, until all the drummers were drumming.

Often what makes a really good joke a really good joke is that a number of ideas come together simultaneously. The moment that the first drummer hit his drum, he brought together several amusing notions. First, that, for whatever reason, I clearly had serious qualms about dancing. Second, that those qualms had something to do with my fear of being made fun of. Third, that I thought those fears would magically disappear if everybody agreed not to make fun of me after I left. And finally, that number three was based on my mistaken assumption that I would be dancing along with everyone else and not *by myself in front of the entire crowd*! Plus, cell phone cameras.

So, it was a really good joke. And it was on me.

Everyone in the bleachers was laughing at the drummer's very clever joke. And staring at me, waiting for me to start dancing.

How did I get myself into this? I thought. The drummers kept up the beat, the crowd grinning expectantly.

Fortunately, I had paid attention after I told the gentleman that I might dance. And so I began: two shuffles from my left foot, two shuffles from my right, trying to stay in rhythm. As I started around the circle, I kept my head down, trying unsuccessfully to block out the crowd's reaction, which I would describe as delighted amusement. I looked up to the bleachers and gave a smile, as if to share in the merriment and show that I was a good sport. But I'm afraid I wasn't successfully hiding my embarrassment and, as I recall, self-loathing. My own cultural heritage was on display as well.

About a quarter way around the circle, a little girl, I'd say four or five years old, jumped up and bailed me out. She grabbed my hand and the two of us danced a little farther until another child came in and took my other hand. And then another and another and another. The night was beautiful again. The adults came in and we all danced under the moon and stars.

I became kind of a dancing fool.

Four or five dances later, a woman sidled up to me and said, "You dance like a white guy."

"What about the deal?" I asked.

"The deal was *after* you leave," she smiled.

*   *   *

At the end of the powwow, Buck approached me. "I talked with the rest of the tribal council. And they all agreed that we've never had a politician here who knows how to read a crowd as well as you."

I was flattered. Of course, it was a good bet that I was the only politician to visit Red Lake who had spent thirty-five years in show business. But also, I had to laugh, because the whole thing had lurched so badly out of control before landing on its feet.

Buck took me by the arm and said, "I'd like to introduce you to my son and his friend, who's in the Army." We walked out to the parking lot, where we found the two young men leaning up against an old beat-up car.

We all shook hands, and I asked the friend, "How long have you been in the Army?"

"Oh, I was only there about a month," he shrugged. "I got kicked out, 'cuz I can't see very well."

I was puzzled. "You're not wearing glasses."

He just shrugged. "The Army was gonna make me glasses. But they didn't."

I was very confused. "What's wrong with your eyesight?"

"I don't know," he said.

All of this was well outside my life experience. I asked an obvious question. "Have you gone to the eye doctor?"

"Oh, we don't have an eye doctor," he said.

One of the best things about running for office is that, if you do it right, you learn a lot about stuff you very likely would never have discovered otherwise. One of the worst things about running for office is that, if you do it right, you're constantly switching gears. As soon as you're done with one thing, you're off to another. Which leaves you almost no time to process the stuff you just learned about.

Leaving the powwow, I was overwhelmed—both

with gratitude at how welcoming and generous Buck and the Red Lake community had been, and with shame at the conditions in which so many First Americans were living. But as Kris was in charge of reminding me, even in the car, there was more work to do: more phone calls to make, more notes to write, more events to prepare for. A candidate who's sitting around and thinking is a candidate who's losing.

In fact, the day after that powwow, I had to fly right off to New York for a couple of fund-raisers in the richest place in America, the Hamptons. The Hamptons are the summer home of the top one-tenth of the top one percent. The ones with the waterfront estates are the members of the top one-tenth of the top one-tenth of the top one percent. The ones with the nicest, biggest waterfront estates in the richest Hampton of them all, Richhampton, are the members of the top one-tenth of the top one-tenth of the top one-tenth of the top one percent (the top one-thousandth percent). Every one of these people can go to an eye doctor pretty much anytime they want. Or, more likely, have an eye doctor brought to them for a full examination.

There, at this lovely home in Richhampton, with delicious food and wine and surrounded by people with flawlessly corrected vision wearing the latest designer regalia, I felt that my donors needed to hear about Red Lake. So I told them the story I've just told you.

I didn't tell them the ending to the story, though, because the ending hadn't happened yet. When I got to the Senate, I got a seat on the Indian Affairs Committee—because, in the Senate, anyone who wants to be on Indian Affairs gets on Indian Affairs.

One of the things I fought hard for was allowing Indian tribal courts to prosecute non-Indians who commit acts of domestic violence. I was also able to get funding to replace a dilapidated, structurally unsafe high school on the Leech Lake Reservation in Minnesota. We passed a new Indian Health Care Improvement Act.

And Red Lake now has an eye doctor.

But conditions in Indian country in terms of education, infrastructure, housing, and health care are still by and large disgraceful.

The good news is that folks in Richhampton are doing better than ever.

Chapter 18

Tax-Dodging, Rape-Joking Pornographer for Senate

Norm Coleman had a problem.

When he'd first gotten to the Senate in 2003, President Bush was extremely popular. That's why, when he apologized for saying he was a 99 percent improvement over Paul Wellstone, Norm explained that he had meant a 99 percent improvement *in terms of supporting George W. Bush.* He happily fell in line as a loyal Bush ally, supporting the president's agenda at every turn and serving as one of his attack dogs in the so-called "truth squad" during the 2004 campaign against John Kerry.

But then Democrats had taken back Congress in the wave election of 2006. And with President Bush's approval ratings circling the drain, Coleman had begun eagerly seeking out opportunities to vote with Democrats on meaningless procedural matters. Tip

O'Neill had a line about politicians like Norm who feigned at bipartisanship: "He's always there when we don't need him."

The upshot of all this was that when it came time to face the voters again in 2008, Norm's record consisted of four years of sucking up to President Bush, two years of running away from him, and not much in the way of actual accomplishments on behalf of the people of Minnesota. But that was okay. Because Norm's best argument for being reelected—the core message of his campaign—wasn't about him. It was about me. Specifically: "Al Franken is an angry, divisive, profane, tax-dodging, rape-joking pornographer."

* * *

Winning the DFL endorsement had been a sixteen-month marathon from my announcement to the convention. The general election, on the other hand, would be a twenty-one-week sprint to election day. And while earning the support of DFL delegates had been a slow, methodical process of building and organizing, the race was about to turn into a chaotic festival of mud-slinging.

For Stephanie Schriock, getting our campaign ready for the nastiness to come started with establishing her authority, which she did instantly with her mere presence.

Being a campaign manager, I've come to realize,

isn't just about managing a staff and a budget. It's about managing a candidate. Indeed, the most important cubic foot in any campaign is the one inside the candidate's skull. And as messed up as that cubic foot had been during what I unaffectionately call "porn and rape joke week," the calm aura of order Schriock created reshuffled my emotional deck. And just in time, too.

You see, the DSCC had gotten cold feet in the wake of the near disaster at the convention. In early July, Schriock got wind that someone had been polling in Minnesota, testing the names of two other potential DFL candidates: attorney Kathleen Flynn Peterson and former governor Arne Carlson, who was actually a moderate Republican but had been left behind when his party lurched to the right.

Yes, I already had the DFL endorsement. But anyone who filed for the race by the deadline on July 15 would appear on the primary ballot in September. And the fact that this poll was in the field suggested that someone was interested in finding out whether a DFLer who took the extraordinary step of jumping into the race at the last minute could successfully knock off the party-endorsed candidate in the primary.

When Chuck called me to acknowledge that, indeed, the DSCC was shopping for a new candidate, I happened to be in San Francisco, helping to raise money for…yup, the DSCC. I didn't really know what to say. But it was some serious chutzpah on Chuck's part, and Schriock went appropriately berserk. "If you ever do anything like that again," she told the DSCC's executive director, J. B. Poersch, in a phone call, "I will destroy you. It may not be now. But someday."

Schriock can be scary. But the truth was scarier. As the general election got under way, I was down by anywhere from eight to fourteen points, depending on the poll.

Schriock and I flew out to D.C. for another awkward meeting with Chuck and Harry. Harry was in a bad mood. But when we showed him a poll we'd done—which suggested that telling voters about some of Norm's ethics lapses, such as the sweetheart deal he'd been getting from a Republican fixer on his D.C. apartment, could bring me back to a tie—he grumpily acknowledged that it was a pretty good hit.

Then he departed, leaving us with Chuck.

We could pull to within five points by Labor Day, we promised him. But it would take everything we had—we would have to empty our war chest just to get close. Would the DSCC be willing to then carry us over the finish line?

Chuck wanted to say yes. But what if our strategy didn't work? What if I *wasn't* within five by Labor Day? Would I be willing to drop out?

I said I had to call Franni, and stepped into another room.

She was pissed. I told her, "Honey, it's okay. They haven't even asked Kathleen or Arne whether they're interested in running. No one's going to jump in by the fifteenth. Even if I don't get within five by Labor Day, they're still going to be stuck with me."

"So it's a bluff?" she asked.

"Exactly."

"Okay. And who's bluffing—us or them?"

Good question. "I think both of us," I answered.

"I'm very proud of you, honey," Franni laughed.

And then I went back in the room and made the deal.

That summer, for the first time, our campaign started to look like a normal campaign: stump speeches, press conferences, rallies, and lots and lots and lots of fund-raising. We ran some positive ads talking about my work on behalf of the troops and my ideas for reforming Washington, and many more negative ads beating up on Norm for being such a stooge for President Bush.

And it worked. On August 22, Minnesota Public Radio released a poll showing me leading the race by one single, beautiful, life-affirming, Chuck-reassuring point.

Republicans realized that in order to stop my momentum, they would need to double down on their strategy of destroying me and dragging the corpse of my character through the city square. And as soon as the state fair was over, that's exactly what they set out to do.

* * *

In mid-September, Minnesotans were treated to this ad, courtesy of the National Republican Senatorial Committee (NRSC):

> Is Al Franken fit for office? Franken writes about committing rape. Writes pornography so vile Democrats denounced him. His profanity-laced anger...followed by violent outbursts. He physically assaulted a protestor. Then there's the $70,000 in unpaid taxes. Al Franken, degrading to women...to us all. Al Franken, frankly unfit for office.

It was a masterpiece. Forget about the DeHumor-izer™—this was the work of a DeHumanizer™, portraying me not just as a foulmouthed comedian, but as an actual monster.

After all, "Franken writes about committing rape" sounds an awful lot like I committed rape and then wrote about it.* And "physically assaulted a protestor"

---

* Or, given its use of the present tense, that writing about committing rape remains a hobby.

sounds kind of unsenatorial, too.* To really drive home the point, the ad depicted my face with parallel lines running across it, a subtle suggestion of jail bars, as if I had done time (or should do time) for my history of raping women and beating up dissenters.

There were a lot of ads like this as Coleman realized his only chance of winning was to reduce me to a small pile of smoking rubble. One of my favorites made use of this underrated joke from "Porn-O-Rama":

> The Internet is going to be a fabulous learning tool for kids. For example, my son used the Internet to do a great sixth grade report on bestiality. He downloaded a lot of great visual aids, and the kids in the class just loved them. Because, you know, at that age, they're just sponges.

The point of the joke, of course, was that parents should consider monitoring how their children use the Internet. A pretty conservative, pro-family idea, don't you think?

But then the DeHumorizer™ got ahold of it. And

---

* It's a reference to an incident during the 2004 New Hampshire primaries in which I stopped a Lyndon LaRouche fanatic who was charging the stage where Howard Dean was speaking. Two weeks later, the mayor of Manchester gave me the key to the city for helping to stop the guy.

to the litany of horrors featured in Republican ads was added the word "BESTIALITY," zooming in at you from infinity while scary horror movie music droned over a disgusted narrator. My mother-in-law, Fran, cried when she saw that one.

* * *

Meanwhile, we were trying to keep the focus on Norm's record. On September 22 (the same day the NRSC ran its "Franken writes about committing rape" ad), we released an ad taking Coleman to task for his oversight failure as chairman of the Permanent Subcommittee on Investigations, an ad that began with the ominous message, "This may be the worst thing Norm Coleman's done."

I held a press conference to show off the ad. We were desperate to get reporters to pay attention to the story, which I thought was a perfect illustration of how Coleman had abdicated his responsibility in favor of being a lickspittle for the Bush administration. But the press still shrugged.

Somehow, the lurid intimation that I was a rapist proved more effective than my indignation over Norm's failure to perform oversight. On September 17, we had run our first internal tracking poll. It showed me with a one-point lead: Franken 41, Coleman 40. Independent candidate Dean Barkley, who had actually served in the U.S. Senate for a few weeks in 2002 after Governor Jesse Ventura appointed him to finish Paul Wellstone's term, was at 14 percent.*

But just one week later, on September 24, the same poll found me three points down: Coleman 41, Franken 38, Barkley 17.

Still, I knew I had the debates. I was relishing the chance to get on a stage with Coleman. But once we started preparing, I found that the debate format— ninety-second answer, thirty-second rebuttal—felt horribly unnatural to me. To make things worse, these debates weren't going to be the two-man debates between me and Coleman that I had been dreaming about for years. Barkley would be on the stage as well. *Senator* Barkley. Along with *Senator* Coleman. And *Mr.* Franken.

My team explained to me that attacking Norm was just going to give Barkley an opportunity to say, "There they go again. Aren't you sick of all this partisan rancor? That's why Minnesota needs an Independent in Washington."

So we came up with a strategy. I would play golf, not tennis. In tennis the idea is to beat the other guy. In golf, it's just about you. My goal would be to show

---

* Minnesota has a proud tradition of third-party candidates. With me and Norm pounding each other daily, Barkley had a particular appeal to voters who were disgusted with both of us.

Minnesotans who I was and that I understood who they are. I would talk about how to replace No Child Left Behind, about getting to universal health care, about a clean energy economy, about a stronger middle class. I would pick spots to contrast what I wanted to do with what Norm had failed to do, waiting till a round where I was the last to speak.

Meanwhile, we were still feeling the impact of Norm's character attacks. Our October 1 tracking poll had me down six: Coleman 40, Franken 34, Barkley 18.

And that's when Franni saved the campaign.

Chapter 19

Franni Saves the Campaign

Franni had never discussed her alcoholism publicly. Part of the disease is the shame that comes with it. She had shared her story only with a few close friends, including those she had met in AA. It's called Alcoholics *Anonymous* for a reason.

Traveling around the state, Franni could see the toll that all the attack ads on my character were taking, and it was making her mad. She knew very well that the guy they depicted was not the guy she had married and raised two children with. Franni wanted to tell Minnesotans who I really was.

So she insisted on sitting down with Mandy and a camera crew.

Mandy interviewed Franni in our living room for over an hour, and Franni spoke honestly and openly about her disease. And while the vicious attack ads from the Republicans had made Franni's mom cry, the ad Mandy and her team cut together still makes *me* cry whenever I see it. In fact, when Chuck Schumer saw it, he called me to say that *he* had cried. And also that he thought it would win me the election.

The ad is very simple. Franni sitting on a couch, talking to an off-camera Mandy, intercut with photos of me and Franni as we've gone through the years, with photos of our beautiful daughter and son and our family. Here's the text:

> I first met Al at a freshman dance in college, and it was love at first sight. We've been married now for almost thirty-three years and we've been so blessed in so many ways. But we also had some bad times. And at one point in our life I struggled with alcohol dependency. How could a mother of two fabulous, healthy children be an alcoholic? When I was struggling with my recovery, Al stood right by my side and he stood up for me. After what we went through, Al wrote two beautiful movies, and he wrote them because he wanted to help people. And they're used in rehabs all over the country. The Al Franken I know stood by me through thick and thin—so I know he'll always come through for Minnesota.

It was a sixty-second ad, which meant it was twice as expensive to run, but *you* try editing that down.

What blew me away the most was the line "How could a mother of two fabulous, healthy children be an alcoholic?" It was so honest about the shame she had felt, and the shame that so many women, especially, with chemical dependency feel. "This ad is the best political ad of the season," wrote local TV anchor Esme Murphy on her blog, "because it might just help one person see in themselves the need to get help."

Two days later, Coleman, Barkley, and I had a debate in a gymnasium, with a big crowd sitting in the bleachers and in chairs on the gym floor. When Franni entered the room, she got a standing ovation.

There is no question that I would have lost the election if Franni had not made that spot. The courage that it took amazes me. A couple years later, a book came out about the eight-month recount and legal battle, entitled *This Is Not Florida*. If you go to the index and look under "Franken, Franni," the first entry is "and alcoholism."

People often come up to me and tell me that I have a thankless job. But as Lorne Michaels used to say, "The thing about a thankless job is that nobody thanks you." And people thank me all the time. I think it's Franni who has a thankless job. Which reminds me. I really ought to thank Franni one of these days for making that ad. And all the other stuff.

* * *

In that debate, the one in the gymnasium, Norm brought up my "assault" on the protester in Manchester, New Hampshire. When I told the crowd about getting the key to the city, they laughed. I had played a good game of golf, but by the next debate the course had changed dramatically.

All summer long, the housing market had been in turmoil, and on September 29 the financial crisis reached a climax in the wake of Lehman Brothers going under. It took about a week for a $700 billion–plus bailout package to work its way through Congress. Coleman immediately came out for the bailout, telling voters in North Mankato that "the government could make 10 or 20 times what it pays on this, possibly."

"It shows how out of touch he is," I told the *Star Tribune*.

I admit that I had the luxury of not having to cast a vote during a rapidly escalating crisis. But I felt that the bailout as proposed did little to protect taxpayers and nothing for homeowners who were the victims of the malfeasance of so many of those who were being bailed out. I said I'd vote for a package that had ownership stakes for taxpayers in companies seeking relief, the creation of a financial product safety commission, protections for homeowners—like allowing bankruptcy lawyers to adjust mortgages in order to prevent foreclosures—and no bonuses or golden parachutes for executives.

At that next debate, which was televised nationally, the bailout became the centerpiece of discussion. Norm asked how I could have opposed a bailout that Senators Amy Klobuchar and Barack Obama had both voted for? "I guess maybe," I offered, "I'm just, I don't know, a maverick."

As the audience laughed, Norm responded, a little uncomfortably (and more oddly, considering that his party's nominee that year was Senator John McCain), "I guess Minnesota should decide if they want a maverick in the Senate."

* * *

Franken Internal Poll, October 1: Coleman 40,
    Franken 34, Barkley 18.
Franken Internal Poll, October 8: Franken 40,
    Coleman 32, Barkley 22.

It's certainly possible that Norm's decision to support the bailout of Wall Street—and my decision to oppose it—was a factor in this swing. But in the October 1 poll, only 33 percent of Minnesotans reported that they had a favorable opinion of me. Then came Franni's ad. And a week later, it was up to 41 percent favorable, with a lot of the difference coming from women.

Still not exactly "beloved" territory. But it was a real turning point in the race.

The Frankens: Joe, Phoebe, Owen, and Alan. Guess what decade I grew up in.

Franken family photo

Believe it or not, I was kind of a nerd.

Franken family photo

Me and Franni in 1971. Pretty cute, huh? She looks good, too.

Franken family photo

bogus productions presents

The Franken & Davis Show

NBC's Saturday Night Emmy Winning Comedy Team
Featuring Mary McCusker

Limited Engagement
Aug 5,10,11,12 - 8PM
Aug 6,7,8,13,14,15 - 8 & 10:30PM

Dudley Riggs' ETC.
reservations: 377-2120 or »» 1430 Washington Ave. So.

Poster for an early Franken
and Davis show.

Tom and I played the two
finalists in our "Mr. USA"
pageant sketch on *SNL* in 1977.

Me and Tom and Jane Curtin and
Gilda Radner. Laraine Newman
loves us, too, she just isn't in this
picture.

Me and Franni with some walleye we caught in the St. Croix River.

Franken family photo

Me and Franni with some kids we had in the 1980s.

Franken family photo

Danny as Julia Child in a sketch Tom and I wrote. Tom is under the table controlling the pressure on the fake blood with the pump from an insecticide sprayer. The video of this now plays at the Smithsonian.

Copyright Owen Franken

Me as Stuart Smalley, healing nurturer and member of several 12-step programs.

Campaigning with Paul and Sheila Wellstone in 1996.

In happier times.

Me and future president Barack Obama on "The Al Franken Show" in 2006.

Me and Karri Turner performing at a USO show in Iraq a couple of weeks after troops complained to Secretary Rumsfeld about having to rely on "hillbilly armor." "I've got some good news and some bad news," I told the troops. "The bad news is, no cheerleaders this year. The good news is, I've got a hundred more of these."

USO tours are the best thing I've ever done.

Me at a bean feed in 2006.

In this bean feed shot, you can actually see some bean residue!

Me and my young staff at a DFL dinner early in the campaign. L-R: Andy Barr, future senator Al Franken, Jess McIntosh, Jon-David Schlough, David Benson, Jackie Bateman, Dusty Trice.

A frame from my first campaign ad, featuring my fourth grade teacher, Mrs. Molin.

An unhinged Brian Heenan whips up the crowd as TeamFranken arrives in Rochester for the DFL state convention in 2008.

Me and Stephanie Schriock, without whom this book would have come to a sudden and disappointing ending about halfway through.

Marlin Levinson, Copyright 2008, Star Tribune

Norm Coleman, Dean Barkley, and me at a debate in 2008. You can tell from my body language how annoyed I am with whatever it is Norm is saying.

Research director Matt Fuehrmeyer and communications director Andy Barr backstage at the debate. You can tell from their body language how confident they are in whatever it is I'm saying.

Mandy Grunwald

In happier times.

Cory Ryan/Getty Images

Another came that very day, October 8. All summer, we'd been making the case that Norm was kind of shady, pointing to the sweetheart deal he'd gotten on that apartment in D.C., as well as a long litany of trips he'd taken to exotic destinations like Paris and the Bahamas, all paid for by special interests with business before the government.

This was technically legal. But nearly fifty trips over his first term—at a cost of nearly $100,000—spoke to a guy who was way too close to powerful interests. In fact, the Center for Responsibility and Ethics in Washington awarded him an Honorable Mention in their list of the "Most Corrupt" people in Washington (a list that, by the way, included both Democrats and Republicans).

In early October, a reporter from *Harper's* magazine had started digging into rumors that a businessman named Nasser Kazeminy, who had flown Norm around the world on his private plane, had also bought Norm some suits. The Senate requires you to report gifts from friends; Norm had not reported being gifted any suits. It was curious, to say the least.

On October 8, when Coleman campaign manager Cullen Sheehan called a press conference to attack me for some unrelated nonsense, a reporter pounced, asking whether there was any truth to the rumor.

"The senator," Sheehan said, "has reported every gift he's ever received."

"That wasn't my question," the reporter responded, but Sheehan gave the same exact answer: "The senator has reported every gift he's ever received."

"So Senator Coleman's friend has not bought these suits for him? Is that correct?"

"The senator," Sheehan repeated, "has reported every gift he's ever received."

Cullen Sheehan never actually answered the question of whether Kazeminy had bought Coleman any suits. But over the next few minutes he would go on to repeat this same oddly legalistic answer nearly a dozen times. It couldn't have been more clear that something was up.

The video went viral, making a round of the national blogs.

*   *   *

I was as curious as anyone as to whether there was some big scandal lurking here. But I was also looking forward to what we had planned for the next day, October 9.

Many of the Republican ads that summer had featured a particular clip of me, my face contorted, my arms waving. I'm practically jumping up and down. I look like I'm having a temper tantrum. It's not my best look.

But I recognized that clip. And I knew exactly where they'd gotten it.

Paul Wellstone had been an amazingly passionate guy, with extraordinary energy. He'd always end speeches with an astounding burst of enthusiasm that brought crowds to their feet. Democrats in the state loved it and always waited in eager anticipation for him to rock it at the end. The closest thing I've experienced has been at Grateful Dead shows.

Now, during the campaign, my friend David Wellstone, one of Paul and Sheila's sons, spent some time touring the state with me. One day I asked David a question that had been on my mind for a few years.

"David, I've heard this thing about your dad, and I wanted to ask you. I heard that he had so much energy that when you kids played soccer, he'd run up and down the sidelines following the ball back and forth up and down the field. Is that true?"

"Yeah." David nodded. "But get this. I ran cross-country." He paused for effect.

He didn't…!?

David nodded again. "My dad used to run alongside me just off the side of the course. About three hundred yards from the finish, I'd be about ten yards behind the leader and totally out of gas, and my dad would start yelling, 'You can take this guy! You can take this guy! You can do it! You can take this guy!!!'"

Now imagine how weird that was for the *other* guy.

I started telling that story in my stump speech. And I'd end with running in place, wildly gesticulating, screaming, "You can take this guy! You can take this guy!!!" and then I'd tell the end of the story.

Which was David saying, "And wouldn't you know it, I'd take that guy!"

Then I'd exhort the crowd, "I need you to be my Paul! Will you be my Paul!? Will you be my Paul!!?"

Crowds loved the story, so I started doing it at the end of rallies. And Republicans had taken their tracker's footage of this and run it through the DeHumorizer™ (which apparently could process body language just as efficiently as it could words). Without the sound, I looked pretty crazy.

So our ad, another Saul Shorr joint, simply explained what they'd done. It opened on a picture of Paul. No music. "Paul Wellstone used to run alongside his son David when David was running cross-country races," began the narrator, an elderly gentleman who sounded like the guy from Pepperidge Farm commercials. "Listen to Al Franken tell the story."

And then the video of me telling the story, with David Wellstone sitting right there and a charmed crowd grinning and chuckling at the memory of Paul. And when I got to the "You can take this guy!!!" part, the narrator pauses the clip. "Look familiar?" he asks, as a few frames from the Republican ad that had taken me out of context slid onto the screen next to me. "That's right. Ads for Norm Coleman used footage of Al Franken telling this story about Paul Wellstone and his son, and tried to make it seem like he was angry."

It's not uncommon to see one ad debunking another ad. But this one felt different, with no music, no hyperventilating narration, no flashy graphics, and a tone that suggested it was more in sadness than in anger. It was, in a way, an ad not just about one deliberate mischaracterization, but about the entire rotten campaign Republicans had run against me. If they could lie about me telling a story about my late friend, a story that was about his positive energy and his enthusiasm and his spirit, then what else were they lying about? Could we trust anything they said? And what did it say about *Norm* that this was how he was hoping to keep his job?

* * *

"Minnesota deserves better," the ad concluded, and I think Coleman must have realized Minnesotans would agree. Because the very next day, he announced that he was going to pull down all of his negative ads and run a purely positive campaign the rest of the way. He explained that he had come to his decision over the recent Yom Kippur holiday. Yom Kippur, the Day of Atonement, is the holiest day on the Jewish calendar, and Norm had evidently had an epiphany.

I decided I was not all that interested in returning to Washington for another six years based on the judgment of voters that I was not as bad as the other guys. I want folks to vote for me, and not against the other folks.

It was probably just a coincidence that a recent poll had shown that, by a more than two-to-one margin, voters blamed Norm more than me for the negative tone of the race. And it was probably just a coincidence that this was happening the day after we'd busted him telling a particularly ugly lie about my Paul Wellstone impersonation. And it was probably just a coincidence that, two days earlier, his campaign manager had signaled to the world that there was likely a major ethics scandal brewing in Norm's closet.

We were incredulous. "It's like an arsonist burning down every house in the village and then asking to be named fire chief," we told the press.

But, incredibly, his claptrap[USS] seemed to be working, and our lead began to dwindle.

Franken Internal Poll, October 15: Franken 39, Coleman 32, Barkley 24.

Franken Internal Poll, October 21: Franken 39, Coleman 35, Barkley 21.

Franken Internal Poll, October 23: Franken 40, Coleman 37, Barkley 18.

Chapter 20

"Has It Gotten That Bad?!"

On October 25, I woke up in a bad mood.

At a debate the night before, I had gone around and around with Coleman and Barkley on the subject of guns. It was the same argument Democrats and Republicans always have: They insisted that I wanted to take everyone's guns away, I insisted that I didn't.

Now, Minnesota is a fairly pro-gun state. A lot of Minnesotans hunt—deer and pheasants in particular. But the Frankens didn't. Dad had taken me and Owen fishing, but not hunting. In fact, the first time I ever shot a gun was during the campaign.

Congressman Collin Peterson from rural western Minnesota, chairman of the House Agriculture Committee, had invited me to go pheasant hunting in October 2007, and I couldn't very well say no. But this was a mere year and a half after Vice President Cheney had shot his seventy-eight-year-old lawyer friend,

Harry Whittington, in the face while hunting quail. If Cheney, an avid lifelong hunter, could shoot a friend in the face while bird hunting, wasn't it possible, even likely, that I could shoot Collin, whom I barely knew, in the face? That wouldn't help my campaign at all!

So I bought a shotgun and went to a range to shoot clay pigeons a couple of times. The day before the hunt, my team gave me a brief:

SHOOT THIS:

NOT THIS:

Mission accomplished. I bagged a couple pheasants that beautiful fall day, and Collin's face emerged entirely intact.

Anyway, I told this story during the debate. But Coleman was still trying to paint me as a gun-grabber—the kind of lie that, as you may recall from my previous books, drives me nuts.

So I was kind of cranky the next morning as I was rushing out the door for a full day of campaigning. Suddenly it occurred to me that there would be media at some of my events. I stopped in my tracks. Playing it out in my mind, I realized that a member of the press might ask me if I really owned a shotgun. And then to trick me, they might ask me the brand of the gun, which I could not remember for the life of me. What if they ask, and I say Remington when I really own a—omigod, I don't even know the name of another shotgun! This could be a disaster! What kind of Minnesotan doesn't know the make of his own shotgun? Certainly not one who expects to represent the state in the United States Senate! Wait! Winchester?!

This kind of confused thinking takes time, and by now I was running late. But I just had to check on my shotgun, which we kept upstairs in the guest-room closet for suicidal guests. My eighty-five-year-old mother-in-law, the one who cried when she saw the commercial that suggested I was into bestiality, was staying with us for the remainder of the campaign. I ran up the stairs and knocked on her door.

"Fran?!" Remember, Franni's a junior. "Fran, are you decent?"

"What?!" Fran is very hard of hearing.

"Can I open the door?!" I yelled. "Are you dressed?!"

The door swung open, my mother-in-law in her robe, looking slightly puzzled.

"I need to find my gun!" I shouted as I passed her, heading to the closet.

"Your tie?"

"No! No! My gun! MY GUN!"

In the closet, I could not find the shotgun, which I had left (unloaded) standing upright in a corner. The shotgun was gone!

"Your gun?" my mother-in-law asked.

"Yes! My gun! I can't find my gun!" I was frantic. Finding my gun was supposed to take seconds. Now my campaign was one question away from crashing and burning *and* I was going to be late for my first event!

I flew past Fran out into the hallway, down the stairs, and out the door.

Moments later my distraught mother-in-law came downstairs and found Franni in the kitchen. "Has it gotten that bad?!" she cried. "Has it gotten so bad that Al has to carry a gun?!"

* * *

By this point, Barack Obama had opened up a significant lead over John McCain, and Democratic Senate candidates around the country were on the rise as well. My race seemed to be one of the few where things were getting hairier and hairier. So a lot of national Democrats volunteered to come to Minnesota to help out by holding big rallies.

Big rallies look great on TV, of course, and guarantee you coverage in the newspaper, which is great. But they're also opportunities to build your get-out-the-vote program. You station volunteers with clipboards all around the room and urge people to sign pledge cards committing to vote. Then, in the days leading up to the election, you follow up and make sure people follow through.

The Clintons were champs. Hillary came to Minneapolis on October 21 for a huge afternoon rally at the University of Minnesota. Then Bill for another at the Minneapolis Convention Center on October 30, the Thursday before the election. That weekend, with our numbers on the Iron Range looking shaky, we called Hillary and asked her to come back. She saw how close the race looked and agreed to come to Duluth for another rally to help get me over the top.

But one person who had no interest in providing that help was Barack Obama.

I believe President Obama has been a hero—one of the best leaders this country has ever had, a man of incredible grace and bountiful intelligence who made real progress for America and deserves to go down in history as one of our very best presidents.

But Candidate Obama, or at least the Obama campaign, was extremely unhelpful. After our Minneapolis rally, Hillary was heading up to the Range for a rally for Obama in Hibbing. Amy and I joined her on the flight. Only the Obama campaign wouldn't allow me on the stage, so Hillary and Amy and Congressman Jim Oberstar would just point to me and say nice things about me, and I'd stand up in the crowd and wave. Awkward.

Over and over again, we asked the Obama campaign to come to Minnesota to hold a big rally, or to hold a small rally, or to land his damn plane at the airport even one time so the newspaper could have a picture of me standing next to the incredibly popular president-in-waiting. No dice. When on October 31 he landed in Des Moines, just a short hop from Rochester, Minnesota, it almost seemed like he was going out of his way to avoid me.

* * *

On October 28, a week before the election, our tracking poll found me up by five: Franken 41, Coleman 36, Barkley 19. The next day, October 29, it was a three-point lead: Franken 40, Coleman 37, Barkley 18.

That day, a weird thing happened. Norm was leaving a campaign event in St. Cloud when, out of nowhere, two men jumped out of the bushes and started chasing him to his car. Does that sound like the kind of Jason Bourne–style action this narrative has been in desperate need of all along? Well, sorry. They weren't secret agents sent to retrieve a microchip. They were reporters—from the *Star Tribune*. In fact, they were *investigative* reporters, guys like the team in *Spotlight* who dig into big scandals. And, boy, did they have a doozy of a scandal to ask Norm about.

Their story ran the next day, Thursday, October 30. It explained that, earlier that week, a lawsuit had been filed in Texas by Paul McKim, the former CEO of an oil and gas services company called Deep Marine Technology (DMT), alleging that the controlling shareholder of DMT had improperly diverted company resources.

That controlling shareholder? Nasser Kazeminy— yep, the guy who had flown Norm around the world on vacation and also bought him suits. And that improper diversion of company resources? A payoff to Norm Coleman.

The lawsuit alleged that Kazeminy had funneled money to Coleman through a Minneapolis insurance firm where Coleman's wife, Laurie, worked in a (no-show) job as an insurance consultant (despite the fact that she had no experience in the field of insurance). McKim said that the chief financial officer of DMT had relayed a conversation in which Kazeminy explained that "U.S. Senators don't make shit" and detailed a plan to send the Colemans $25,000 a month. In fact, according to the lawsuit, three of these $25,000 payments went through before McKim could stop the scheme.

Someone had delivered a copy of the lawsuit to the *Star Tribune* in an anonymous envelope. And now its two ace investigative reporters were waving copies of it at Norm Coleman, who dove into his SUV. The reporters continued to demand answers, pounding on the windows until the car peeled out. The DSCC tracker's video was striking, and so was Coleman's response—he canceled all his events that afternoon.

"Huh," I thought upon hearing about all this. "That doesn't sound *totally* unlike Norm. Probably good for me, right?" But of course, I had no idea whether any of it was true. And I resolved to just keep focused on my own message.

Eventually, Norm emerged to deny the allegations, which came as no surprise. What *did* come as a surprise to me, although I guess it shouldn't have, was that he accused me of being behind the lawsuit in the first place.

"Huh," I thought upon hearing that. "That's *insane*." I'd never heard of the lawsuit, or of Paul McKim, or of Deep Marine Technology. And how exactly had I convinced the Republican CEO of a

Texas company to file a huge lawsuit? It seemed like a kind of desperate accusation.

"Oh well," I thought. "People won't buy that."

* * *

Our tracking poll on Thursday the thirtieth showed me up by two; our tracking poll on Friday the thirty-first showed me up by one.

The final weekend of a campaign is usually all about getting out the vote. Your final TV ads are locked in. Your final rallies are set. It's just a straight-ahead sprint to the finish line.

But not for us.

On Saturday, November 1, Norm did something that even I couldn't believe. He put up a hastily shot last-minute ad featuring him and Laurie sitting side by side on their couch. "Al Franken's eleventh-hour attack," Norm begins sadly. "Phony accusations filled with lies delivered anonymously to a Minnesota newspaper before being filed in a Texas court. A vicious personal attack on my wife. This time Al Franken's crossed the line."

It was Hall-of-Fame-level chutzpah. "A vicious personal attack on my wife." We still had no idea whether anything in the lawsuit was true—but it certainly wasn't a "personal attack," at least not from me, and it wasn't on Laurie. It was a very serious allegation that Norm had accepted bribes—which, again, hadn't come from me.

Looking back at it now, I guess I can see how he might have felt like that was his only move. But at the time, I just couldn't believe the gall. The whole thing felt like a new level of ugly. This wasn't what I'd signed up for.

We quickly put together a response of our own in which I flat-out accused Norm of lying. But stations told us it was too late to "change traffic"—to replace the issue-focused ads we'd been planning with this new response. Schriock bullied them into doing it anyway.

Schriock was doing a lot of bullying that week. As materials arrived at DFL headquarters for the weekend's big get-out-the-vote push, we got a look at the doorhangers that canvassers would leave for voters to discover on election day. Funded and approved by the Obama campaign in Chicago, they featured big pictures of Barack Obama and encouragements to vote for various down-ballot offices on the DFL ticket—but barely any mention of the Senate race. Obama had decided to basically pretend that I wasn't even on the ballot.

Fortunately, the guy running the Obama campaign's Minnesota efforts was Jeff Blodgett. Schriock pleaded with him: If our campaign paid to redo the doorhangers, only this time with me included prominently on them, would Jeff go rogue and use them instead of the ones he'd gotten from Chicago? Jeff agreed. The Franken-free doorhangers vanished.

* * *

Then, on Sunday night, November 2, two days out, we met for our final debate at the Fitzgerald Theater. I got off one good line—"This is not about Norm Coleman's wife. This is about Senator Coleman's political sugar daddy!"—but otherwise tried to keep the focus on the issues. Everyone was on edge. Everyone was exhausted.

Afterward, Schriock and Cullen Sheehan, Norm's campaign manager, found themselves together by the stage as the room emptied. "What's going to happen?" he asked her.

"I don't know," she replied.

"Me, either," said Cullen.

The next day—Monday, November 3—we ran the very last round of our tracking poll:

Coleman 41, Franken 39, Barkley 14.

Chapter 21

"It's Close, It's Very Close"

If you've ever watched a TV show or a movie about an election, you know what election day looks like: forests of candidate signs outside polling places, TV news trucks doing live spots, "I Voted!" stickers on everyone's lapels.

But until you've been a candidate, or worked on a campaign, or been a Hillary Clinton supporter in 2016, it's hard to understand the peculiar kind of anxiety that takes hold as the day turns to evening. You spend two years working yourself to exhaustion, trying to do everything right, and then, at a certain point on a fall Tuesday, it's suddenly no longer in your hands. You still carry all the emotional weight of the campaign. But there's really nothing left for you to do except pester everyone around you with the same question: "What are you hearing?"

One person who was asking that question was

Chuck Schumer. He had called Schriock that morning and said he knew what was going to happen in every Senate race in the country except ours. "So, what's going to happen there?" he had asked her.

"It's close," Schriock had told him. "It's very close."

A friend of mine, who worked with one of the networks, heard in the late afternoon that exit polls from Minnesota were looking good for me. Very good, in fact. Like, *really* good. Of course, this was the same guy who four years earlier had called to tell me that the exit polls looked very good for Kerry.* So as the Frankens arrived at election night headquarters at the Crowne Plaza hotel in St. Paul, silently riding the elevator up to our suite, my optimism was tempered with an equal dose of pessimism. Very fitting for what lay ahead.

* * *

As the polls began closing in the East, with states like New Hampshire, Pennsylvania, and Virginia going for Barack Obama, it was quickly becoming clear that this would be an especially bad night for racists all across the country.†

The networks quickly started calling races, and Democrats were picking up one Senate seat after

---

* Howard Fineman.

† Eight years later, they would make an extraordinary comeback.

another. At 8 p.m., the polls closed in Minnesota, and returns began to trickle in.

"How does it look?" I asked Schriock.

"It's early," she answered. "But it looks close."

Precincts and counties continued to come in. "How we doin'?" I asked Schriock.

"It looks like it's going to be close."

As we scrutinized the Minnesota returns, Democrats continued to gain Senate seats and Barack Obama continued his sweep to victory.

"What's it look like?" I'd ask Schriock.

"It's going to be very close."

The networks agreed with Schriock. "A very close race in Minnesota," they'd say, "between incumbent Republican Norm Coleman and former *Saturday Night Live* comedian Al Franken."

This was beginning to become unpleasant. No joke.

Then, at 10 p.m. central time, as soon as the polls closed on the West Coast, the networks called the presidential race for Barack Obama.

It was a stunning moment. The networks cut to a quarter million people in Grant Park in Chicago going absolutely nuts. We could not take our eyes off the TV. That mass of people—all ages, all races—cheering, jumping for joy, waving sparklers, grinning, laughing, crying. I didn't know whether to laugh or cry myself. *My God! He won! Obama won!*

And then he and his family took the stage. Pandemonium. We had a young, smart, cool, handsome president-elect! And he had a young, smart, cool, beautiful family! And they were black! Holy crap!

I felt lifted. Elated almost. But not quite. "Why?" I asked myself. "Why am I not euphoric?"

Oh. Right.

I was having a rugged night emotionally. I'd say the same was true for pretty much everyone on our team. But Schriock and Dan Cramer, the Wellstone alum who was running our field program, were all business, analyzing the returns precinct by precinct.

"How's it looking?" I asked Schriock.

"It's going to be very close," she said.

I tried Dan, hoping for a better answer.

"*Very* close," he said.

* * *

At least Franni was confident. To this day, she will say, "I just knew you were going to win." And to this day, I will contend that there was absolutely no reason for her to feel that way.

By midnight, it was getting clearer than ever that the outcome would be, in Schriock's words, "very, very close."

When Franni and I went to bed around three in the morning, we were behind by about fifteen hundred votes. There were still votes out from St. Louis

County, which included Duluth and the Iron Range, so there was reason to hope that I'd wake up refreshed three hours later with a lead. There were also votes outstanding in the exurbs of Minneapolis, so there was reason to worry that I'd wake up refreshed three hours later a loser.

When I did wake up three hours later, thoroughly unrefreshed, I was still behind. But the margin had narrowed slightly. It was now very, very, *very* close. About eleven hundred votes. Or about four one-hundredths of a percent.

At 6:30 in the morning, with nine of the state's more than four thousand precincts still left to report, the AP called the race for Coleman. But we knew the race was going to overtime regardless. Under state law in Minnesota, a recount is automatically triggered if an election is within one-half of a percent.

Schriock asked me and Franni if we were willing to go through a recount. We looked at each other and said, "Yeah!"

At 10:30 a.m., with the remaining nine precincts counted, and Coleman's margin now 725 votes, Norm held a press conference and declared himself the winner. When asked what he would do if he were in my place, Coleman was very clear. "I would step back. I just think the need for the healing process is so important. The possibility of any change of this magnitude in the voting system we have is so remote."

So, in the interest of "healing," Norm had decided that were he behind, he would step back. It wouldn't be long before Norm would reverse himself and take the "anti-healing" position.

Chapter 22

The Recount

In August 2012, I went out to Washington state to do a fund-raiser for my colleague Senator Maria Cantwell. After the event, the two of us sat together on some rich person's porch and talked about senator stuff.

Maria was reflecting back on her first race for the Senate in 2000, which she had won after a painful two-week recount. Let me repeat that: a painful *two-week* recount.

As she described her two-week ordeal, I could see the anguish clearly written on Maria's face. Then she turned to me and asked, "How long was *your* recount?"

"Eight months."

"Oh my God. How did you do that?"

"Well," I said, putting things in perspective, "it wasn't the Bataan Death March."

Technically, it wasn't an eight-month recount. The

recount itself actually ended on January 5, in time for me to be seated with the rest of my class on January 6. So it was a *two*-month recount. Worse than Maria's, but still.

On January 6, however, Norm Coleman officially took the anti-healing position, filing what is known as an election contest. In other words, he went to court to try to overturn my victory.

That thing, the election contest? *That* took a while. The contest wouldn't be decided until April 13. And then Norm, doubling down on the anti-healing thing, appealed that ruling to the Minnesota Supreme Court, which ate up another two and a half months.

But, you know. No hard feelings.

* * *

Minnesota is widely and rightly lauded for its civic spirit, which is reflected not just in the high-minded tone of its political discourse (until Norm and I ruined that forever) and its high level of voter turnout (in 2008, as in the previous six federal elections, Minnesota led the nation), but also in its election laws.

Our election officials are transparent and accountable. Our procedures are careful and methodical. We take our time to get it right.

For example: Even before a recount, there's a process called a canvass.

You know the vote totals that you see next to

candidates' names on election night? Yeah. Those are always wrong.

Why? Well, because human beings are fallible. And the people who count votes are human beings.

In Minnesota, the election night count is tabulated by the secretary of state's office based on results they get from precincts across the state, either by computer or by phone. And in that process, little mistakes happen: arithmetic errors, transposed numbers, sevens that look like ones. An election official will say "nine hundred and sixteen" and the person on the other end of the phone will hear "nine hundred and sixty." Stuff like that.

So the election night count is always off. Sometimes by a little, sometimes by a lot. And that's why election officials always do a canvass: a process by which they go back through the precinct-by-precinct data, check their math, and reconcile all the numbers to make sure they've fixed any errors.

This happens after every election, and it can change the margin by tens of votes, hundreds of votes, or thousands of votes. And the reason you almost never hear about it is that even a shift of thousands of votes almost never matters.

But this time, with Norm up by just 725 votes heading into the canvass, it did matter. The canvass reduced his margin to 215 votes.

How? Well, here's an example: In rural Partridge

Township, the tape from the voting machines showed that Norm got 143 votes to my 129. Those results were written on a form and delivered by hand to the county seat, Pine City, where they were to be typed into a computer and submitted to the secretary of state's office.

But the county worker typing in those results accidentally entered just 29 votes for me—he or she missed the "1" key on the keyboard. It was the kind of mistake anyone could have made, especially at the end of a long election day. And during the canvass, when someone checked that 143–29 total against the original forms, the mistake was discovered and corrected. Which meant 100 votes got added to my total.

The entire canvass actually produced a relatively small shift in votes compared to previous statewide elections (for example, in 2006, Amy Klobuchar's margin increased by 2,854 votes during the canvass— no one cared, though, because she had won by more than 400,000 votes). But because it resulted in Norm's already very small margin becoming even very smaller, his campaign freaked out.

Panicking at the realization that Norm's emphatic declaration of victory might have been premature, they immediately cried foul, describing the entirely routine correction of errors like the one in Partridge Township as "statistically dubious and improbable shifts that are overwhelmingly accruing to the benefit of Al Franken."

A tone had been set: The 725-vote lead Norm held the morning after the election would henceforth be treated as the only credible result. Any change to that margin (at least, any change that wasn't in his favor) would be treated as evidence that I was trying to steal the election.

*   *   *

Then we were on to the hand recount, which is just that: Election officials recount each individual ballot by hand.

That's possible in Minnesota because of our voting technology. Optical-scan machines read *paper ballots* that voters mark by filling in a circle, like on an SAT test.

So, much of the process involves looking at a ballot that is clearly marked for a candidate and saying, "Yup, that ballot is clearly marked for that candidate."

But occasionally it can be unclear whether a given ballot should or shouldn't be counted, or which candidate it should be counted for.

For example: A voter might have screwed up the filling-in-the-circle instruction. Or a voter who had changed her mind might have filled out the circle for one candidate, crossed it out, and filled out a circle for another candidate. Or a voter who had brought a hot dog into the voting booth might have gotten mustard on his ballot.

In any event, the election judge makes a call as best he or she can. But each campaign gets to have representatives present who can challenge that call if they disagree. If a ballot is challenged, it gets set aside to be adjudicated by the State Canvassing Board, which for my recount consisted of two Republican appointees, two Democratic appointees, and an Independent appointee.

By the end of the recount, the Canvassing Board was handed a pile of 1,325 disputed ballots (out of 2.9 million cast, counted, and recounted). They examined each one, by hand, in public, during lengthy and tedious sessions live-streamed on the Internet.

In the end, the board split 3–2 on just fourteen ballots. They split 4–1 forty-five times. But they were unanimous on all the rest.

And when they were done, I was up by 49 votes.

One more wrinkle: Some voters had tried to cast absentee ballots, only to have those ballots rejected. And our team discovered that some of those absentee ballots *shouldn't* have been rejected. So we went to court to make the case that wrongly rejected absentee votes should be counted. We didn't know who the votes were for, but we figured we might as well stick with the position we had adopted from the outset: "Count every legal vote." Coleman stuck with his "I won, screw you" position.

In the end, the court ruled that 933 wrongly

rejected absentee ballots should in fact be counted. But by the time they were to be opened, Norm wasn't in the lead anymore. I was. Which made it even more nerve-racking to watch those ballots be opened for the first time, live on the Internet: "Franken ... Franken ... Coleman ... Barkley ... Franken ... Coleman ..."

Fortunately, they wound up breaking in my favor, and my lead grew from 49 votes to 225, which is the margin the Canvassing Board certified on January 5, declaring me the winner. Yay.

* * *

Where the hell was I during all of this? In my house, mostly, calling people for money to pay our bafflingly large and expensive team of lawyers, led by Democratic super-attorney Marc Elias (if you're ever in Washington, check out the Franken Wing of the Perkins Coie law office—it's gorgeous).

True to form, Stephanie Schriock had a plan in place for an eventual recount. And my role in that plan was to raise the money to pay for it, and nothing else.

You see, I learned something very important during the recount: not to trust my instincts. For example, when I heard Coleman suggest that I step back and let the healing begin, my instinct was to respond with something biting and sarcastic. But, wisely, my team told me to shut up. Which I did.

And wouldn't you know it, as the weeks, and then

months, passed, Minnesotans seemed to appreciate it. One day, as I was grocery shopping, a woman came up to me and said, "I like the way you're handling the recount." I held up the avocado I was inspecting and said, "You see this avocado? It's handling the recount the exact same way I am."

In fairness to me, the avocado didn't have to spend six to eight hours a day calling wealthy avocados to raise lots and lots of money to pay for its many, many lawyers.

When the State Canvassing Board declared me the winner, I finally spoke to the press for the first time since the recount had begun. I tried to strike a conciliatory note. "I know this is not an easy day for Norm Coleman and his family," I said, "and I know that because Franni and I and the kids have had plenty of time over the past two months to contemplate the possibility that this election would turn out differently."

Pretty gracious, don't you think?

I wrapped up my remarks and immediately flew to Washington so I could be sworn in with the rest of the new senators the next day, January 6.

Except, of course, that didn't happen. Thanks to the delay caused by Norm's unsuccessful election contest and his subsequent unsuccessful appeal of his unsuccessful election contest, it would be almost exactly six more months before I could get to work in the Senate.

Which meant for six months Minnesota would only have one senator: Norm's term had expired, and with no one there to replace him, Amy Klobuchar's office had to handle double the constituent service duty, which doesn't sound like a big deal unless you're a Minnesotan trying to get help with a late Social Security check.

It also meant that President Obama had one less Democratic senator there to help him rescue the economy (as you'll see in a few pages, Republicans had no interest in helping at all). Which oddly didn't seem to trouble the new president. Soon after Norm filed his election contest, Schriock got a call from a top Obama adviser, who proudly informed her that a check for $20,000 from the Democratic National Committee to help pay our legal bills was on its way.

"Don't you dare do that," Schriock barked. The Coleman campaign had just received a *million dollars* from the Republican National Committee. A check for $20,000 from the DNC would be worse than getting nothing.

She called her friend Jim Messina, who had become the president's deputy chief of staff, to make that point. Sheepishly, he asked, "So, you were expecting something with another zero?"

"Another *two* zeroes," Schriock responded.

Ultimately, we got the one extra zero ($200,000). And when I visited Washington shortly after, I got a promise from that "top Obama adviser" that the new president (whose approval rating was well over 60 percent) would do a fund-raiser for me. He never did. But, again, overall: great president.

* * *

In almost every other state, the governor and secretary of state would have signed an election certificate as soon as I won the recount, and I would have been seated provisionally in the U.S. Senate along with the rest of my Senate class while the legal contest was being resolved.

Not in Minnesota. According to Minnesota state law, Governor Tim Pawlenty and Secretary of State Mark Ritchie could not sign the certificate until all state legal remedies had been exhausted.

But after I won the recount, I learned from my lawyer, Marc Elias, that Harry Reid wanted to find a way for the Democratic-controlled U.S. Senate to seat me anyway.

No way, I told him. It just felt wrong. Minnesotans are big into fairness. We love process. And besides, I told Elias, I might want to get reelected.

"You'd have six years to figure that out," he countered.

But I stood firm. I was totally committed to letting this happen however it was going to happen. After the recount, I knew I had in fact received the most votes, and that it was just a matter of time until I got to Washington, the right way.

And in that sense the six-month delay was actually a lot harder on Norm than it was on me. He had lost, and now his legal team was grasping at straws to find some way to reverse his defeat. For me personally, those six months were the most relaxed and enjoyable period of my life from the moment I announced my campaign to, well, right now.

I still had to raise money like crazy. But Franni and I actually got to go out to dinner once in a while instead of just eating peanut butter out of the jar in our darkened kitchen after getting home from a campaign event at two in the morning, like we'd been doing for two years.

We even took a vacation! Although, actually, it was terrible. Schriock insisted that we get out of town for a while, escaping the Minnesota winter for Key West, home of Margaritaville and key lime pie. But we spent the entire miserable week trying to get the Internet to work and then sitting in front of Franni's laptop watching the live stream of the election contest.

It could have been worse. Poor Norm didn't get to eat any key lime pie. He came to court every day and sat somberly at his lawyers' table, looking somewhat like a husband on trial for murdering his wife.*

---

* Just to be clear: Norm was *not* on trial for murdering his wife, or anyone, for that matter. It was a civil proceeding.

Coleman's election contest made a variety of charges of impropriety and unfair treatment, each of which fell apart under the scrutiny of the three-judge panel appointed to hear the contest (one Democratic appointee, one Republican appointee, and, again, one Independent appointed by Jesse Ventura). But all they succeeded in doing was getting another 351 previously rejected absentee ballots counted (which increased my margin to 312 votes).

The judges threw out Norm's contest in a unanimous tripartisan decision. I emerged from my house to give yet another magnanimous victory speech, and that was that.

* * *

Except, of course, that *still* wasn't that. Coleman appealed the case to the Minnesota Supreme Court, which would eat up another two months. By now, he had gone from throwing Hail Marys to simply delaying the inevitable. Which was actually the point.

In April, Republican senator Arlen Specter announced that he was switching parties, giving Democrats fifty-nine votes in the Senate. Once I was seated, we would have a filibuster-proof sixty-vote majority.

Never mind that nobody thought an appeal would have any chance of succeeding. Republicans may have been disappointed that they didn't win the seat, but they could at least draw this out as long as possible.

It wasn't until June 30 that the Minnesota Supreme Court denied Coleman's appeal. Norm called me that day to concede, which he did with notable grace. "It's the best job you'll ever have," he told me.

"Norm," I said, "it couldn't have been any closer."

Later, I would tell Schriock, "I guess I really don't hate him after all."

"Ha!" she cried. "I knew it!"

Once again, I emerged from my house to magnanimously declare victory. The election had been in the fall. I had won the recount in the winter. The contest had been dismissed in the spring. And now, on a glorious summer day, it was finally over.

*   *   *

The moral of the story? Well, for one thing, if you're going to declare a victory that you know full well might not hold up under the scrutiny it's about to receive, maybe try to underplay it a little. Also, if you're a law student with a lot of debt piling up, might I suggest a career in election law?

But, really, the moral of the story is that, as corny as it sounds, your vote can make a huge difference—and your activism can make an even huger one. When you win a race by 312 votes (out of 2.9 million cast!), it's hard not to think about all the individuals who each literally could have been the one who got you elected. I know a lot of Minnesotans who talked to more than

312 voters, or dropped more than 312 pieces of literature, or gave us twenty bucks so we could run a rural radio ad that reached more than 312 people.

So when I go to DFL events in Minnesota now, I have a lot of people to thank—and I have to thank them effusively, because each and every volunteer could have been the one who made the difference between winning and losing.

Chapter 23

Welcome to the NFL

After Norm Coleman's election contest was thrown out in April, it was obvious to everyone that I was going to be seated sooner or later. And when Arlen Specter switched parties two days later, making me the presumptive filibuster-busting sixtieth Democratic vote, my imminent arrival in the Senate became what Joe Biden would call a big freakin'[USVP] deal.

Specter had joined Biden in the Senate in 1981, so the two had served together for nearly three decades, and it was the vice president who had brokered Specter's party switch. As part of the deal, Specter got to keep his three decades of seniority, meaning he would be well positioned to snag big committee chairmanships over more junior Democrats even if they had been part of the caucus for years. Also a big deal. But something that a lot of Democratic senators weren't thrilled about.

Then, in a May 5 interview with the *New York Times*, Specter, now a Democrat, was asked who he wanted to win in Minnesota. He said Norm Coleman. Evidently Arlen had forgotten that he had changed uniforms. It gave disgruntled Democratic senators a great excuse to strip him of his seniority and send him to the back of the line within the caucus, which they did in an elaborate ceremony involving a sword, a candle, and a silver Masonic trowel made by Paul Revere.

A couple of days later, Schriock, Franni, and I headed over to the White House for a meeting with Vice President Biden, who I'd always been a big fan of.

The three of us were ushered into the vice president's office in the West Wing, where we waited for just a few minutes before Biden walked in and warmly welcomed us. Then, sitting on the couch across from us, he turned very serious.

"I've been in this town forty years," he said. "And let me tell you how you succeed in this town—how I got here." He leaned toward me to bring home the import of what he was about to say.

"Never promise anything you can't deliver. Never. Promise. Anything. You can't deliver."

I nodded. I understood. I wasn't going to do that. I. Wasn't. Going. To do that.

Then he turned to the little unpleasantness regarding Specter. The vice president wanted to make sure I wasn't offended and wouldn't hold it against Arlen.

"Oh, no," I said. "Just tell Arlen that I know it was a rookie mistake."

This brought a small, slightly pained laugh from the vice president. Then, "No, I won't tell him that."

I nodded. Okay.

Then he turned to business. "Listen. You're going to be seated soon. Might be a week. Might be a month. But you're going to be seated. And we've got to get you something. We need to get you something that you can deliver right away for the people of Minnesota."

This sounded good.

"Is there anything you can think of?" he asked.

"Well…" I hadn't prepared for this. "I guess completing the Northstar Line? That's the commuter rail line that's supposed to go from Minneapolis to St. Cloud."

The vice president nodded. It was a brilliant nod, because it was utterly ambiguous. Maybe he knew what I was talking about, maybe he didn't. God, he was good at this.

"But, see, right now it only goes from Minneapolis to Big Lake? Which is about halfway to St. Cloud?"

"Right."

"And, well, right after the stimulus passed, you went to St. Cloud, and you said that we were going to complete the line with the money from the stimulus."

Another nod. Yes, he remembered. "How much is that going to cost?" he asked.

"I think $135 million?" I knew that was a lot. But it was a $787 *billion* stimulus bill.

Biden considered it for a couple of seconds, then nodded decisively. "Then that's what we're going to do! A few days after you get seated, we'll announce that we're going to complete that line—and we're gonna give *you* the credit."

Wow! That's great!

"So, this is how things work," I thought. "Not so hard, this whole senator thing!" It wouldn't be long before I was the crafty veteran, a giant of the Senate in my own right, doling out wise, if slightly patronizing and rather obvious, advice to newbies. The vice president and I shook hands and then he gave Franni and Schriock nice hugs.

We left the veep's office feeling good. As we were headed out, we walked by Ron Klain's office. Ron had been Vice President Gore's chief of staff and was doing the same job now for Biden. Ron popped out and said hi.

"How'd it go?" he asked cheerily.

"Really well!" I said, beaming. "He said we're going to get the Northstar Line finished up to St. Cloud!"

Ron knew exactly what I was talking about. "Hmm. How much is that going to cost?" he asked with significantly less cheer.

"I think about $135 million," I answered brightly.

There was the slightest pause, me grinning from ear to ear.

Then Ron shook his head. "No."

Huh?

"That's too much," he said.

And then Schriock, Franni, and I went home.

Welcome to the NFL.

Chapter 24

I Actually Become a Senator

In addition to calling people for money, traveling to raise money, and complaining about how much money I had to raise, I spent some time during the election contest looking for a chief of staff.

Stephanie Schriock asked a friend named Drew Littman, who had been Barbara Boxer's chief of staff, to help me find someone suitable. Drew introduced me to a number of very impressive candidates. But none was as impressive as Drew himself. Eventually I pulled a reverse Cheney* and just offered him the job.

One of the first, and smartest, things Drew did was to set up a meeting with Tamera Luzzatto, who had been Hillary Clinton's chief of staff when Hillary served in the Senate.

---

* Dick Cheney was the head of the search team that, after an exhaustive search, chose Dick Cheney as George W. Bush's running mate.

It had occurred to Drew that I might be facing some challenges similar to those that Hillary had faced: Republicans might be particularly wary of me, considering that I had spent so much time heaping scorn and ridicule upon them, while Democrats might be concerned that, as something of a celebrity, I might steal some of their camera time. Hillary had navigated those challenges with notable success, not just earning the respect of her colleagues on both sides of the aisle, but getting a whole lot done for the people of her state. "Wow," I thought, "she should be president someday."

So we sat down with Tamera, who spelled out the "Hillary Model."

Simply put, it's: Be a workhorse, not a showhorse. Go to all your hearings. Come early, stay late. Do your homework. Don't do national press. Be accessible to your state media and to your constituents.

That sounded smart to me. I'd be available to Minnesota press and Minnesota constituents. I'd be knowledgeable about Minnesota issues. I'd be Minnesota's senator and nobody else's.

*   *   *

I finally actually *became* Minnesota's senator on July 7, 2009.

Normally, there are thirty-three or thirty-four senators being sworn in on the same day—the first day of the new Congress that is convened in January.

Because there are so many, each one only gets three or four tickets for family and friends to sit in the gallery, where they can watch the new or reelected senators take the oath of office from the vice president, three at a time.

In my case, though, waiting six months really paid off. Because I was the only senator being sworn in that day, the entire Senate gallery was filled with my family, my friends, my supporters, and, of course, my lawyers—who, in a touching nod to the historic moment, had agreed not to bill me for the 1.3 hours they would spend in the Capitol that day.

Many of my new colleagues did me the honor of showing up on the floor for the occasion. Looking around, I saw a lot of my Democratic friends, of course, but also a good number of Republicans, who used the occasion to attach a rider to my swearing-in that would defund Planned Parenthood. Who says Republicans don't have a sense of humor?

My friend Vice President Walter Mondale had flown in from Minnesota. He and Senator Klobuchar walked me down the aisle to take the oath of office on Paul Wellstone's family Bible. As soon as I finished, the gallery erupted in sustained applause.

I looked up and blew a little kiss to Franni and the kids, then scanned the rows to see all my friends and supporters—even Mrs. Molin was there, grinning from ear to ear and clapping madly for her fourth-grade student. Pretty much everyone who had been a key player in my election was there cheering me on (with the exception, I suppose, of Norm Coleman).

My new colleagues stopped by to offer congratulations. I was especially gratified that so many Republicans turned out: Orrin Hatch, Richard Lugar, Sam Brownback, and even Minority Leader Mitch McConnell himself. And whether it was out of respect for the institution or simply an acknowledgment of the ordeal I'd been through, their congratulations were sincere and heartfelt. I took it as a hopeful sign.

I even engaged in some friendly banter with arch-conservative Jim DeMint. "How are things on the far left?" he asked me cheerily.

"They're great," I responded. "How are things on the nutcase right?"

We both laughed. And went on to build a cordial relationship based entirely on giving each other crap.

That afternoon, I got on the Senate subway, the Disneyland-style tram that runs between the Capitol and the Senate office buildings, and happened to sit down across from Chuck Grassley, another old-school Republican.

"You look just like you look on TV!" he greeted me.

"There's a reason for that," I replied. "But, actually, people say I'm shorter than I look on TV."

"Ya," Chuck said in his distinct midwestern twang. "Guess what they say about me?"

"That you're taller than you look on TV?"

"Ya! How'd you know that?"

"Well, you're taller than you look on TV."

"Ya. Guess what else they say about me?"

"That you're friendlier than you seem on TV."

"Ya! How'd you know that?"

"Because you're friendlier than you seem on TV." This was becoming a real meet-cute. "You know," I said, taking a chance, "it wouldn't hurt to smile every once in a while."

"Well," Chuck said dubiously, "normally what I'm talkin' about is pretty serious."

"Well, you could smile at the beginning. Then talk about the serious stuff. Then smile again at the end."

"Oh, ya!" Chuck grinned. "That's a good idea!"

I was already making friends! And in fact, Chuck would go on to cosponsor more of my legislation than any of my other Republican colleagues.

* * *

Later that day, I cast my first vote, for which I was strongly rebuked by John McCain (widely considered one of the Senate's strongest rebukers), because it had been a vote to defeat an amendment of his that would have stripped antiterrorist funding for commercial bus lines.

But, hey, it was a start.

Chapter 25

My First Big Win*

It can take new senators months or even years to pass their first piece of legislation. It took me two weeks. Although, to be fair, I'd had a long time to work on it before I got there.

I first met retired Army captain Luis Montalvan at an event for the Iraq and Afghanistan Veterans of America at the Obama inaugural. I also met Tuesday, his beautiful golden retriever. Luis told me he wouldn't have been able to come to the event if it weren't for Tuesday.

Luis had served as an intelligence officer in Iraq, and was seriously wounded in Al Anbar Province. He returned with two Bronze Stars, a Purple Heart, and severe PTSD, which manifested itself in panic attacks, nightmares, and acute agoraphobia (the fear of leaving your home), all of which he self-medicated with alcohol.

Then a nonprofit organization contacted Luis and offered to partner him with a service dog. Desperate for any possible solution to his mounting problems, he went to a training facility in upstate New York, where he met Tuesday.

I asked Luis how Tuesday had changed his life.

"Well, Tuesday can anticipate my panic attacks by observing changes in my breathing or smelling my perspiration. So he'll nuzzle me and prevent me from having a panic attack."

Wow.

"If I'm having a nightmare and start thrashing around, Tuesday will jump on the bed and wake me up. And he broke my isolation. You know, you have to take a dog out a couple times a day. And I learned something. People don't like going up to scruffy-looking wounded vets. But they do like coming up to a scruffy-looking vet who has a beautiful dog."

Luis told me that, thanks in large part to Tuesday's help, he had turned his life around, enrolling in journalism school. After graduating, he went on to write a number of bestselling books about his experiences, including a couple of children's books about him and Tuesday, and became an advocate for other veterans. My grandson, Joe, just loves his book, *Tuesday Takes Me There.*

* * *

In the period between the inauguration and my swearing-in, I learned as much as I could about service dogs. I spoke with a couple who now could go to the mall with their autistic son, who loved taking care of his service dog, even as his service dog was taking care of him. I met a veteran who told me his dog kept track of when he was supposed to take his medication and would tug him by his sleeve to remind him if he hadn't taken it as scheduled. I visited a training facility in Minnesota where I saw a German shepherd pick up a nickel with her teeth.

Wow.

As soon as I got to the Senate, I had my staff draw up a bill that would fund a three-year Department of Veterans Affairs study pairing two hundred dogs with veterans suffering from invisible wounds, and measure the benefits to each veteran against the costs of training each service dog, which were not insubstantial, even when offset by all the stray nickels they could pick up. If it worked, we'd have the evidence to argue for expanding the program more widely.

A few days later, Drew and a couple of other staffers walked into my office with a sheaf of paper. There it was, my first piece of legislation! It was kind of a Moment. Everyone was beaming.

I sat down with the pages and began to scan them, making a few notes in the margins where I thought the amendment could read a little snappier.

"Al," someone said. "What are you doing?"

"Just punching it up a bit." Blank stares from the

team. "Making it sing a little bit. You know. So it'll be more fun to read."

There was an awkward silence until Drew said, "Um, no, Al. You don't do that."

"Oh."

"Yeah."

"Well, that'll save me a lot of work," I said, putting down my pen.

In fact, as it turns out, not only do senators not do punch-up, they don't write legislation at all. And neither do their staffs. You may have seen a filmstrip in sixth grade on how a bill becomes a law, but the way a bill becomes a *bill* is via the Office of the Legislative Counsel. Senate staff (from both parties) bring in their bosses' ideas, and then a team of nonpartisan lawyers carefully translates them into unintelligible legalese in order to make sure that bills actually do what their authors want them to do.

Can you even begin to *imagine* how depraved their holiday party must get?

Anyway, I needed a Republican cosponsor, so I called Johnny Isakson from Georgia, who serves on the Veterans' Affairs Committee. Johnny immediately said he loved the idea. Later, he told me why.

Johnny's mother had always hated dogs. When he was growing up, the family dogs were never allowed in the house. But Johnny and his wife, Dianne, had a mutt named Sox (mostly black Lab, but with four white paws—hence the name). Sox was an inside dog who loved to jump up on the couch. And when Johnny's mom would come over to visit, that would always make her furious.

But after Johnny's mom developed Alzheimer's, her mental state deteriorated to the point where she was in a near-constant state of agitation. And when she would stay with Johnny and Dianne, there was just one thing that could calm her down: sitting on their couch, snuggling with Sox.

So Johnny signed on, and the bill sailed through as an amendment to a defense authorization bill.

A week after we broke for August recess, senators gathered in Boston to honor an actual giant of the Senate, Ted Kennedy, who had died after a long fight with brain cancer. Johnny approached me at the memorial. "Al," he said, "I've been getting a great reaction back home for that dog bill of yours. Even from nonveterans. If you ever have another bill you want cosponsored, you let me know."

"Oh, I've got one, Johnny. It's a bill for gay marriage and abortion on demand."

Johnny nodded politely and said, "I'll get back to you."

And you know what? He hasn't.

* * *

I know that's kind of a fun ending to the story. But that's not the actual ending to the story.

Even after Johnny and I got the amendment into the defense authorization bill, and even after the defense authorization bill passed the Senate, I had to find a member of the House to make sure the provision stayed in the final version of the bill.

And even then, an authorization bill doesn't actually fund anything. It just authorizes stuff. Hence the name. The actual funding has to come from an appropriations bill. So we had to then make sure that the defense appropriations bill had money for the study that had been authorized by the authorization bill.

That's a much less fun ending to the story. And even that's not the actual ending.

Did you notice the asterisk at the end of the title of this chapter? You see, it's been more than seven years since my amendment passed. And that three-year study still isn't finished yet.

How is that possible? Well, first the study had to be designed. And since it involved both human beings and animals, it took a lot of extra time to clear both sets of compliance hurdles.

And then once the study finally began in Tampa, it almost immediately hit some speed bumps. First of all, they can't do anything right in Tampa.* It turned

---

* Including, now that I've made this joke, my book signing at Tampa's finest bookseller, the Hudson News at the airport. No, I'm sorry, I've never been to Tampa. I'm sure it's great. I'm just cranky about the study.

out that one of the service dog providers picked for the study shouldn't have been accredited. After a couple of false starts, the Tampa study eventually wound up being scrapped.

I continue to meet periodically with the three-person team from the VA in charge of the study. As frustrated as I was when things went wrong, they were more so. After they learned about the flawed accreditation system for service dogs, they redesigned the study, and as I write this, they've matched nearly two hundred veterans with service dogs in three cities across the country—except this time the dogs are being trained by VA trainers.

Meanwhile, Purdue University has conducted a similar study. And their preliminary results are promising: Veterans who have been matched with service dogs have experienced less depression, less anxiety, a greater sense of satisfaction, and a reduced feeling of isolation.

We're losing twenty veterans a day to suicide. I think my service dogs idea could help. I hope I'm right. And I hope that the VA's three-year study will bear that out—when it's finally finished in 2018, nine years after I got it approved.

* * *

The story of my first bill is, in some ways, a story about politics at its best: I met a heroic American who gave me a good idea, I reached out to experts to craft legislation, I found bipartisan support, and we got it done. Nobody filibustered my bill, or lied about it, or sank it with a poison pill, or hired sleazy lobbyists to stop it from becoming law.

But this is also a story about how, even when everything goes right, politics can be full of setbacks and frustrations.

And sometimes, it's even full of heartbreak: As I was putting this chapter to bed, I got the unfathomable news that Luis Montalvan had taken his own life in a hotel room in Texas.

I guess I should say something here about how, despite this tragedy, I still believe in the potential of the idea he and Tuesday (who wasn't with Luis at the time and is doing fine) inspired—or maybe about how it's a reminder of just how imposing this challenge is, even if we all work together and do our best to address it.

And that's all true. But mostly, I'm just sad. As we worked together on this issue, Luis became more than just a symbol, more than just an ally in an important cause. He became my friend. And even as I work to carry on the fight we shared, I'm going to miss him.

Chapter 26

What Gets Me out of Bed in the Morning

Not long after getting to Washington, I started noticing the overuse of certain clichés. Which I suppose is why they're clichés.

For example, how often have you heard a politician say, "Growing up in [STATE WHERE I GREW UP], I learned the value of hard work"? As if kids in the other forty-nine states grew up learning to slack off. By the way, I use this one *all the time*, but only because, growing up in Minnesota, I really did learn the value of hard work.

Here's another one that drove me crazy. It's just the word "robust." As in "robust funding." Which just means "a lot of funding." Or as in "a robust response." Which just means "a strong response." No human being uses this word in casual conversation. But everyone in Washington uses it all the time.

That's why I issued a fatwa against it in my office. No "robust" in speeches, no "robust" in press releases, no "robust" in *robust* letters calling for *robust* funding to *ensure* (another cliché) a *robust* response to a *pressing* (ugh) problem.

This policy held until I was trying to get a Republican colleague to sign on to a letter I'd written to get stronger funding for Section 8 housing. My colleague reviewed the letter and agreed to sign on, with one condition: that I change the word "strong" to "robust." That's when I gave up the ghost. So if you ever happen to see me giving a speech and I use that word, just know that I deeply hate myself in that moment.

Speaking of existential angst, another thing I noticed was that a lot of people in government kept saying things like, "What gets me out of bed in the morning is making sure our veterans have good jobs," or "What gets me out of bed in the morning is seeing to it that every child in America has a world-class education," or "What gets me out of bed in the morning is doing everything I can to see that our electric grid is secure."

I thought to myself, "Why is everyone in this town so depressed?"*

What gets *me* out of bed in the morning is having

---

* Remember, this was pre-Trump. Now, of course, I don't have to wonder why everyone I talk to is so depressed.

to pee. Sometimes that's also what gets me out of bed in the middle of the night. In either case, I always go right back to bed. The next thing that gets me out of bed in the morning is Franni saying, "It's morning and it's time to get out of bed."

But I never get up right away. My first thought is usually, "Oh, I wish I could sleep some more." Then it's, "Man, I love to sleep." Then I think, "These covers are really nice. And warm, too. I like how it's cool on the underside of the pillow. That's a nice contrast."

Then Franni will come in and say, "C'mon, you really have got to get up. I brought you some coffee."

Then I think, "Mmmm, coffee. How long can I wait to get up before the coffee gets cold?"

Then Franni comes back and says, "C'mon, Al. Really. You're being picked up in half an hour. And I brought you another cup of coffee."

And then I think, "Crap! I have to pee again." So I get up and start to tell Franni about the dream I was having about trying to get someplace but not being able to find it.

"Everyone has that dream," Franni will say, handing me a towel. "Now get in the shower."

The shower usually wakes me. That and the coffee. And as I'm getting dressed in my suit, I start thinking to myself, "It's great to be alive. Now I get to go to the Senate and fight for the uniquely hardworking people of Minnesota!"

Chapter 27

The Case of Perry Mason's
Lost Case

In the Senate, the lion's share of your work gets done through the committees on which you serve, and you get your committee assignments from your party leader. A couple of weeks before I was sworn in, I met with Harry Reid. Harry told me he thought I'd be great on the Judiciary Committee. I pointed out that there are a lot of lawyers in the U.S. Senate and that I wasn't one of them.

"That's why I want you there, Al. We need members with that perspective on Judiciary. You'll be great!"

Of course, Harry was just B.S.ing. I was the last senator to arrive and he had a spot to fill on Judiciary.

During my first week in the Senate, the Judiciary Committee began the confirmation hearings of Judge Sonia Sotomayor for her nomination to the Supreme

Court. As the most junior of the twenty members of the committee, I sat at the end of the dais, next to Senator Arlen Specter of Pennsylvania. Arlen had *presided* over the most recent Supreme Court confirmation hearing, for Samuel Alito, as the Republican chairman of the committee. But as you will recall, when he switched parties and became a Democrat, the Democratic caucus had stripped Arlen of his seniority because he had made intemperate remarks about yours truly. It had to be more than a little galling for the former chairman of the committee to have to sit next to me.

In an attempt to lighten what must have been an uncomfortable moment, I turned to Arlen when he took his place on the first day of the hearings and said, "I'm sorry you have to sit next to a *pisher* like me." *Pisher* is Yiddish for pisher.

Arlen smiled graciously, appreciative of my humility and my appeal to our kinship as members of a people traumatized by centuries of persecution. At least I think that was what was going on.

I was the last member to make my opening ten-minute statement, becoming the first person in American history to have both participated in a Supreme Court confirmation hearing and also played a senator in a sketch about a Supreme Court confirmation hearing.*

---

* I played Senator Paul Simon in a very substantive *SNL* sketch about the Clarence Thomas hearings.

I used the time to develop my thesis that the Roberts Court was an *activist* Court, making one 5–4 pro-corporate ruling after another. That's a pretty common critique now, but I was actually the first Judiciary member to make it. Court watchers were a little startled that this was coming from the Comedian.

As Republican members spent hour upon hour obsessing over Sotomayor's "wise Latina" remarks, Democrats picked up on my activist Court theme. When it was time for my thirty-minute round of questioning, I was set to bring it home.

But I began by referring back to something Amy Klobuchar had asked Judge Sotomayor about earlier in the hearing, which is why Sotomayor had chosen to become a prosecutor. Sotomayor had answered that she had been inspired by watching *Perry Mason* as a kid.

I, too, had watched a lot of *Perry Mason* as a kid. And so I started my questioning by asking her why she was inspired to become a prosecutor by a show in which the prosecutor, Hamilton Burger, lost every case.

And she said, "Actually, Perry Mason lost one case."

Now, I wanted to get to my substantive points, so I said, "Well, we'll return to that later," not actually intending to do so. And I went into my questions.

But with about two minutes left, I didn't really have the time to develop my next line of questioning, so instead I just said, "Judge Sotomayor, you said that Perry Mason lost one case."

"Yes," she responded.

"Which case was that?" I asked.

"I don't know."

I waited a beat and said, "Didn't the White House prepare you?" Big laugh.

My time had now run out, which meant the committee's questioning was over, and the senators on the committee went off to a separate room to receive a classified members-only briefing on the nominee's FBI background check.

Meanwhile, the Web was blowing up about my groundbreaking critique of the Roberts Court. No. It was blowing up about what case it was that Perry Mason lost.

As we filed into the room where we were to receive the briefing, I was still sort of feeling like the new kid in school standing alone in the lunch line. I didn't really know any of the Republicans on the committee, beyond some passing niceties with Lindsey Graham and the subway meet-cute with Chuck Grassley. And then Tom Coburn of Oklahoma walked in and announced authoritatively, "Actually, Perry Mason lost *two* cases."*

---

* "The Case of the Deadly Verdict" and "The Case of the Terrified Typist."

And then Jeff Sessions drawled, "You know what I liked? *Dragnet*!"

Then John Cornyn of Texas chimed in, "I liked *Highway Patrol*."

So, looking for a chance to bond, I said, "I worked with Broderick Crawford." Crawford had been the star of *Highway Patrol*, but was also an iconic tough-guy movie star who won the Oscar for Best Actor in *All the King's Men*.

And *boom*, every Republican in the room just *stopped*. "You worked with Broderick Crawford?!!!"

And I said, "Yeah. He hosted during the first season of *Saturday Night Live*."

I told them about how, the Thursday of that week, I'd been assigned to mind Crawford because it was Saint Patrick's Day and he'd started drinking very early in the day.

Thursdays were the days we taped promos, usually around one in the afternoon, and I'd written a promo for Broderick and Gilda Radner where he had five lines and she had one. But Broderick was already really soused at this point, so I took a line away from him, and he had four lines and Gilda had two. Then I had to make it three and three. By the end, Gilda had five lines and Broderick had one. And we got the thing on tape.

Anyway, I'm telling this story, and suddenly all my

Republican colleagues are going, "You really *were* in show business! You worked with Broderick Crawford!"

So this was my first big breakthrough with my Republican colleagues.

My point is, the Senate is filled not just with lawyers, but with old white men.

Franni thought
she saw Norm
Coleman with a
fruit basket.

Meeting with Vice President
Biden. You can tell from
my body language how
aware I am that there's a
camera in the room.

White House photo

This photo of me and Vice
President Mondale was taken
moments before I was sworn in.
ME: Can I do this?
MONDALE: I don't know.

Franken.senate.gov

Me and Mrs. Molin share a nice moment at my swearing-in party.

Drew Littman, my first chief of staff, fitting right in at the Minnesota State Fair.

Amy Klobuchar and I both sit on the Judiciary Committee. Here, she shows me the ropes. Specifically, where to get the best tuna sandwich in the Capitol.

Me and Lindsey Graham sharing a light moment before impugning each other's integrity.

At President Obama's 2011 State of the Union address. See if you can spot the Republicans in this picture.

I often draw sketches of colleagues during hearings. Here's one of my favorites. Favorite sketches, I mean.

Me letting my
id out.

In happier times.

Alana Petersen, the
only state director I've
ever had.

Current and former chiefs of staff Jeff Lomonaco and Casey Aden-Wansbury, two of the only people on Earth who know the pressure of having your finger on the DeHumorizer™ button.

Ed Shelleby

Tom Williams/CQ Roll Call

Me, communications director Ed Shelleby, and energy staffer Bidisha Bhattacharyya reviewing a speech draft. Guess which one of us isn't a Minnesotan. Hint: It's Ed. Bidisha's from Rochester. Ed's from Cincinnati.

Me and Franni on the campaign trail in 2014.

Glen Stubbe, Copyright 2014, Star Tribune

Me, Franni, Joe, and Thomasin as I'm about to give my victory speech on election night 2014. This is us when we're *happy*.

A precious moment with my grandson Joe at the swearing-in reception for my second term.

Joe, a couple of years later, using his little sister Avery as a prop.

Avery without her brother
torturing her.

My grandson Jacob
with his brother
Charlie.

Partners in crime.

Politicians have to send out Christmas cards. Here's ours.

From our Family to Yours

Heather Ryan

Muna Abdulahi giving the class speech at the Willmar Senior High graduation.

West Central Tribune, Willmar, Minn.

West Central Tribune, Willmar, Minn.

Muna's sister Anisa being crowned homecoming queen.

Chapter 28

The Angel and the Devil

Actors often claim not to read their own reviews. I don't know much about actors, other than that they are all liars, but I can say that most senators do look closely at their press coverage. And not just out of vanity. It's important for us to know exactly how our constituents and the general public see us. Also: vanity.

The incisive critique of my questioning of Judge Sotomayor in *Slate* was particularly gratifying. Regarding my argument on the Roberts Court's judicial activism, Mr. Slate wrote:

Some of the only questioning along those lines came from Sen. Al Franken, who made Sotomayor very uncomfortable as he grilled her on the Roberts Court's tendency to overreach. In this term's Voting Rights Act case, the court came close to striking down an act of Congress, and in an age-discrimination case, it decided an issue that was never briefed. Franken politely asked Sotomayor, "How often have you decided a case on an argument or a question that the parties have not briefed?" He wondered whether that constituted judicial activism.

Good question. Why was the junior senator from Minnesota—the one sworn in only a week ago—the first one asking it?

Mainly, though, the press coverage of my performance focused on another question: what to make of my use of humor during the hearing. Was it an example of appropriate levity? Or an early indication that I was going to be the Senate's class clown? The next day, *MinnPost*, Minnesota's online newspaper dedicated to public policy, ran a think piece on just this question entitled "Franken's Senate Debut: Appropriate Levity or Class Clown?"*

It was, I suppose, a balanced thumb-sucker, with weighty analysis from various experts. Larry Jacobs, an oft-quoted political science professor at the University of Minnesota, asked, "So, why did he throw in the Perry Mason thing? Why did he not just go into his very reasonable questions about judicial activism?

---

* I feel like they missed an opportunity by passing up "No Joke: Franken Tells Joke."

Instead there seems to be a very driven need for cleverness...That is what set alarm bells off for me." Alarm bells!

On the other hand, Guy-Uriel Charles, a Duke law professor with a suspicious hyphenated first name, "argued that the Perry Mason bit was a 'positive thing'":

> "Obviously, the risk is that he won't be taken seriously, that he will be viewed as a clown," Charles said. "But, oddly enough, it seems that if he played it as a straight man, without any humor, he would have been taken less seriously."

Quite a needle to thread, don't you think?

David Schultz, a political science professor from Hamline University in St. Paul, provided a secondary layer to the customary journalistic navel-gazing. "'The danger is that the main story becomes about his discussion with [Sotomayor] on Perry Mason,' said Schultz."

This was irritating—a pundit punditing about how other pundits might pundit—but it was also dead-on.

"And indeed," the piece continued, "the Perry Mason segment reverberated through headlines, stories and TV clips throughout the evening and into the next day."

My team took this all very seriously. They, too,

were well aware that a lot of onlookers were waiting with bated breath for me to screw up, and they felt a lot of pressure, probably even more than I did, to stop it from happening. And in the wake of the *Perry Mason* incident, they became what I can only describe as hypervigilant, a concerned Paul Drake or fretful Della Street, if you will, to my cavalier Perry.

Thus, new rules: I could be funny in the office, but only with members of the staff, not in meetings with visitors. It was also okay to be funny on the floor with my colleagues, as long as I wasn't loud enough to be picked up by the C-SPAN microphones. And, for God's sake, no physical humor!

After a few months of utterly humorless behavior in public, a reporter desperate for something to write about approached Jess McIntosh, who had come with me to Washington to be my press secretary in the Senate. "Why isn't your boss funny anymore?"

"Because of you guys," she replied.

* * *

Doing a good job as a senator was important enough to me that I was willing to restrain my urge to occasionally be funny around people who didn't work for me. But that doesn't mean it was easy.

In fact, after a couple of months, this was all driving me kind of nuts.

Which brings me to a November 5, 2009, hearing

of the Health, Education, Labor, and Pensions (HELP) Committee, on which I also sit.

We were discussing ENDA, the Employee Non-Discrimination Act, which prohibits discrimination against LGBT people in the workplace. As of this writing, there are still thirty states that don't have laws on the books protecting lesbian, gay, bisexual, or transgender workers. Gay couples can now enjoy all the rights and responsibilities of marriage, but if you get married on Saturday and then you both get fired for being gay on Monday morning, that's a pretty crummy way to start a new life together, don't you think?

In 1993, Minnesota became the first state to ban employment discrimination on the basis of either sexual orientation or gender identity. At the very beginning there were a few bathroom kerfuffles of the sort that might be a highlight in a Madea movie. But soon everyone figured out that everybody has to go to the bathroom occasionally at work, and, more important, that firing people because they're gay or lesbian or bisexual or transgender is really cruel and dumb. Nothing bad has happened because of Minnesota's law, unless you're an employer in another state who lost a smart, hardworking, and very talented employee to a Minnesota company like 3M, or General Mills, or Target, or any of our state's seventeen Fortune 500 companies because of your state's intolerance and stupidity.

The room was packed full of LGBT advocates there to observe the hearing. And of course, a number of my Democratic colleagues, including Chairman Tom Harkin, were there to talk about this important issue.

But the Republicans on the committee didn't seem ready to discuss ENDA that day, because no Republicans, not even ranking member Mike Enzi, had shown up. This was pretty unusual. In my four months in the Senate, I'd never been to a hearing without at least one member of the minority present.

As Chairman Harkin gaveled the hearing to order, a thought occurred to me. Wouldn't it be funny, I thought, if, when I was called on, I said, "I think it's a shame that none of the gay members of the committee showed up today"?

I knew, of course, that telling the joke was a really bad idea. It would undermine everything I had been working toward: to be seen as a workhorse and not a showhorse, and yada yada.

The "yada yada" came from the Devil as he popped up on my right shoulder.

"C'mon!!!" the Devil yelled. "Tell the joke! It'll kill!!!"

"Now, Al," the Angel appearing on my left shoulder said calmly, if a bit sanctimoniously, "you worked way too hard for far too long to do this, and you know it."

"It'll kill!!!" the Devil screamed, hopping up and down. "The room is full of LGBT activists!!! It'll get a HUGE laugh!!!"

I tried to ignore the Devil as Chairman Harkin gave his opening statement. A passionate champion of civil rights, Harkin had authored the 1990 Americans with Disabilities Act, which changed millions of lives and our nation for the better. "Qualified workers should not be turned away or have to fear losing their livelihood for reasons that have nothing to do with their capabilities, skills, or performance. Such practices are un-American, and it's time for them to stop," he said.

At least that's what the transcript says he said. The Devil was drowning him out.

"C'mon!!! Everyone will love it!!!" The Devil was positively vibrating with excitement.

"Al," the Angel warned, "you remember the reaction to Perry Mason."

"Screw the press!!! People loved it!!! Besides, this is much funnier, with much broader appeal!!!"

"And will be much worse," said the Angel. "The other side will accuse you of saying that all the Republicans on the HELP Committee are gay."

"It's a joke!!!" the Devil snarled at the Angel. "Everyone will know it's a joke!"

"Of course they will, Al. But you know how this works," warned the Angel. "They will all pretend they're deeply offended."

"Screw 'em, I tell ya!!! It'll kill!!!"

Now Jeff Merkley, the author of the bill we were

considering, was quoting Martin Luther King Jr.: "Human progress is neither automatic nor inevitable. Every step toward the goal of justice requires sacrifice, suffering, and struggle, tireless exertions, and passionate concern of dedicated individuals."

But the cacophony coming from my left and right trapeziuses was making it hard for me to pay attention. And, frankly, both the Angel and the Devil were making valid points.

The Devil pointed out that this was a very different situation from the Sotomayor hearings. Everyone had been watching those. But no one was paying attention to the ENDA hearing. Wasn't it possible that by getting an enormous laugh, I might bring more attention to this issue? And maybe help a lot of LGBT people? And hadn't some of my most passionate supporters insisted that it would be refreshing for me to use my comedic talent for just this kind of thing?

The Angel did his best not to scold, but he did point out that if I said the line, my entire staff might bolt from the Hart Senate Office Building and never be seen again.

I started experiencing a kind of vertigo. You know that feeling you get when you're on the balcony of a very tall building and you start to panic because you realize you could just throw yourself off? For a moment or two I had that feeling. I could just blurt, "I think it's a shame that none of the gay members of the committee showed up today." And then see what happens.

Then things got worse—because, all of a sudden, the Angel and the Devil each sprouted their own Angel and Devil!

The Angel's Angel was talking about losing my chance to feed the hungry and house the homeless. The Devil's Devil was talking complete nonsense about how Victoria's Secret models love to laugh.

Merkley was wrapping up. It was my turn in a matter of seconds.

Fortunately, the Angel's Devil and the Devil's Angel were hashing things out between themselves.

"I know what your boss is worried about," the Devil's Angel said to the Angel's Devil. "But all our side is saying is that this place could use a little lightening up."

"Sure," replied the Angel's Devil. "And, believe me, I've been making that case on my end. But we have to pick our spots."

"No doubt," agreed the Devil's Angel. "No one over here is saying we go for the joke every single time."

"Well, the Devil's Devil is."

"Oh, nobody listens to him."

"Uh-huh," said the Angel's Devil, not really believing that. "Well, look. Bottom line: I think we can work together, but we've gotta look for the right opportunity, and this ain't it."

"Fair enough," nodded the Devil's Angel. "I'll take it to my boss, and I guarantee you I'll get reamed out."

The Angel's Devil rolled his eyes at this little bit of posturing.

"But," the Devil's Angel continued, "I think he'll live with it if you promise me that you'll get your boss to look for some opportunities to be funny that are less high-risk."

The Angel's Devil put out his hand. "We've got a deal."

I was relieved. This was very good staff work. And just in time.

"Senator Franken," said Chairman Harkin.

I turned to my prepared remarks.

Growing up, my kids read in history books about a time in our country when it was perfectly legal to fire somebody or refuse to hire somebody because they were black or a woman. For them it was a concept that they couldn't understand. I hope that my future grandkids will only read about when it was legal to fire someone because they're gay or transgender.

As I read my opening statement, I thought of my actual staff up in our office blithely watching their boss on TV with no inkling of the anguished psychodrama I had endured and how, for the moment, anyway, my reputation, and their jobs, were secure.

When it came around to me for my five minutes of questioning of Tom Perez, then assistant attorney general for civil rights and eventually labor secretary and DNC chair, I thought back to the deal that the Angel's Devil and the Devil's Angel had struck. I decided it was finally time for a little good-natured humor.

> ME: I've also seen a real change in attitudes about gay and LBGT people. I'd say my kids' generation—I have kids in their twenties—thinks whether someone is gay or not is about as interesting as if they're left-handed.* I think it's more interesting than being left-handed,† but—
> [Laughter.]
> TOM: I'm ambidextrous.
> ME: Yes.
> [Laughter.]
> I'm not going to touch that.
> [Laughter.]

And from that day forward it was okay for me to be mildly funny. In spots. Also, the Devil's Angel got fired, but sometimes you have to stick up for what you believe in.

---

* I stole this line from comedian George F. Will.

† This wrinkle is my little spin on Will's amusing (but not really funny) joke. And he calls himself a comedian!

Final note: Four years and two days later, on November 7, 2013, Merkley's ENDA legislation passed in the Senate on a 64–32 vote, with ten Republicans voting in favor.

The Republican-controlled House, of course, refused to even consider the bill. And a majority of states still don't have protections against discrimination for LGBT employees on the books.

And as for the deal the Devil and the Angel made? Well, the Angel got what he wanted. I behaved myself and resisted the self-destructive impulse to tell a joke regardless of consequences. And the Devil got what he wanted: this book.

Chapter 29

Never Give the Staff Credit

When I was in Iraq and Afghanistan with the USO, I found myself paying particular attention to defense contractors and their employees. Many of these men and women serve with incredible courage and distinction, but there definitely seemed to be something of a rough-and-tumble culture among contractors. And of course, as civilians, they are not subject to military discipline. That's why, in addition to the widespread waste, fraud, and abuse that contributed so egregiously to the chaos in Iraq and Afghanistan, it didn't surprise me when I heard reports that many female employees of those contractors had been the victims of sexual assault.

If women in the military had little recourse in that horrific situation, their sisters who worked for contractors had even less. They had signed employment contracts that contained mandatory arbitration clauses. A mandatory arbitration clause requires the employee to resolve any employment dispute through a private arbitrator, often one selected by the employer.

This meant that a female employee of a defense contractor who had been raped by a fellow employee in a war zone could not go to court against the contractor, even if the contractor had been grossly negligent in allowing the assault to happen. Her only recourse would be to go before an arbitrator *selected by* the contractor.

Which brings me to Jamie Leigh Jones, an employee of Kellogg, Brown, and Root (better known as KBR), who alleged that she had been drugged and gang-raped in 2005 by a group of KBR employees at the base in Iraq where she'd been quartered along with dozens of men.

When I got to the Senate, she had been trying for four years to take KBR to court—despite the mandatory arbitration agreement she had been forced to sign as a condition of employment. The Fifth Circuit in Texas had ruled in her favor, but KBR was appealing to the Supreme Court, which, in a number of 5–4 decisions before and since, had voted to expand the power of mandatory arbitration agreements and limit the rights of employees (and consumers) to get justice through the court system.

Drew had the idea of introducing an amendment to a defense bill currently on the floor that would prohibit the Defense Department from hiring contractors who enforce arbitration agreements in cases of sexual assault, wrongful imprisonment, and other civil rights violations.

Great idea, Drew. Let's do it!

I rounded up a number of cosponsors and brought the amendment to the floor, where we got word that the Republicans opposing it, led by Jeff Sessions, were planning to argue that the amendment was unconstitutional.

So my Judiciary counsel quickly got letters from three eminent law scholars—one conservative, one liberal, one middle-of-the-road—arguing for the amendment's constitutionality, and I asked the Senate pages to place copies on every member's desk in the chamber before the debate.

In the end, we won the vote, 70–30, with only (male) Republicans voting against it. Defense contractors would no longer be able to enforce mandatory arbitration agreements against employees who claimed they had been sexually assaulted.*

* * *

Immediately following the vote, I held an impromptu press conference with a crush of press.

"How'd you get the idea for the amendment?" a reporter asked.

---

* After more than four years of fighting to get into court, Jamie Leigh Jones finally had her case against KBR heard by a jury. Though she lost the case, she had her day in court, as have other women who have been, or claimed to have been, sexually assaulted while working for defense contractors.

"My chief of staff, Drew Littman, came up with it." I turned to acknowledge Drew, only to notice that his bald head was turning an angry shade of red.

When we got back to my office, Drew calmly asked if he could have a moment with me alone.

As soon as the door closed, he wheeled and bellowed, "Never give the staff credit! *NEVER!*"

I was taken aback. "But I was asked a question..."

Here's the concept Drew explained to me that day. The senator is elected to office by the people of his or her state. Everything emanates from the senator. Every accomplishment belongs to the senator. Every once in a while, there is something called "staff error," where a staffer can be blamed for something you screwed up. But any positive achievement? That came from you.

So, the idea of "never giving the staff credit"? That was all mine.

* * *

When my grandson, Joe, was just thirty minutes old, I held him in my arms for the first time, looked down at his angelic face, and told him, "It's all staff."

Let me explain what I mean to you, who might understand what I'm talking about. Because the point was completely lost on Joe.

As a senator, my main focus is on my committee work. For example, I serve on the Health, Education, Labor, and Pensions Committee. That committee is only important if you care about your health, or your family's health, or your education, or your kids' education, or your grandkids' education, or if you work, or if you plan to work someday, or if you plan to *stop* working someday and retire.

That's one of my committees. Then there's the Judiciary Committee, which involves everything from Supreme Court confirmation hearings to immigration reform to law enforcement oversight to civil liberties and privacy issues, all of which are fascinating. And then there's patent law.

I'm also on the Indian Affairs Committee, which covers a whole range of neglected and very thorny issues. And, oh yeah, Energy and Natural Resources, which deals with everything from water policy to nuclear labs to land management to the electric grid to, you know, climate change. That thing.

Yes, so my "main focus" is on literally all of those issues. I also have to cast votes on *other* issues. Like whether or not to bomb Syria.

And for every issue, there aren't just two sides, there are dozens of sides. And each of those dozens of sides has advocates making the case who deserve to be heard and whose perspective I need in order to make the right decision. Plus, each issue has a ton of experts out there who have spent their entire lives learning about it—as opposed to me, who perhaps once wrote a funny sketch that sort of touched on it.

Sometimes people ask me, "How do you keep track of all this information? How do you keep up on all these issues?" And the answer is, I don't.

You only have time for so many meetings in a day. And you (or, at least, I) only have room in your (or, at least, my) brain for so much information at once.

So your staff takes all the meetings you can't take, and knows all the stuff you don't know. They're not just your eyes and ears, not just your representatives—they're the external hard drive for the computer or, in some of my colleagues' cases, the old-fashioned mechanical adding machine in your brain.

On top of that, keep in mind that when you're a senator, you aren't just a senator. You are the public face of the Office of the Senator. That office is its own entity that communicates with the press, answers correspondence from the public, helps constituents with problems like delayed Social Security checks and visas for relatives living overseas, determines where you need to be and how you're going to get there, and a million other things that you have neither the time nor the expertise to do personally.

You need people to do all this stuff, and people to *manage* all the people who do this stuff, and make sure they get their paychecks on time, and that there's paper in the printer, and also, in addition to your office in D.C., you have offices back in your state, and perhaps by now you're beginning to understand why I have more than forty people working for me.

Congressional staff are chronically underpaid and underappreciated, and, frankly, I don't have time to deal with either problem right now. I'll try to remember to put someone on it.

But if you've ever been watching C-SPAN and seen two senators engaging in a colloquy where they graciously thank each other for the long hours of work they'd each put in hashing out a compromise and hammering out the details of a piece of legislation, remember: They probably didn't do much of that. All the hashing and hammering was probably done by a handful of people in their mid-to-late twenties with hundreds of thousands of dollars in graduate school debt.

It's possible that the two senators supervised their respective staffs every step of the way, getting into the weeds on the policy, receiving constant updates on progress, and giving strategic guidance at every turn.

It's also possible that at least one of the senators needs his chief of staff to remind him whether his staffer's name is Jennifer or Jessica.

The point is: It's all staff.

* * *

On the other hand.

When you're the senator, you're the only one who

has to know at least something about *everything*. Your energy staffer is an expert on utility regulation, and knows way more about it than you do, and that's great.

But you still have to know *enough* about utility regulation to have a conversation with thirty members of the Rural Electric Co-op Association who are coming to see you at 10:00. And *also* enough about Medicare payments to Critical Access Hospitals to have a conversation with the Crow Wing County executive, who's got an appointment with you at 10:30. And *also* enough about patent law to not look like an idiot when the president of the University of Minnesota and the CEO of 3M drop by at 10:45 to hear the latest on the very complicated patent reform bill that is somehow the single most frustratingly complex subject the Judiciary Committee deals with.

Oh, and you still have to decide whether you want to vote to bomb Syria.

You're the only one who has to know something about all of these issues and take all of these meetings—and not just in Washington, because you're also the only one who constantly goes back and forth between D.C. and your state, and travels to every corner *of* your state.

You're the only one in the caucus lunches with the other senators in your party. You're the only one in the classified briefings down in the SCIF (the Sensitive Compartmented Information Facility, a secure room where you can't even bring your cell phone in). You're the only one who makes calls to the parents of service members who have died. You're the only one who has to cast the tough votes.

And, by the way, you're the only one who's responsible for getting reelected every six years so that everyone else doesn't lose their job and have to go make twice as much money in the private sector.

So, yeah, it's all staff. But actually, as I tell my staff, it all comes from the top.

Chapter 30

Letting My Id Run Amok

It didn't take long for me and Franni to establish a routine in Washington. I'd walk home from my office to the little house we had rented on Capitol Hill—Franni found it on Craigslist—where, during a quick but always delicious dinner prepared by Franni, we would discuss each other's days and muse about our hopes and dreams for our children, our country, and the world.

But mainly I would complain about how much work I had to do.

You see, after dinner, I would go to my den to do my homework. Mostly, that's reading.

Every night, I go home from the office with a binder. Inside the binder is a schedule for the next day, usually loaded up with a wide variety of meetings, along with briefings for each one so I know what I'm talking about when I sit down with those labor leaders, or those activists for Alzheimer's research, or some guy who wants to pitch a new postage stamp honoring Danish pianist Victor Borge.*

That's my binder. Well, it's one of them. The "daily" binder. In addition to that one, I have a binder for each hearing I'm going to attend the next day.

One thing I didn't know before I got to the Senate is that witnesses customarily submit testimony in writing before the hearing itself—which means we senators get to read it the night before we question them!

Not long after the press conference where I stupidly gave Drew credit for his—I mean, *my*—idea on mandatory arbitration, Judiciary Committee chairman Pat Leahy scheduled a hearing on the issue. At hearings, each side gets to invite witnesses. Not surprisingly, Republicans had invited a witness who would testify in *support* of mandatory arbitration agreements: a lawyer representing the U.S. Chamber of Commerce.

The night before that hearing, I opened my Judiciary binder and flipped directly to the testimony from the Chamber stooge who was going to try to defend these indefensible agreements, a guy named Mark A. de Bernardo.

A passage immediately caught my eye: The employee actually *benefits* from mandatory arbitration

---

* How did that guy get a meeting with a senator? Staff error.

clauses, Mr. de Bernardo argued, because under arbitration the employee prevails 63 percent of the time, compared to prevailing just 43 percent of the time in court.

Hmmm, I thought. As a trained lie-spotter, I had become intimately familiar with the right wing's most common techniques—including the deceptive use of statistics. And that one seemed downright suspect, especially since he used a very particular word like "prevails." What exactly did that word mean in this context?

I decided to dig a little deeper. In a footnote, de Bernardo had cited a source for his statistic: page 30 of a Congressional Research Service study. I called my Judiciary Committee staffer and asked him to track down the study so I could take a closer look. He found the study. It was only ten pages long. Kinda hard to analyze a statistic that appears on page 30 of a ten-page report.

The next morning, I woke up with a song in my heart and adrenaline in my blood. I took my seat at the end of the dais and waited patiently for my chance to question de Bernardo. Finally, it was my turn.

Would a rape victim, I asked him, be deemed to have "prevailed" in an arbitration proceeding if she was awarded fifty dollars?

De Bernardo started fumfering.

"Please answer yes or no," I instructed him.

He paused uncomfortably. "I say no."

I had him.

Okay. Would a rape victim, under his definition of "prevailing," be considered to have "prevailed" if she was awarded . . . one hundred dollars?

"You know, I think this is a distinction without a difference. What we are talking about—"

By now, I recognized a pivot when I saw one. Nice try.

"Answer yes or no, please, sir."

He knew he was cooked. "The question is, 'What is the number that counts as prevailing?'"

"I think that is sort of the question, isn't it?" I said, trying not to flash my incisors.

De Bernardo stammered a bit more before giving up: "I don't know."

Aha. "So when you said no, you didn't know whether that was true or not, did you?"

"Well . . ."

"Did you? Did you!? DID YOU!?!?!?"

Okay, the last two "did you!?"s were silent.

Now, I'll bet Mark A. de Bernardo is a good husband and father, who just wants to provide for his family by defending a corporation's right to heartlessly exploit its employees and rip off its customers. But I was enjoying this. Perhaps a little too much.

Truth be told, I recognized the feeling. It was the same feeling I had gotten back in the old days when I realized just how far up Liar's Creek Bill O'Reilly was, claiming he had won two Peabody Awards and then claiming he hadn't said that. I can't help it. I love getting these guys.

But now, instead of simply exposing the mendacity of a right-wing lying liar, I was standing up for everyone who had been the victim of a mandatory arbitration clause. The family who had to go before an arbitrator chosen by the nursing home that had allowed Grandma to die of dehydration. The women employees who had been paid less than their male counterparts at Walmart but couldn't file a class action lawsuit because the Supreme Court had decided (in another 5–4 Roberts Court decision) that they had to go into arbitration as individuals.

Maybe I wasn't allowed to be funny anymore. But I could still let my id out once in a while by eviscerating some right-wing jerk.

"It's not enough for you to kill these guys," Mandy Grunwald observed after one such evisceration. "You have to set them on fire."

* * *

Would you like another example? I bet you would. And I would *love* to relive it.

As I mentioned in the powwow chapter, I made it onto the Indian Affairs Committee in the face of some stiff competition from no one. One day, we were considering an amendment to the Indian Health Care Improvement Act that would allow dental therapists to provide oral health care to American Indian and Alaska Native children in woefully underserved Indian country.

Children in Indian country have twice the rate of tooth decay as the general population. Sixty-eight percent have untreated cavities. One in three report missing school because of dental problems.

More than fifty developed countries outside the United States have a licensed trade called "dental therapist"—midlevel oral health providers, whose scope of practice is somewhere between a dental hygienist and a dentist. Guess who doesn't like that idea? Dentists.

In 2006, the American Dental Association opposed (unsuccessfully) an experimental program that paid for Alaska Natives to train as dental therapists in New Zealand and then return home to provide oral health care to isolated Alaskan villages—many of which are accessible only by air, and which would receive dental care just once a year, when a dentist would fly in and stay for all of a week.

The Alaska experiment had been successful. Alaska senator Lisa Murkowski (a Republican), who had cosponsored a new Indian dental therapist amendment with me, invited one of the dental therapists from Alaska to testify about the difference it made for kids to have an adult from their own village reminding them to brush every day and take care of their cavities. And a pediatric dentist from Minneapolis testified that peer-reviewed studies showed that dental therapists "improve access, reduce costs, [and] provide excellent quality of care."

But the American Dental Association didn't want the competition from dental therapists, and so they opposed our amendment. They sent their president, Dr. Ronald Tankersley, to testify against it. The night before the hearing, there I was with my binder, reading his testimony, getting that old familiar feeling as my lie-dar began to tingle.

"This year alone," he was planning to say the next day, "there will be seventy additional dentists providing care in tribal areas. With one more year of similar recruiting success, the shortage of dentists in IHS (Indian Health Services) could actually be eliminated."

That couldn't be right, I thought. I called my staffer on Indian Affairs and asked for some real data. How many dentists are there in Indian country? What's the shortfall? What's the attrition rate?

He called back a few minutes later. Here was my end of that conversation: "Uh-huh. Uh-huh. Uh-huh. Oh, man—this is going to be fun!"

The next day, after Dr. Tankersley read his testimony, I asked him, "Shouldn't everyone have access to dental care?"

"We believe they should," he answered.

I repeated back to him what he had just said about the seventy new recruits this year, and about how if there was similar success the next year, the dentist shortage could actually be eliminated.

Was that his testimony?

"Yes."

"Do you know how many dentists there are in the IHS?"

"No, I don't."

"There are six hundred dentists in the IHS. Do you know how much the shortfall is?"

"Yes. The shortfall at this point is about another seventy dentists."

"No, it is not." The shortfall, I told him, was about 25 percent—or around 150 dentists. And did he happen to know the rate of attrition?

"I don't know the statistics," he said, blanching a bit. "But the turnover rate is high."

"So when you said that 'with one more year of similar recruiting success, the shortage of dentists in the IHS *could* be eliminated,' why did you use the word 'could'?"

"Because there is no way we *know* that it will be eliminated."

"Why did you even bother to say it? Because the turnover rate is about 30 percent."

I did the math for him. The current shortfall was

150 dentists. Turnover would add another 180. That made a shortfall of 330. Seventy new recruits would still leave Indian country about 260 dentists short.

I asked him again if he agreed that everyone should have dental care.

"We do."

"It doesn't seem to me," I said, "that your testimony is convincing at all. And what I want to do is make sure that kids in Indian country don't have rotting teeth. That is my responsibility."

Of course, I have failed in that responsibility. Yes, our amendment passed, which means that dental therapists can serve in Indian country—but only in the two states where dental therapists are licensed to practice at all: Alaska and Minnesota.*

American Indians receive less than half per capita what we spend on health care for the average American. And that's a disgrace, one that even the most satisfying takedown can't eliminate. But at least that day I got my Indian name from a Minnesota Ojibwe friend of mine: Yells at Dentist.

* * *

It's one thing to take on a professional association president who didn't prepare and doesn't know what

---

* Nine other states are now looking at licensing midlevel oral health providers.

he's talking about. It's way more fun to take on a right-wing ideologue from a conservative think tank.

In 2011, Tom Harkin, chairman of the HELP Committee, called a hearing to talk about how we can build and strengthen the middle class.

There is a classic philosophical divide between the two parties on how the economy works, and on the government's role in creating jobs. The night before the hearing, I read the testimony of Kenneth Green, a resident scholar at the American Enterprise Institute and the Designated Conservative on the panel. Green's written testimony ended with the sentence, "In conclusion, the idea that the government can create jobs in the economy is a myth."

Mm-hmm.

The next day, I began my questioning by noting a few government projects that had created *millions* of jobs.

Had Mr. Green heard of the Erie Canal? It opened European markets to midwestern agricultural goods and timber and made New York the Empire State.

The hearing itself, I noted, was being carried on C-SPAN, the Cable *Satellite* Public Affairs Network. Was Mr. Green aware that the Defense Department had sent up the very first satellites?

The hearing was also being streamed on the Internet. Did Mr. Green know that the Internet had been created by the government?

How about rural electrification? The interstate highway system? Don't a lot of companies rely on the interstate highway system to ship their goods? And what about Mr. Green himself? His bio said that he had received his graduate degree from UCLA—a public university. Did any of his professors believe that they had jobs? Did any of them teach him *anything*?

"It would be absurd," Green finally conceded, "to say the government can't create jobs."

I got in one last swing. "When we receive testimony here in the United States Senate," I pointed out, "we really like the testimony to say what it means and mean what it says."

* * *

These hearings quickly emerged as one of my favorite parts of the job. The only problem was that there was a fine line between showing up a jerk and being one myself—between letting my id out and letting it run amok.

And every so often, I'd go overboard.

In 2011, we had a hearing in the HELP Committee to talk about chronic disease prevention, and one of the witnesses was a guy named Tevi Troy from the Hudson Institute, a right-wing think tank in Washington, who was there to complain about the Affordable Care Act.

At one point, he was arguing that the ACA would force employers to drop health insurance for their workers because it would be cheaper to just pay the penalty than to pay for coverage. So I asked him about Massachusetts, where the *reverse* had happened under Romneycare—the percentage of companies insuring their workers had actually gone *up*, the only state in the country where that had happened.

He cited a statistic from "a study in the *Wall Street Journal* that showed that AT&T, for example, spends about $2.2 billion annually on covering its workers"— whereas it would have cost only $600 million to drop the coverage and pay the penalty instead.

Of course, AT&T *hadn't* dropped coverage, because offering health insurance makes you a more attractive place to work and also keeps your workforce healthier and more productive, which was why *more* companies had chosen to offer insurance in Massachusetts, not *less*, which was *the entire point*.

There might have been an interesting argument to be had there, but I got a little sidetracked by the words "*Wall Street Journal.*" You see, the *Journal* has a serious and trusted newsroom, but its editorial division pumps out a steady stream of absurd piddlepaddle,[USS] and right-wing hacks love to borrow credibility from the news department to support the nonsense on the op-ed page. So anytime I hear someone cite it, I get a little suspicious.

"Did the *Wall Street Journal*," I asked the witness, "have a study? Or an editorial?"

"It was a statistic cited in the *Wall Street Journal*," he answered, a little nervously.

Oh, man.

"Cited *where* in the *Wall Street Journal*?"

"It was, um, on the editorial page," he stammered.

I had him. "On the *editorial* page."

"It was an op-ed."

"Okay," I said. "It was an op-ed. In the *Wall Street Journal*."

"Yes."

"That's interesting," I said, or, if I'm being honest, smirked.

"The statistic remains accurate," he offered lamely.

"You know," I sneered, "it's funny. The *Wall Street Journal* op-ed page sometimes—I don't know if you know this—uses statistics in misleading ways." There was laughter in the room as the witness squirmed, but my health care staffer, Hannah Katch, quickly pushed a note in front of me: "You're being an asshole."

She was right. Not only was I focusing on the wrong thing (the editorial credibility of the *Wall Street Journal*), but I was badgering this poor guy.

Immediately after the hearing, I thanked Hannah. Then I went straight to our office and called an all-staff meeting. Everyone piled into the conference room wondering what this could be about.

"Hannah just handed me a note while I was questioning a witness," I said. I read the note aloud. "Hannah did me an enormous favor. I don't want anyone in this office ever to be afraid to call me an asshole."

Blank stares, a few nods.

"Okay. Meeting over."

Chapter 31

I Screw Up

As minority leader, Mitch McConnell constantly used—and, I'd say, abused—the rights of the minority in the Senate to slow things down. Things like nominations to the federal bench. Or important diplomatic posts like ambassadors to Turkey (while jihadists were using it as a base to invade Syria) or Sierra Leone (during the time it was gripped by the Ebola outbreak) or South Korea (which is located just south of North Korea). Or key national security positions like under secretary for personnel and readiness at the Department of Defense, under secretary for nuclear security at the Department of Energy, and, oh yeah, secretary of the Department of Homeland Security.

Now, it's one thing to stand up and filibuster something or someone you oppose. This was something else. On hundreds of occasions, the minority would use a parliamentary procedure called "forcing a cloture vote" simply to waste everyone's time. They did it more than ever before in history; in fact, four out of every ten cloture votes in the history of the United States Senate up to 2014 came in the eight years that Mitch McConnell served as minority leader.

If you don't know what a cloture vote is, here's the deal. If the minority won't consent to proceed to a vote, the majority has to file a cloture motion to end debate. Passing a cloture motion requires sixty votes. So when you hear people talk about a "filibuster," more often than not it isn't Ted Cruz or Rand Paul talking for sixteen hours. It isn't an exhausted Jimmy Stewart as Mr. Smith, his voice rasping from speaking through the night, collapsing as the gallery gasps. It's just the minority leader refusing to allow a bill or nomination to move forward. He doesn't have to say anything except "I object" when the majority leader asks unanimous consent to go to a vote.

The filibuster can be (and is) used to kill proposals that don't have strong bipartisan support. Mitch McConnell's innovation was in using it constantly to slow down things that *did* have bipartisan support, just to make sure as little as possible happened that Obama could get credit for.

You see, once a cloture motion is filed, it can't be voted on at all until an intervening Senate day passes.

So if you file a cloture motion on a Monday, you can't vote on it until Wednesday. And even then, you're still voting on the cloture motion, not on the actual thing you wanted to vote on. If you get those sixty votes and the cloture motion passes, the Senate then has to wait for *another* thirty hours of "debate" to elapse before we can go ahead and vote on the dang[USS] bill or nomination. I put "debate" in quotes there because, again, it's not like we spend thirty hours actually debating the topic. It's just a way of saying we have to kill a bunch more time.

And in fact, in most of the situations there wasn't actually anything to debate. McConnell would force cloture votes on ridiculously noncontroversial stuff.

So it was not uncommon for us to file a cloture motion on a Monday for a vote on, say, a noncontroversial district court nominee, only to have the nominee confirmed with an overwhelming majority (in one case by a 98–0 vote) late on Thursday evening. That's right—Republicans would routinely filibuster things that they'd then turn around and *vote for*.

This wasn't just a thumb in the eye of that poor nominee who had to wait forever to become a judge or a postal regulatory commissioner or a member of the Chemical Safety and Hazard Investigation Board. It was a deliberate strategy to prevent the Senate from moving to important issues we really needed to address. (For a more in-depth discussion of how the filibuster is used to eat up time, check out my forthcoming seventh-grade civics textbook, *How a Bill* Doesn't *Become Law.*)

What made it worse was that McConnell had made his intentions clear by actually saying, "The single most important thing we want to achieve is for President Obama to be a one-term president." Not making sure that kids get a great education, not creating millions of good jobs, not even getting our deficit under control. No, his first priority was about Republicans winning the next presidential election. I wasn't shocked that he thought that. I just was appalled that he actually said it.

* * *

Mitch was really good at antagonizing the Democratic majority, which I think he'd take as a compliment. And perhaps that helps explain my first really big mistake in the Senate, which came during the debate on Elena Kagan's nomination to the Supreme Court. I was presiding over the Senate, which means I had to listen to speech after speech from conservative Republicans explaining why Kagan, who had been a clerk for Justice Thurgood Marshall and White House counsel in two administrations and dean of Harvard Law School and solicitor general under President Obama, was the least-qualified Supreme Court nominee in our nation's history.

As the Republican leader, Mitch McConnell gave the final speech against Kagan. It was awful. And at one point during his awful, awful speech, Mitch said:

No one has any doubt that Ms. Kagan is bright and personable and easy to get along with. But the Supreme Court is not a social club. If getting along in polite society were enough reason to put someone on the Supreme Court, then we wouldn't need a confirmation process at all.

And, I am truly embarrassed to report, listening to Mitch's awful speech, I rolled my eyes.

Now, rolling my eyes at this patronizing sexist dreck about this extremely brilliant legal scholar that made her sound like a promising debutante might have been a very reasonable reaction for the ordinary observer. Certainly for the ordinary Democratic observer. But I was not the ordinary observer. In fact, at that moment, I had the distinct privilege of presiding over the United States Senate.

It is the duty of the presiding senator to listen to each and every colleague with respect, or, short of that, work on thank-you notes or read press clippings. Rolling my eyes at McConnell was a huge breach of Senate protocol, which I compounded by shaking my head once or twice and, worse, smirking at stuff I found particularly objectionable. In my defense, I was tired.*

Fortunately, C-SPAN always stays on the speaker

* This is not a good defense.

during Senate sessions, so there is no visual record of what was a very serious transgression. But as soon as Mitch had finished his speech, he marched up to the podium and let me know he was furious, as he had every right to be.

"This isn't *Saturday Night Live*, Al!" he said, loud enough for the press to hear.* Mitch is very smart, and for his purposes that was exactly the right thing to say—after all, the political press had been itching to write something about Senator Yuk-Yuk causing trouble by reverting to his old ways. I came back lamely with something about how offensive I had found his speech, which didn't impress Mitch at all. He informed me that if I ever did anything like that again, he'd call me out on it right there on the Senate floor.

The Senate then moved to a vote on the Kagan nomination, and as I presided over the process, it quickly began to register that I'd really screwed up. I got to declare that Elena Kagan had been confirmed as a Supreme Court justice, which should have been a pretty fun moment, but my heart wasn't in it, and as soon as I finished my duties, I left the chamber and went directly to the minority leader's office. Mitch wasn't there, but I told his aide that I had come to

---

* They sit in the balcony directly behind the podium.

apologize. And then I walked back to my office, feeling terrible.

By the time I got there, it was clear just how deeply I had stepped in it. I learned a couple of things that day. First: Don't smirk at a colleague, let alone the minority leader, when you're presiding. Second: When you're the senator and you really screw up, the job of the staff is to support you and not to tell you that you're an idiot and then leave the office in disgust. For that, I thank Drew, who went right into "let's figure this out" mode.

I handwrote a note of abject apology to Mitch and walked back over to his office to deliver it personally. Then Drew and I and the press team composed a statement admitting my mistake, acknowledging that I had been completely in the wrong, and expressing my desire to apologize directly to the minority leader.

The statement made the press accounts, and so did a statement from a McConnell aide: "Senator Franken apologized and that's a perfectly appropriate way of handling the situation."

Both statements helped limit the damage, but especially the one from Mitch's office, which of course wouldn't have gone out without Mitch's okay. He had done me a real solid. And so I guess I actually learned three things that day, the third being that Mitch McConnell can actually be kind of a mensch—once in a while.

That day was the last day of a long work period (hence me being tired), and afterward, we immediately broke for the August recess. The night we returned to D.C. was especially nice, so I took a few staff members out to dinner at a Mexican place on Capitol Hill that has a little patio. Then I spotted Mitch and his wife, former labor secretary (and current transportation secretary) Elaine Chao, dining alfresco at the restaurant next door.

I walked over to them and started with some small talk about how much Franni had enjoyed getting to know Elaine through the spouse club meetings, which had the virtue of being true. Then I thanked Mitch for the statement his office had released.

"Well," said Mitch, "we all make mistakes. What counts is that we learn from them."

And from then on, I made it a point never to have an interaction with Mitch unless I had something nice to say. Usually, that meant complimenting some speech he gave in a setting that was completely bipartisan: "Mitch, that 9/11 commemoration speech you gave on the Capitol steps yesterday was really moving."

Every year, the spouse club holds a dinner at which the majority leader and minority leader both speak. Mitch's remarks at these are always great, which gives me at least one annual opportunity to compliment him. One year, he gave an especially beautiful speech, quoting from legendary former majority leader Mike

Mansfield (a true giant of the Senate) about how we senators owe everything to our spouses. The next day, I approached him on the floor and said (meaning it), "That was just a lovely speech last night."

"Well, you can't go wrong quoting Mansfield," he replied modestly.

We were standing alone, and for some reason, I felt enough of a connection to take a risk. "Mitch," I said, "I have to say, I really like your speeches better that aren't in the service of evil."

Mitch favored me with his best Grinch smile. Then he said, "I like the evil ones better."

I laughed, and he seemed pleased. Now we're very close, and even though he and I may disagree, when we're off the clock, we're the best of friends— sometimes we go to dinner and Mitch will laugh so hard that milk shoots out of his nose.

Chapter 32

Operation Curdle

Frankly, being civil with Mitch isn't always so easy. The fact is that his campaign of obstruction wasn't just obnoxious. It was deeply cynical—and ultimately proved to be downright dangerous.

During his presidential campaign, Barack Obama had offered a refreshing and even inspirational vision of what our democracy could be. We needn't be trapped by our old partisan divides, he told Americans. We can change the tone in Washington. We can set aside our differences and recognize our common humanity. The cynics be damned—we should dare to hope for something better from our politics.

"On this day," he declared in his inaugural address, "we gather because we have chosen hope over fear, unity of purpose over conflict and discord. On this day, we come to proclaim an end to the petty grievances and false promises, the recriminations and worn-out dogmas that for far too long have strangled our politics."

To which Mitch McConnell basically responded, "Oh yeah? Well, screw you, buddy!"

Even before the inauguration, Republicans had decided that they were going to prevent the new president from keeping his promise to move the country beyond the rank partisanship that had consumed Washington. McConnell had laid out the strategy to his caucus at a resort in West Virginia that winter: Instead of working with the popular new president to pass his agenda (or trying to find areas of compromise), Senate Republicans would focus on *making the new president less popular.*

Journalist Alec MacGillis, who reported on the summit in his book *The Cynic: The Political Education of Mitch McConnell*, summed it up this way: "In other words, wait out Americans' hopefulness in a dire moment for the country until it curdles to disillusionment."

* * *

The way I see it, Republicans had three options for how to deal with the new political reality they faced in January 2009.

Option 1: Recognize that the new president was hugely popular and had a mandate from the

American people to deal with a series of pressing crises, and ask, "How can we help?"

Option 2: Recognize that the new president was hugely popular and had a mandate from the American people to deal with a series of pressing crises, and say, "Congratulations, but we have some political standing, too, and we're going to make you come to the table and negotiate. So let's sit down and work out something we can all live with."

Option 3: Focus on reducing his popularity, refuse to respect his mandate, and as for those pressing crises? Not only are we not going to help him solve them, we're going to do everything we can to prevent him from solving them, and then we're going to blame him for failing to solve them. In fact, after a while, we're going to start blaming him for *creating* the problems in the first place!

Democrats and Republicans had faced this dilemma many times before, but never before had anyone ever chosen Door Number 3.

In part, Republicans were able to get away with "Operation Curdle" because of timing.

When Franklin Delano Roosevelt took office in 1933, the country had been suffering with the Great Depression for almost four years. The message from the American people to the new president was loud, clear, and universal: Do something! Anything! Standing in his way would have been an act of political suicide. Even Option 2 would have taken some real chutzpah.

President Obama, on the other hand, took office just as the economic meltdown was beginning to peak. The day he took the oath of office, George W. Bush shook his hand, saying, "The economy's losing eight hundred thousand jobs a month. The stock market's in free fall. The foreclosure crisis is out of control. Businesses are closing their doors across the country. I'm going home to Texas. Good luck!"

Then he left, only to pop his head back in: "Oh, and there's still a war going on. Maybe a couple? Not sure." Then he headed for the helicopter. "Oh, hey!" he shouted over the roar of the propellers. "That bin Laden guy? Never gonna find him. Anyway, I'm outta here!"

Then he and Laura flew away, waving goodbye to an economy he had left in ruins.

The timing mattered not just because the most devastating effects of a recession caused by Bush's policies were about to be felt under Obama's watch, but because the delay in the impact of the recession gave Republicans just enough wiggle room to play politics with it.

Of course, while ordinary Americans were just

beginning to realize how bad things were getting, economists had already issued dire warnings that if dramatic action wasn't taken, the Great Recession could turn into Another Great Depression. The numbers were scary. And the solution was clear: an emergency stimulus package that could put people back to work quickly, build shovel-ready infrastructure projects, and rescue state and local governments that were shedding teachers and other workers who were delivering desperately needed services.

Economists agreed that in order to be effective, this stimulus would need to be massive—at least a trillion dollars. But political scientists agreed that Democrats only had fifty-nine votes. And one of those votes (me) was, at the time, stuck in recount hell. Which meant in order to get the sixty votes necessary to break Mitch McConnell's filibuster and proceed to an actual vote on the stimulus, President Obama would need *two* Republicans.

Desperate to find just two Republicans willing to help him save the economy, President Obama had to make compromise after compromise, eventually reducing the total package to $787 billion. On top of that, a couple hundred billion was diverted away from the direct spending economists were calling for and instead used to cut taxes for individuals and businesses. That's what it took to get Arlen Specter (who would soon defect to the Democratic caucus) and

Maine's two moderate senators, Olympia Snowe and Susan Collins, on board.

Thanks to those three—and not one other Republican—the stimulus package barely broke Mitch McConnell's filibuster and passed in the Senate over the hysterical denunciations of the rest of the Republican caucus.

And then, when it went to the House, Speaker Nancy Pelosi and the Democrats had to pass it all by themselves. It received not one single Republican vote, which Republicans celebrated like they'd just won the Super Bowl (a few of them even lit a cop car on fire).

And *then*, having enjoyed making a big show out of refusing to help the president succeed, Republicans then turned to making a big show out of complaining that he had failed.

In reality, he hadn't. The stimulus kept us from falling into Another Great Depression, and created millions of jobs. But it took a while to kick in, and it wasn't as strong as President Obama and Democrats wanted (or as economists had called for). It's hard to get people excited about avoiding a hypothetical depression when you're slowly muddling through a huge recession. The economy didn't *feel* very stimulated. So it was very easy for Republicans to win the "messaging fight."

At a caucus meeting months later, Harry Reid reminded us Democrats that the stimulus had included the biggest middle-class tax cut in history (true). Sherrod Brown leaned over to me and grumbled sarcastically, "Yeah, I get thanked for that every day." People had no idea. Because while the Bush administration had celebrated its 2001 tax cut by mailing taxpayers a letter (at taxpayer expense) announcing it, this time Americans simply had a little less withheld in every paycheck.

Meanwhile, the construction jobs, the infrastructure upgrades, the "shovel-ready" projects all across the country? The Obama administration put up signs at all these sites—but the signs read, "Funded by the American Recovery and Reinvestment Act." The *what*?

Democrats always have a disadvantage in messaging—not because we're idiots, but because we have complex ideas and, sometimes, a hard time explaining them succinctly. Our bumper stickers always end with "continued on next bumper sticker." And by the time I got to the Senate in July, Republicans were giddily (and successfully) blaming the still-sluggish economy on "Obama's failed stimulus." Which didn't stop them from simultaneously taking credit for stimulus projects in their districts, grinning widely for photo ops at groundbreakings and, later, ribbon-cuttings.

Not long after I got into office, I went to a groundbreaking ceremony in Maple Grove for a three-mile, $47 million extension of Minnesota State Highway 610 made possible by an infusion of $27 million in stimulus funds. There were about a dozen public officials there—a few state legislators, a mayor or two, some county commissioners, and Senator Klobuchar and me. I was surprised to see Minnesota's 3rd District Republican congressman, Erik Paulsen, who, like every House Republican, had voted against the stimulus, smiling under his hard hat.

When I got up to speak, I said, "Well, I certainly don't deserve any credit for this. I got to the Senate after the stimulus was passed. I guess we should thank the members of Congress here who voted for the stimulus."

I looked down the line of hard hats, and said, "Okay, there's Amy Klobuchar. Let's hear it for Amy!" Applause. "And...let's see," I continued, looking directly at Representative Paulsen. "Well...I guess just Amy."

Meanwhile, presiding over the Senate, I heard Republican senators claim that the only jobs created by the stimulus had been for federal bureaucrats. Presumably these included federal bureaucrats who had moved to Minnesota to operate the excavators, bulldozers, compacters, and pavers to build the three-mile extension of Highway 610.

* * *

The stimulus had been a successful test run of the Republican strategy: Abdicate their responsibility to govern, obstruct the president's agenda, complain that things weren't getting better, and wait for Americans to get fed up so they could profit politically at his expense. Operation Curdle was well under way. And any notion of building a better politics, any hope of "changing the tone in Washington," was quickly erased.

Soon after I walked into this mess, I asked a few of my veteran colleagues if it had ever been this bad. Sure, a couple of them said. Remember that guy who almost got caned to death on the Senate floor?

"Charles Sumner?"

"Yeah. That's the guy."

So the one time that anyone could think of when it was this bad was the near-fatal beating of a sitting senator in the lead-up to the Civil War and the deaths of more than six hundred thousand Americans?

But then again, that was the summer of 2009. It actually got worse from there.

* * *

That September, a South Carolina Republican congressman named Joe Wilson interrupted President Obama during an address to a joint session of Congress, shouting, "You lie!"

It was a pretty shocking breach of protocol. But over the next four days, Wilson took in a million bucks in campaign donations. Stuff like this was already becoming par for the course. Republicans had already

decided to disregard President Obama's mandate—
and some were even going so far as to question his
legitimacy.

After listening to one too many examples of a sitting congressman fanning the flames of the "birther"
myth, I told Drew that I wanted the Capitol Police to
install a special metal detector before the State of the
Union address for any member of Congress who didn't
believe the president was born in the United States.

Drew thought I was joking. I was—I think. But I
made a serious case. If you believed that Obama wasn't
born in Hawaii, I reasoned, it meant two things: One,
you were generally insane, and two, you believed that
the president was a usurper. Exactly the sort of people
who should get wanded before being allowed into a
room with the guy.

"You can't do that," said Drew.

"Okay," I said. "But if one of these guys plugs the
president, you're going to feel pretty stupid."

* * *

Republicans made huge gains in the 2010 midterms,
seizing the majority in the House and picking up six
seats in the Senate.

Worse, these gains were powered, and the new
House majority controlled, by the ascendant Tea Party.
These folks weren't just extremely conservative. They
were openly uninterested in actual governing. They

saw themselves not as legislators, but as revolutionaries. More than a few of them were just plain nuts. All year, they'd been raising hell at town hall meetings, complaining about everything from the Affordable Care Act (more about this in a bit) to the president's secret Muslim heritage (more about this, I'm guessing, in Donald Trump's presidential memoir). Now they had come to Washington—and, what's more, they were clearly running the show.

At the 2011 State of the Union, I walked in with Rand Paul, the libertarian new senator from Kentucky who had chosen me to be his mentor.* I gave him some mentorly advice: "Rand, if the president says something you don't like, your job is to stand up and yell, 'You lie!'"

He laughed—but then added, "Actually, you know, that would be pretty good for fund-raising."

The chamber was crowded, and I had to scramble

---

* After the 2010 election, I called all the winners on election night to congratulate them and welcome them to the Senate, including the Republicans. I thought that was what you do. It isn't. I guess I was the only Democrat who called Rand, and we had a nice conversation. So Rand picked me to be his Democratic mentor (he picked Texas senator Kay Bailey Hutchison for his Republican). I hadn't even been aware that there *was* a mentor program, because I had been seated so late. Long and short of it—I was a terrible mentor. I advised Rand to be a workhorse and not a showhorse, not realizing that he was planning to run for president at the first opportunity. Every once in a while, I'd ask Kay, "Is he listening to any of your advice?" "No!" she'd say, slightly bemused.

to find a seat. Winding up next to Marco Rubio, another new Republican senator, I tried my joke again. "Marco, some advice: If the president says something you disagree with, get up and yell, 'You lie!'"

Chuckling, Marco responded, "That'd be great for fund-raising."

I turned to my other side and poked Saxby Chambliss, a veteran Republican. "Saxby," I said, "I just told Marco that if the president says something he doesn't like, he should get up and yell, 'You lie!'"

Saxby laughed and said, "Not a bad fund-raising tactic."

The message had clearly gotten through to Republicans, even the noncrazy ones. Not only were they not being punished for the strategy they'd embarked upon at the beginning of President Obama's term, but they were being *rewarded* for it by a conservative base hell-bent on destroying the guy. And so instead of trying to tamp down the most extreme elements of their party, Republicans indulged them time and time again, sometimes even egging them on by promising victories that they knew were impossible, just to keep them on board and engaged.

This dynamic manifested itself in years of ugly brinksmanship. For example: Raising the debt ceiling had always been relatively routine, but with the Tea Party pulling House Speaker John Boehner's strings, it became an opportunity to take the fiscal future of the country hostage. Sign Paul Ryan's radical austerity budget into law, they threatened, or we'll force America to default on its debt for the first time ever.

That's what these guys were about. As my friend Norm Ornstein (the guy who played "Norm Ornstein" for *Indecision '92*) and his less funny colleague Tom Mann would later write in their book *It's Even Worse Than It Looks*, this new Republican Party was "an insurgent outlier—ideologically extreme; contemptuous of the inherited social and economic policy regime; scornful of compromise; unpersuaded by conventional understanding of facts, evidence, and science; and dismissive of the legitimacy of its political opposition."

Even after they failed to defeat President Obama in 2012, Republicans had gone too far down this path to turn back. They had trained their base to respect nothing and expect everything: While the GOP's official post-election autopsy urged moderation on issues like immigration, the activists who ran the show concluded that Mitt Romney had lost because he wasn't extreme *enough*.

By the end of President Obama's second term, Republicans had failed to keep any of the promises they had made to keep the Tea Partiers on board and engaged—they hadn't repealed health care reform or defunded Planned Parenthood or proved that the president was born in Kenya.

All they had done was break the damn government.

With Republicans putting up a unified front of opposition, we made no real progress on big issues like immigration or tax reform. Even after the massacre at Sandy Hook Elementary School in Newtown, Connecticut, we couldn't get an extremely mild gun safety bill through the Senate. And of course, they shut down the government for sixteen days in 2013, costing the U.S. economy $24 billion.*

And the thing of it was, ordinary Americans who weren't themselves rabid partisans saw all this happening and blamed *both sides*. I was always amazed when I would go around Minnesota and meet people who didn't follow national politics that closely but who knew that Republicans had been extremely uncooperative during the Obama administration. "I know," I'd say, "it's awful."

"Yeah," these people would often respond. "But that's Washington for you."

I never fully understood this "a pox on both houses" mentality until I read an article by Jonathan Rauch in the *Atlantic* last summer. He was talking about a study by a pair of political scientists in which they'd found that "between 25 and 40 percent of Americans...

---

* According to an estimate from Standard and Poor's. The estimate could be wrong, though—remember, these were the guys who gave AAA ratings to all those junk financial products, helping to cause the economic crisis.

have a severely distorted view of how government and politics are supposed to work."

Rauch calls these people "politiphobes":

> [T]hey see the contentious give-and-take of politics as unnecessary and distasteful. Specifically, they believe that obvious, commonsense solutions to the country's problems are out there for the plucking. The reason these obvious solutions are not enacted is that politicians are corrupt, or self-interested, or addicted to unnecessary partisan feuding.

These folks didn't reach that conclusion without some help. Many political reporters can't seem to write a sentence about a problem without casting at least some blame onto both sides. Congressional Republicans knew that, and made hay with it. McConnell and his friends consistently blamed *Obama* for the partisanship of the Obama years, managing to suppress their giggles all the while.

And too many journalists bought it. Take, for example, this bloodcurdling artifact of Operation Curdle—a piece in *Time* magazine by Mark Halperin from December 2009 identifying the root cause of Obama-era partisan rancor:

> *Once the new President cast his lot with his party in passing an economic-stimulus measure rather*

than seeking bipartisan agreement, rival Republicans started digging in.

Fortunately, the press cleaned up its act before 2016. Sigh.

* * *

Speaking of which. As the 2016 presidential campaign unfolded and it became clear that Donald Trump might actually become the Republican nominee, pundits searched their pundit brains for answers to where the Trump phenomenon had come from, pinning the blame on everyone from Sarah Palin to Richard Nixon to Kim Kardashian.

But the answer was right there in front of us the whole time. Yes, Donald Trump's takeover of the Republican Party had roots in the fact-free right-wing media bubble and in Newt Gingrich's pioneering of the politics of personal destruction in the 1990s. But his campaign grew directly out of the strategy Mitch McConnell implemented beginning at that retreat in West Virginia after Barack Obama won the White House in 2008, a strategy of total war against a Democratic president, a strategy in which no attack, no matter how false or outrageous, was out of bounds. When Republicans chose Door Number 3—when they chose to become "insurgent outliers"—they unwittingly opened the door for Trump.

"For the fat-cat donors, special-interest lobbyists, and elected officials who usually run the Republican show," wrote David Corn of *Mother Jones*, "Trump is an invasive species. But he has grown large and strong in the manure they have spread across the political landscape."

And after eight years of refusing to help the president govern—in fact, eight years of actively trying to make the country ungovernable—Republicans hadn't just created a monster within their own ranks. All that inaction and gridlock helped to create a nation of politiphobes, people who (correctly) felt like they were being left behind in the economy and (correctly) felt that the political system was broken and rigged against people like them and (extremely incorrectly) felt that everyone who had anything to do with politics was more or less equally to blame.

Rauch writes that these voters are inclined toward "leaders who will step forward, cast aside cowardly politicians and venal special interests, and implement long-overdue solutions."

These leaders "can be politicians, technocrats, or autocrats—whatever works," Rauch adds. "Whether the process is democratic is not particularly important."

Chapter 33

Health Care: Now What?

Donald Trump's health care plan, as expressed during his campaign, was as follows: "Repeal Obamacare and replace it with something terrific."

Okay, that's not the entire plan. Trump later elaborated on "something terrific," explaining that his plan would be "so much better, so much better, so much better."

When he was elected, it became clear that "repeal" was now a real possibility. The "replace" part, however, was as much of a mystery as it had always been. Over the previous six years, Republicans had voted more than sixty times to repeal the law. They had offered zero plans to replace it.

That's not to say they didn't have ideas related to health care. For example, Republicans have always been big on "tort reform," which means making it harder to sue for malpractice. Then there's the one actual idea Trump offered during the campaign, which is to allow health insurance companies to sell insurance plans across state lines.

Here's the thing about that, by the way. There is no federal law that prevents it. It's up to the states to decide which health insurance companies can sell within their borders. In fact, since the ACA passed, six states have allowed insurance companies from outside their borders to offer policies to their citizens.

And guess what: *No health insurance company has done it!* Why? Because in order to offer coverage in a given state, you need more than a license to do so. You need to learn the state, assess the health care needs of its population, and set up a network of providers willing to accept your insurance.

So that barely counts as an idea. And more important, it has nothing to do with the central challenge of health care reform, which is making sure that nobody in America goes bankrupt because they get sick or hurt—or, worse, goes without care they need because they can't afford it.

By the time you read this, Republicans may well have succeeded in repealing some or all of the Affordable Care Act. But I'm willing to bet they won't have succeeded in replacing it. Because the truth is, they've never been interested in addressing that central challenge. And they've been proving just how uninterested they are since the very beginning of this debate.

* * *

Let's go back to 2008, when Barack Obama first ran for president and I first ran for the Senate. Getting to universal health care was at the center of our respective campaigns. And for good reason: Every developed country in the world had some form of universal health care except the United States, providing care for all their people and doing it at about half the cost and with better outcomes.

During one of our debates, Norm Coleman had insisted that the United States already had the best health care system in the world, pointing to the Mayo Clinic in our home state.

True, Mayo provides health care that is second to none on the planet, which is why Mayo is such a point of pride in Minnesota. The problem was that great health care delivered by a number of world-class hospitals and clinics doesn't make a health *system*.

As T. R. Reid pointed out in his 2009 bestseller *The Healing of America*, the United States didn't *have* a health system—we had a *number* of health *systems*. If you were in Medicare or Medicaid, you were in the Canadian system: single-payer. If you were in the military or the VA, you were in the British system: socialized medicine. If you got your insurance through your employer, as most Americans did, you were in the German system.

But if you didn't have any health insurance, you were in the Cambodian system, where one illness or injury could literally ruin or even end your life. More than half of all personal bankruptcies in America were caused, in part or entirely, by a health care crisis. And that statistic doesn't even count all the people, like Margie Hogan's young lupus patient, who were going without care they needed because they didn't have insurance to pay for it.

One reason so many people were trapped in the Cambodian system was that before Obamacare, insurance companies could turn you down (or charge you outrageous, impossible premiums) for coverage if you had a preexisting condition like cancer, heart disease, or diabetes.

I know. It's hard to believe. But way back in 2009, that's the way it was.

Nowadays, of course, pretty much everyone agrees that this is cruel and wrong. Even Donald Trump agrees! If you want everyone to have the security of health insurance, you can't let insurance companies deny coverage to people who have preexisting conditions.

But here's the catch: If no one can be turned down (or charged more) for having a preexisting condition, then there's no incentive to actually *get* health insurance until the moment you need to use it. You might as well wait until you develop lupus or get a light bulb stuck up your butt before buying a policy.

This is known as the "free rider" problem: If only sick or light-bulbed people have insurance, then insurance becomes impossibly expensive to provide, and thus impossibly expensive to afford. So if you want sick people to be able to get insurance without the insurance market collapsing, then healthy people have to have insurance, too.

Of course, some people in the Cambodian system didn't have insurance not because they couldn't get an insurance company to cover them, but rather because they didn't have a job that provided insurance and didn't have the money to buy a policy on their own. So if you're going to require that everybody get insurance, you have to subsidize it for people who can't afford it otherwise.

Hey, wait a minute. A lifeline out of the Cambodian system for people who didn't have insurance…an individual mandate to avoid the "free rider" problem… subsidies to make sure that people can afford the insurance they're required to have—this sounds an awful lot like Obamacare! And of course, that's exactly the three-legged stool that formed the foundation of the Affordable Care Act.

Here's what's important to understand about this model: The stool only works with all three legs. Without the subsidies, you can't have the mandate. Without the mandate, you can't have the ban on discrimination against people with preexisting conditions. And without those protections for the most vulnerable Americans, you're right back where you started.

If this sounds like a complicated way to solve the problem, well, it is. A simpler solution would have been to just go to a national single-payer plan like Canada's: Medicare for everyone. And many progressives, like Bernie Sanders, thought that's what we should do back in 2009. Unfortunately, we needed sixty votes to pass anything, and we were, oh, about fifty votes short.

What would a conservative solution to the "Cambodian system" problem look like? Well, actually, a lot like Obamacare. The three-legged stool model, in fact, had originated with the very conservative Heritage Foundation, and had been enacted in Massachusetts under a Republican governor with the improbable name of Mitt. Where, by the way, it worked extremely well: Romneycare now covers 97 percent of Bay Staters, and both Democrats and Republicans there intend to keep it intact, no matter what Trump and my Republican colleagues do to Obamacare between the time I finish this book and the time you read it.

* * *

So if Republicans had had any interest in getting people out of the Cambodian system, they could have supported the conservative framework in the Affordable Care Act. Or they could have offered some other alternative plan. But they refused to do either.

Max Baucus, chairman of the Senate Finance Committee, was determined to get a bipartisan bill, and in April 2009 he'd put together a Gang of Six (three Democrats, three Republicans) to start negotiating. Every Tuesday, when we met for our caucus lunch, he'd report that they were getting closer to an agreement. This went on for months.

Finally, at a lunch in late September 2009, Max acknowledged that the Gang of Six was at a complete impasse, and that he had finally concluded that Republicans never had any intention of reaching an agreement, no matter what was in it.

At this, former Republican Arlen Specter interjected, "Well, I could have told you that!"

Then why didn't you?! I thought to myself.

By then, however, a tiny window had opened to allow us to get it done on our own without any help from the Republicans.

Remember, when President Obama was sworn in, he had fifty-eight Democratic votes. In April, Arlen Specter made it fifty-nine. But by the time I got there in July to make it sixty, Ted Kennedy was bedridden in Hyannisport in the final stages of his battle with brain cancer, so we *still* really only had fifty-nine.

Senator Kennedy passed away in late August. On September 24, Massachusetts governor Deval Patrick appointed Paul Kirk to fill his seat until a new senator could be picked in a special election the next January. Finally, for the first time, Democrats actually had the sixty votes we would need to move forward on health care.

The bad news was that we would need every single one of those sixty votes. Which meant every single one of us had a veto. Good luck, Harry Reid!

Fortunately, Harry was exactly the right guy for this impossible job. Harry grew up in the hardscrabble Nevada mining town of Searchlight. He put himself through law school as a Capitol Police officer. As chairman of the Nevada Gaming Commission, he had taken on the mob (his wife, Landra, once famously found a bomb attached to their car). Simply put, Harry Reid is a hardass.

As a young man, he had been a boxer. I once heard President Obama repeat what Harry told him about his career in the ring: "I wasn't the most talented guy. I wasn't very fast. I wasn't big, obviously. But I could take a punch."

Harry's job on health care was to take punches— for President Obama, and for everyone who was counting on him to deliver on the promise of reform. And, boy did he take a lot of punches. But he got it done. And that's why Harry Reid will always be a hero to me.*

Still, the math was the math, and it forced us to make some tough compromises. A handful of moderate-to-conservative Democrats were opposed to the public option, which would have increased competition in the insurance market. Gone.

Someone floated the idea of lowering the age for Medicare to fifty-five. Hmmm. Not a bad idea. Makes both pools healthier (Medicare adds some people between fifty-five and sixty-five who are, on average, healthier than people over sixty-five, while the private health insurance market loses its oldest members). Okay. Let's do it! But then Joe Lieberman announced on *Face the Nation* that he was against it. Gone.

In November, we hit another hurdle: Ben Nelson told us he had decided he needed tighter restrictions on federal funding for abortions. Great.†

Barbara Boxer, the Senate's staunchest supporter of

---

* I've also learned that Harry's a lot funnier than people think. After a 2011 speech by the president to a joint session of Congress, I headed back with Harry to the Senate chamber through Statuary Hall. On either side of us was what seemed to be the entire Washington press corps. The din was so loud, I knew no one could hear us. So, in full view of the news cameras, I whispered into Harry's right ear, "Harry, talk to me like I'm important." Without a beat, Harry turned to me and said flatly, "That would be impossible."

† Friends of mine ask me why we tolerate Democrats like Ben Nelson. I tell them he's the only kind of Democrat who can get elected in

a woman's right to choose, bit the bullet and negotiated a compromise with Ben: Women would have to make a separate second payment to their insurer to get coverage for abortion. We didn't like it, but we didn't have a choice.

Finally, on Christmas Eve, we passed the bill through the Senate. Phew.

Then, suddenly, things got even harder. In January, the not whip-smart Scott Brown, a Tea Party Republican, won the special election for Ted Kennedy's seat in Massachusetts.

Democrats *freaked out.* Many saw Brown's victory as a sign that the Republican strategy was paying off so handsomely that it could give them control of Congress in that November's midterms and set the president up for a defeat in his 2012 reelection campaign.

On top of that, our math problem had just gotten a lot worse, because once Brown took office in early February, that would be the end of our sixty-vote, filibuster-proof supermajority.

"Wait," you're thinking, "I thought you had already passed the bill." We had. And so had the House. But there were some differences between the two bills.

Ordinarily, this wouldn't be a big deal. We'd convene a conference committee, hash out the differences,

---

Nebraska, and we need as many Democrats as we can get. Besides, I like Ben.

and then both chambers would vote to pass the unified bill that came out of the conference.* But Republicans were still hell-bent on stopping us from passing health care reform, and now that they once again had forty-one votes in the Senate, they could stop us from voting on that unified bill.†

So a conference committee would be out of the question. There was only one solution: The House would have to pass the exact same bill we had just passed. Guess who didn't like that idea? House Democrats. Liberals wanted provisions from the House's more progressive bill, and Democrats from more conservative districts were now spooked by Brown's victory in Massachusetts.

We were stuck. And we needed the most important Democrat in the country to decide on a plan.

---

* Look, I could explain what a conference committee between the House and Senate is, but it should be clear from the context, and at some point in this book you're going to have to accept some of the responsibility to figure stuff out for your own damn self.

† During the 2012 campaign, Republicans and their lackeys in the media liked to claim that Obama "owned the Congress for the first two years. They did everything he wanted." That was Mitch McConnell. Chris Wallace of Fox News put it this way: "The first two years, he had a filibuster-proof majority in the Senate." I think they kept using this talking point specifically to drive me insane. The truth is that we held a filibuster-proof majority from September 24, 2009 (when Paul Kirk was sworn in), until February 4, 2010 (when Scott Brown was sworn in)—all of four months and ten days.

No, not Rachel Maddow. President Obama! Unfortunately, many of the Democrats who were freaking out about Scott Brown's victory worked for the president. And some, most notably Obama's chief of staff, Rahm Emanuel, wanted to scale down the bill or even abandon health care reform altogether.

It all came to a head on February 4, 2010, the day Scott Brown was sworn in. That day, President Obama spoke to Senate Democrats at a one-day emergency retreat at the Newseum, urging us to "finish the job" on health care. Except he didn't explain how he thought we could do that.

When the president finished, the press left the room with him. Paul Begala, Tim Kaine (then chair of the Democratic National Committee), and David Axelrod were set to speak for about five minutes each and then take questions. "Okay," I thought. "Here comes the plan."

Begala spoke for five minutes. Nothing about health care. Kaine spoke for five minutes. Again, nothing. "Okay," I thought. "I guess they're having Axelrod do it. After all, he's the president's chief political adviser, his guru, his guy. He's gonna tell us the plan."

David started talking. First minute, nothing on health care. Saving it for the end. Classic.

Second minute, still nothing. Same with the third.

Between minute four and minute five, it occurred to

me that one of two things was about to happen. Either Axelrod was going to run over his allotted time, or he wasn't going to tell us the friggin' plan. And indeed, when he finished his five-minute remarks, there was not one word about how we were going to solve the intractable political crisis facing the most important legislation in a generation.

"Questions?"

My hand shot up.

"Senator Franken?"

I exploded. "I've been doing a slow burn for the last five minutes. I cannot believe we're not talking about health care. This is the president's signature legislation. We've been working on this for a year now. The House obviously has to pass exactly what we passed, word for word. What is the plan to make that happen?"

That's exactly what I said, except that I dropped the F-bomb maybe fifty times. For instance, before "slow burn," "minutes," "believe," "health care," "legislation," "year," "House," "passed," "word," and "word." And also "plan" and "happen."

Axelrod responded that I wasn't being fair to the president, and that if I could tell him how to get 218 votes in the House, he'd be happy to pass along my advice.

"That's the president's job!" I yelled, inserting a single F-bomb before "job."

After some more back-and-forth, Bill Nelson and

Carl Levin raised their hands. Each pointed out to Axelrod that he hadn't actually answered my question, although they managed not to swear at him. Which was probably easy for Bill, a very devout Christian.

And later that evening, President Obama announced at a Democratic National Committee fund-raiser that he wanted the House to move forward with the Senate bill.

Finally, after a few hair-raising weeks of negotiations and arm-twisting, the House passed the Senate bill as it was by a 219–212 margin.* And the president signed the bill into law.

For Axelrod's part, he didn't take my outburst personally. I think it probably helped that after the bill finally passed, I wrote him a nice note. It read, "You're welcome."

* * *

The story of how the Affordable Care Act passed, then, goes something like this:

Democrats looked at all the people who were one car accident or cancer diagnosis away from disaster, and all the people who were getting sick or even dying because they were trapped in the Cambodian system,

---

* We would later be able to make some minor adjustments through a complicated parliamentary procedure called "reconciliation," which requires only fifty-one votes.

and they saw it as a moral crisis. And they were willing to do whatever it took to address that moral crisis. Navigating a narrow path through a political maze. Voting for elements of the bill that they felt were imperfect, or even counterproductive. Opening themselves up to demagoguery and maybe even losing their jobs. Swearing at David Axelrod.

And Republicans? Well, I'm sure many of them felt bad for people like Margie's lupus patient. But I just think they cared more about winning the political fight: catering to the free-market ideologues and conspiracy theorists in their base and continuing to put up that unified front against President Obama. I don't think they were willing to do the work or make the sacrifices necessary to solve the problem.

And I don't think there's any reason to believe that's changed since 2010. Because they've spent the last seven years trying to stop the Affordable Care Act from working the way it was intended.

For example: A group of Republican state attorneys general filed a lawsuit claiming that the individual mandate—the second leg of the stool—was unconstitutional, because the federal government didn't have the power to force people to buy something. For two years, as the case worked its way through the court system, we were treated to constant rhetoric about Obama's unconstitutional overreach, and nobody was sure if the law would be allowed to stand.

This, of course, was despite the fact that the Republicans' argument was ridiculous.

You see (and this is important!), the Founding Fathers wrote a constitution that gave almost all power to state governments and very, very little to the federal government. That constitution was called the Articles of Confederation, and it was a disaster, which is why I didn't capitalize the "c" in "constitution" there.

Then the Founders wrote the United States Constitution, the one we have been living under since 1789. Article I, Section 8, Clause 3 of that Constitution grants Congress the power to regulate interstate commerce. Gee, you think the pharmaceuticals and medical devices used in health care involve any interstate commerce?

That's why, as expected, when the Court ruled in June 2012, its four liberal justices correctly voted to uphold the individual mandate under the commerce clause. But after a series of earth-shatteringly, mind-blowingly partisan 5–4 rulings, everyone had worried that the five conservative justices would swallow the Republicans' insane argument. And, believe it or not, they did!

But Chief Justice John Roberts, custodian of the Court's reputation, knew that killing health care reform with a third highly partisan, legally dubious, and immensely impactful 5–4 decision on the heels of *Bush v. Gore* and *Citizens United* might undermine any remaining confidence in the Court's integrity once and for all. So Roberts voted with the liberals, agreeing that the mandate was constitutional. But he picked a *different* rationale, concluding that the mandate was allowable because the penalty it imposed on people who didn't buy insurance was really a *tax*, which Congress is empowered by the Constitution to implement.

Roberts's reasoning was so weird that Supreme Court reporters from both CNN and Fox News initially reported the ruling wrong.

Also, critically, Roberts's decision included a drive-by shooting: It eliminated the requirement that states use federal dollars to expand their Medicaid programs, which would have helped cover millions more low-income Americans.

An expert marksman, Roberts had aimed directly at the ACA's foot, weakening the law before it could go into effect. Republicans hadn't succeeded in getting the Court to block Obamacare, but they could take solace in the fact that Chief Justice Roberts had made it less good.

* * *

The fact that the Affordable Care Act isn't perfect isn't *entirely* Republicans' fault.

For example, there was the day in October 2013 when the new health insurance exchanges went live and HealthCare.gov—the website where people could shop for different policies—immediately crapped[USS] the bed. This was a really bad unforced error by the Obama administration, and people were right to be mad about it. I was furious.

Another thing that really cheesed[USS] me off was the phone number. The administration had set up an 800 number for people to call to get help finding the right insurance plan for them. Great idea. What was the number? 1-800-GET-CARE? 1-800-ACA-HELP? 1-800-NOT-SICK?

No. It was 1-800-318-2596. What does that spell? Nothing. If you added an extra digit to the end, you could get to 1-800-318-A-LYN(x). But come on! You know how earlier I said that the reason Democrats are bad at messaging isn't that we're idiots? Well, sometimes it is.

And, yes, some people have gotten the short end of the stick when it comes to the new law.

Just a few weeks before the 2016 presidential election, voters learned that the average premium on the health insurance exchanges established by the Affordable Care Act was about to go up by nearly 20 percent.

These premium hikes presented a real hardship for many Americans, especially those in rural communities where the insurance markets feature less competition and offer consumers fewer choices in health insurers. Anyone who has to pay unreasonably high premiums or copays and whose income is just a little too much to qualify for a subsidy that could help has every right to be angry.

But ask yourself who you should be angry *at*.

That premium hike happened in no small part because fewer healthy people than expected signed up for health insurance through the exchanges, meaning the overall pool of people in the exchanges was sicker than expected, meaning that insurance companies participating in the exchanges were losing money, which led those insurance companies to bail on the exchanges.

Why did fewer healthy people than expected sign up? Well, it probably didn't help that the Koch brothers ran ads featuring a demented Uncle Sam performing a gynecological exam on a Millennial to scare young people away from the exchanges. Also, Republican state health commissioners did "everything in their power to be an obstructionist," which is in quotes because those words were actually spoken by Republican insurance commissioner Ralph Hudgens from Georgia.

That's not the only way Republicans sabotaged the exchanges. They also deliberately changed the law to more or less guarantee that this would happen.

You see, when we set up Obamacare, we'd anticipated exactly this problem: that the people signing up for insurance might be sicker than expected. So we built into the law several programs to mitigate the risks insurers faced when they entered this new market, helping to make up for initial losses and keep them in the insurance market. One important program was called "risk corridors," another example of Democratic messaging genius. But Republicans, led by the wilier-than-you-might-have-expected Marco Rubio, snuck a rider into a spending bill that killed off risk corridors, which meant insurance companies wound up only getting compensated for about 12 percent of what they were owed. Thus a bunch of insurers waltzed, premiums shot up, and Rubio and his friends rubbed their hands together while cackling gleefully.

Of course, we could easily be working on fixing the problem that caused these premium increases in the first place: perhaps by giving people more incentive to sign up for the exchanges, perhaps by changing the formulas for how insurance is subsidized for low- and middle-income people, perhaps by bringing back the idea of a public option to increase competition. As recently as November 7, 2016, I was very excited about implementing these ideas as part of the new Democratic Senate majority under President Clinton.

In fact, from the moment the law passed, Democrats have been open—even eager—to talk about how to improve it and address problems that have arisen as the law has taken effect. *Because figuring how to improve laws and address problems is kind of Congress's job.*

But Republicans have shown no interest in fixing Obamacare. And while it may be easy to dismiss their intransigence as politics as usual, that isn't how things usually go.

For example, many Republicans vehemently opposed the creation of Social Security and then of Medicare. But that didn't stop them from supporting, and in some cases even *suggesting*, ways to improve those laws as it became clear where they needed improvement. One of President Bush's signature domestic programs was an *expansion* of Medicare!

That's how things are supposed to work. If you are privileged enough to have a job as a lawmaker, part of your job is to *make laws*. And if you don't like the way a law is working, your job is to help make it *work better*.

But that's not what Republicans thought their job was. Just like with the stimulus, they first tried to stop health care reform from happening at all, which was their right. But then they tried to make it as ineffective as possible so they could complain that it wasn't working. Since then, they've voted more than five dozen times to repeal it, even shutting down the government over health care reform in an effort led by Ted Cruz, about whom I'll have a word or two later in the book, neither of them good.

And, of course, they've lied about it the whole way.

Before it passed, they confidently predicted horrors that never wound up happening. *Obamacare is going to force more Americans into working part-time so their employer doesn't have to provide them health care. Employers are going to stop covering their employees and dump them into the exchanges.* Nope. That didn't happen.

And after it passed, they started inventing horrors to complain about.

"Obamacare has killed millions of jobs!" they've said, millions of times. In fact, since the ACA passed, our economy has created more than sixteen million new jobs.

And even though some people have had a bad experience with the new law, the fact is that, for most Americans, the law is unquestionably a net winner. Most Americans, around two-thirds of workers, continue to get their insurance through their employer. In the decade before Obamacare became law, their premiums rose at an average of 7.1 percent per year. In 2016, their premiums rose by an average of 2.9 percent. As for the 4 percent of Americans who get their insurance through the exchanges, roughly 80 percent of them receive subsidies, and nearly three out of four have the option of purchasing coverage for less than $75 a month.

* * *

As for our health care system, it's on steadier footing than it's ever been.

Before the ACA, the growing cost of health care had become unsustainable, more than doubling over the previous ten years and even threatening the long-term future of Medicare. That's why the law included measures designed to try to *restrain* that growth—what's known as "bending the cost curve."

This isn't the most exciting part of health care reform (except to me), which is why we had to sex it up with an exciting catchphrase like "bending the cost curve," but it's important, so bear with me for a minute.

Early on in the debate, I became fascinated with an article in the *New Yorker* by Atul Gawande, a surgeon, public health researcher, and professor at Harvard's School of Public Health who had been a frequent guest on my radio show.

His piece compared Medicare spending in McAllen, Texas, with Medicare spending at the Mayo Clinic in my home state. McAllen was spending three times more per person than Mayo was, even as Mayo was delivering far better outcomes.*

Huh. Clearly, Mayo was delivering health care more efficiently and effectively than McAllen. If

---

* Of course, the demographics are very different: McAllen is near the Mexican border and its population is poorer. But the study also included El Paso, which has the same demographics as McAllen but spends half as much per patient.

we could figure out how, and spread those methods to other places, we could improve outcomes even while—here it comes!—bending the cost curve.

One of the methods Mayo used was something called "coordinated care." By the time people get into Medicare, they usually have more than one thing wrong with them. As a seventy-something woman told me at the Minnesota State Fair that summer, "At my age, everything is preexisting."

So the Mayo Clinic has every specialty—cardiology, orthopedics, oncology—in one location. Smart!

Another thing: At Mayo, all the doctors are on salary. What they get paid doesn't depend on how many tests they order or how many procedures they perform. Doctors at Mayo see their patients as patients.

In McAllen, on the other hand, doctors were paid by the procedure, which meant they were incentivized to see patients as profit centers. For example, as Gawande reported, doctors in McAllen owned the imaging centers, so they made money on every CAT scan and MRI they ordered—and, no surprise, they ordered a lot of CAT scans and MRIs. Meanwhile, a doctor in a system like that gets nothing if a patient avoids getting diabetes, but there's a big payday for a surgeon if he gets to remove a diabetic's foot!

No wonder so much money was getting spent on health care that didn't actually make people healthier.

Because of screwy incentives, doctors in McAllen, like in much of America, weren't delivering health care. They were delivering "sick care."

If we could get more places to do health care like Mayo, and not like McAllen, we could make a big difference. This area of focus is known as "delivery reform," and there's another reason I was so focused on it: As it turns out, Minnesota is really good at delivering quality and cost-effective care, consistently leading national rankings. If every state did health care as well as Minnesota does it, we'd spend less and have better outcomes.

I've always seen it as part of my job to bring the best of my state to Washington. And I was able to bring two Minnesota innovations to the health care debate that made it into law. One is called the National Diabetes Prevention Program, and it offers nutritional instruction and physical training to prediabetics, reducing the odds that they'll develop diabetes (which is far more expensive to treat than it is to prevent). The other is called medical loss ratio, or MLR, which mandates that insurance companies spend at least 80 cents of every dollar you pay in health insurance premiums on actual health care (as opposed to administrative costs, marketing, CEO salaries, or profits)—and that if an insurance company fails to meet that standard, it has to rebate the difference to policyholders.

Thanks to these reforms and many others, the law

has been hugely successful in bending the cost curve. Since it passed, the cost of health care has indeed continued to rise—but it has been rising at about half the rate it had during the previous decade.* And in four of the last five years, the growth in health care spending has been slower than at any other time in the last half century.

As for McAllen, Texas? The city that had the highest Medicare spending per capita in the country? McAllen brought down the cost of its health care for Medicare recipients by nearly $3,000 per capita because of incentives in the ACA to reward coordinated care and other health care delivery reforms.† Forget about *bending* the curve—this was reversing it altogether.

* * *

Repealing Obamacare means wiping out all that progress: not just the delivery reform, but the 20 million people who didn't have insurance and got it thanks to the ACA, and the 153 million people with preexisting conditions who were saved from worrying that

---

* According to the Bureau of Economic Analysis's index of health-related personal consumption expenditures, my personal favorite index of health-related personal consumption expenditures.

† Two primary care groups each formed Accountable Care Associations, dramatically lowering emergency room visits and hospital readmissions and saving Medicare a total of $26 million in their first year.

they'd be discriminated against, and all the young adults who gained the ability to stay on their parents' insurance, and every American who got a flu shot or a long-overdue checkup and didn't get handed a bill at the end.

All these people have a lot riding on whether Republicans really mean it when they say they're going to replace Obamacare with something that protects them.

After Trump won the presidency, "repeal and replace" was itself replaced with "repeal and delay." The idea was that the Affordable Care Act would be repealed immediately, but the repeal wouldn't go into effect until after the 2018 midterm elections, thus buying Republicans some time to think of an idea for how to replace it. The only way this isn't the dumbest idea in the entire world is if the thing you care most about is the politics—being able to boast to your base that you've succeeded in repealing Obamacare, while making sure that you can get reelected in the midterms before the rest of the country figures out how devastating repeal would be.

And even then, they still have to come up with a plan! But if it doesn't cover people with preexisting conditions, guarantee that people won't get bankrupt if they get sick, and continue to "bend the cost curve," then it isn't a replacement at all. In fact, President Trump has gone on record promising that the

Republican replacement will cover every American, give them the same or better benefits, and cost less.

I'm all ears, guys!

The truth is, I don't really believe that Republicans are *ever* going to come up with a *real* replacement for the Affordable Care Act. Because it seems to me that they don't actually care about making sure that every American has access to quality, affordable health care.

What *do* they care about? They want insurance companies to be able to sell you junk policies. They want drug manufacturers to be able to gouge people who rely on medications to stay healthy. They want to make it harder for people who've suffered from medical malpractice to get their day in court. They want rich people to not have to pay for health care for poor people.

And, most of all, they want to keep using this issue to rally their base, reward their donors, and punish Democrats.

I don't know what's going to happen going forward. Heck, I don't even know what's going to happen between the time I finish this book and the time you read it. But what I do know is this: Anyone who trusts this Republican Party with the future of our nation's health care system simply hasn't been paying attention.

Chapter 34

I Meet George W. Bush

Hey, how about a palate cleanser?

Here's an interesting story. Or at least a story, at any rate. In the spring of 2015, I was invited to a Major League Baseball dinner at the Hay-Adams Hotel, right across the street from the White House. Dinners in D.C. are an enormous time-suck, so I try to avoid them if I possibly can.

But a number of the team owners, including Jim Pohlad of the Minnesota Twins, were going to be there, so I accepted the invitation to sit at his table. Mitch McConnell and Speaker Boehner came as well, because the owner of the Cincinnati Reds was there. And Dianne Feinstein was seated with the owner of the San Francisco Giants.

It was a nice evening, about fifty people. After cocktails and dinner, the new commissioner of baseball, Rob Manfred, welcomed everybody. Mitch and John

Boehner gave nice remarks about being lifelong Reds fans—Boehner's from Cincinnati, and Mitch's hometown, Louisville, Kentucky, is right down the Ohio River from, well, Riverfront Stadium, where the Big Red Machine dominated the National League during most of the 1970s. And then Dianne got up to the podium to talk about the importance of the Giants to San Francisco.

As I listened to Dianne, I noticed a slight change in the sound of the room. I turned around and saw former President George W. Bush and his wife, Laura, standing at the back, smiling. Dianne acknowledged the president and Laura and wrapped up. Then the new commissioner invited the former Texas Rangers owner (and commander in chief) to make a few remarks.

As Bush walked to the podium, we all gave him a standing ovation. I thought he was a terrible president, but he had been the president, and I wanted to show respect for his office. He seemed really loose and happy, and started with a joke. "Usually, I do this for money." A good laugh. "I hope Bill and Hillary don't ruin that for me." Big laugh. He was referring, of course, to recent headlines about the craploads^{USS} of money the Clintons had been raking in for public speaking gigs. Funny *and* topical. Not bad!

He spoke for five minutes. Another standing ovation. I said good night to the folks at my table and made my exit, heading toward the door farthest from the podium in order to avoid running into the former president, whom I had savaged to great comedic and commercial success.

But as I turned around and headed in that direction, I suddenly saw him standing directly between me and the exit, engaged in a conversation with two people I also didn't want to talk to. I couldn't very well skirt past the former president without it seeming like I was snubbing him, so I stopped and stood awkwardly/respectfully a few feet away.

Bush saw me and suddenly made a beeline right toward me.

"Remember where we were the last time we saw each other?!" he asked.

"Uh, yeah," I said. "Iowa." I had been covering the Iowa straw poll for *George* magazine in August 1999, and met Bush at a small event in someone's backyard in Indianola.

"Do you remember what I asked you?" I asked him.

"No."

"Okay. It was when the cocaine stuff was coming out, and I said I wasn't interested in that, but since we were in Iowa, I wanted to ask whether you had ever manufactured any crystal meth."

He nodded, perhaps wondering where I was going with this.

"And you outsmarted me," I continued.

Now he had it. "I didn't answer, did I?"

"No. And that was smart. Because if you had, I would have said, 'Then why won't you answer the cocaine question?' "

He nodded. I decided to change the subject.

"You know, what I always liked about you is that you like comedy."

"I do," he confirmed enthusiastically.

"I remember you said that your favorite movie was *Austin Powers.*"

"Still is!"

"And also, I remember your taking a risk by going on Letterman via satellite."

He remembered that. "That was a mistake."

"Staff error, sir."

I could tell he appreciated that. I continued, "And you told a very risky joke that I admired you for, because I can't imagine anyone on your team thought it was a good idea. Do you remember it?"

"No."

"Well," I said, "Dave asked you, 'You say you're a uniter, not a divider. What does that mean?' And you said, via satellite, 'Well, if you had open-heart surgery, I'd sew you back up.' " This had been just a few months after Dave's open-heart surgery.

"And that got a big laugh, right?"

"No! Oh, no. See, because you were on satellite, you didn't see it, but Dave turned to the audience and completely sold you out."

I'm not sure if he understood that I was giving him a compliment for taking the risk, rather than reveling in how badly he had bombed, but in either case, he came back with an upbeat comment. "Well, you were always my favorite comedian on *Saturday Night Live*."

I made a face, clearly indicating that I wasn't buying that for a moment.

"Okay," he said with a big grin. "I was lyin'."

"Well," I responded, "you're my favorite president."

He laughed and gave me a big high five. Holy mackerel, I *liked* him. Now I understood how he got elected twice. Or once, if you're one of the people who constantly called in to Air America.

Chapter 35

The 64 Percent Rule

In order to be an effective Democratic senator, you have to be able to hold two inherently contradictory ideas in your head at the same time without suffering a cerebral hemorrhage.

One: Republicans are just awful. They're beholden to corporate special interests, they're dishonest and/or crazy, they're so cynical that they'd willingly thwart badly needed progress for the sake of their own selfish political motivations. And they've broken Washington irrevocably. So if we care about making progress in America, we need to fight them at every turn.

Two: Republicans exist. And they care about our country just as much as we do, if not always exactly in the same way we do. We do not have a monopoly on power (how's that for an understatement?). And the truth is, neither do we have a monopoly on good ideas.

So if we care about making progress in America, we need to work with them.

My friend Mike Enzi, a Republican senator from Wyoming, has what he calls the 80 Percent Rule. Republicans and Democrats, Mike says, actually agree on 80 percent of any given piece of legislation. So if we focus on that 80 percent, and ignore the 20 percent where we disagree, we can get a lot done.

I think Mike may be a little too optimistic. Some issues, there's just no common ground. If some of us believe that you should be allowed to bring military-style assault weapons onto public transportation, and others of us think that's insane, there's no 80 percent there.

We just have to argue about it, and then take a vote, and live with the outcome, at least until we win some more elections.

Mike's 80 Percent Rule, in my estimation, only applies to, charitably, about 80 percent of what we do in the Senate. Hence, Franken's 64 Percent Rule.

*　*　*

The good news is that there's a lot you can get done in that 64 percent. Take one of the issues where we have actually made some bipartisan progress during my time in the Senate: education. Everyone agrees that there is nothing more fundamental to our nation's success than education. One hundred percent of politicians say that, one hundred percent of the time.

Now, there are some basic fault lines between Democrats and Republicans on this issue. Generally speaking, Democrats support teachers' unions, public school systems, and a strong federal role in education, while Republicans believe in more local control of education, and believe that competition in the form of school vouchers will improve the quality of schools. Also, some conservatives used to secretly support the voucher movement because they wanted to *undermine* public education in order to "advance God's Kingdom" by diverting funding from public schools to religious schools. I say "used to" because, with Betsy DeVos now running the Department of Education, they no longer bother keeping it a secret.

Anyway, those fault lines were scrambled in 2002, when George W. Bush signed into law his signature education bill—called, with unintended irony, No Child Left Behind (NCLB).

Passed with strong bipartisan support, NCLB sought to improve our nation's K–12 education system by setting high standards and imposing an extensive testing regime on public elementary and secondary schools, along with draconian measures if the schools failed to achieve federally mandated progress.

By the time I came to the Senate, there was a bipartisan consensus that NCLB was a disaster.

*   *   *

During my 2008 campaign, I'd often say in my stump speech, "I have not met one teacher in Minnesota who likes No Child Left Behind."

Then, in early October, a teacher took me aside. "I like No Child Left Behind," he said quietly, "because it disaggregates the data."

Under NCLB, test data was broken down, and each subgroup of students at a school—black, Hispanic, Asian American and Pacific Islander, American Indian, English Language Learners, students in special education—had to succeed in order for the school to be considered to have made "adequate yearly progress."

The teacher continued, "That guarantees that schools are finally interested in how their black and Hispanic kids are doing."

And he was absolutely right.

You see, NCLB was a reauthorization* of the origi-

---

* Congress has frequent opportunities to revisit issues like education, because many bills that spend money must be periodically reauthorized—that is, their provisions are set to expire after a certain number of years, forcing legislators to come back to the table to adjust things that aren't working, make improvements, or reopen the underlying argument altogether. More civics class materials on the legislative

nal Elementary and Secondary Education Act (ESEA) signed into law by President Johnson. And like the 1964 Civil Rights Act, which made my dad (and me) a Democrat, and the 1965 Voting Rights Act, ESEA was a civil rights bill, giving the federal government a bigger role in K–12 education to ensure that states were providing a decent education for *all* of their students.

So the disaggregation of data became the second thing I liked about No Child Left Behind, the first being the name.

Otherwise, the law was a disaster. If a school failed to make "adequate yearly progress" for four years in a row, it would have to undergo a federally mandated restructuring—in some cases, schools would be forced to fire and replace 50 percent of their teachers and their principal. This made no sense, for example, in rural areas, where there are teacher shortages. A number of rural school superintendents told me about two "failing" schools in their district which just swapped their two principals and half their teachers—showing the sort of problem-solving ingenuity that I dearly hope they passed on to their students.

NCLB had a whole host of wildly stupid rules. For

---

sunsetting process, including study guides and suggested discussion topics, are available at—what's that? We've eliminated civics from nearly every school nationwide? Never mind.

example, students would take their NCLB tests in late April, which meant that the school wouldn't get the results until well after the school year had ended, at which point it was too late to use the results to actually help the students. Hence, educators referred to the test results as "autopsies."

Another stupid thing: Schools were judged by what percentage of students met or exceeded "proficiency." That created a perverse incentive for teachers to focus on kids in the middle—students right below and right above this arbitrary "proficiency" benchmark. Teachers in Minnesota called this a "race to the middle." They could ignore the kids at the top, because they knew those kids would never fall below proficiency. And they could ignore the kids at the bottom, because there was almost no chance that those students would reach proficiency that school year.

This "proficiency" thing was nuts. A sixth-grade teacher who takes a kid from a third-grade level of reading to a fifth-grade level of reading is a hero, not a failure.

More stupidly, the tests were not allowed to measure students' ability outside their grade level. A fifth-grader could only take a test designed to show whether or not he could read at a fifth-grade level. If your son couldn't read at a fifth-grade level, wouldn't you want to know whether he was reading at a *fourth*-grade level, as opposed to a *second*-grade level? Tough. The

NCLB test didn't do that. It only measured for fifth-grade "proficiency," and gave no answer more detailed than "pass" or "fail."

That's why many Minnesota schools started administering a computer adaptive test in addition to the mandated NCLB test.

These tests were far more useful. For one thing, they were on a *computer*, meaning teachers could get the results for each kid right away, and use them to inform their instruction. For another, they were *adaptive*, meaning that if a child was answering questions correctly, the questions would get harder, and vice versa. That way, the teachers could see at exactly what grade level each student was testing. Teachers, principals, and superintendents in Minnesota all told me they preferred the computer adaptive test.

But this meant students had to take *both* tests, and because the stakes were so high, that meant a lot of test prep, or what teachers referred to as "drill and kill."

It reminded me of the McNamara fallacy, named for Robert McNamara,* Kennedy and Johnson's data-driven secretary of defense during the Vietnam War. The McNamara fallacy is this: What can be measured

---

* McNamara was CEO of Ford when Kennedy nominated him for defense secretary. A journalist asked an executive at Ford if he thought McNamara was a good choice. "Yes," the executive answered, "because he doesn't make small mistakes."

will be measured, and what cannot be measured won't be measured. And only things that are measured are deemed important.

Hence the drilling and killing. Teachers spent all their time trying to get their kids to learn the certain discrete skills they knew would be tested. Not on the test, and therefore not in the lesson plans, were things like critical thinking, creativity, the ability to work with others, and love of learning. All of which are kind of important. Or at least I'm told. By employers.

* * *

By the time I got to the Senate, everyone knew that NCLB needed to be reformed. We held lots of hearings and talked to lots of witnesses. There was a lot of agreement on what wasn't working, and we all took turns vehemently agreeing about it. In other words, we did a lot of what we in Washington call "admiring the problem."

So why did it take seven years to get it done?

Well, that whole "two contradictory ideas" thing works both ways. Even as we were finding ourselves in agreement on what we needed to do, Republican leaders were working to prevent us from actually doing it. The entire time Democrats held the majority in the Senate, we couldn't break through to even bring a K–12 education bill to the floor.

But after Republicans took the majority in the 2014 election, we started to see some things move. Ironic, you might think. But not really. As minority leader, Mitch McConnell's goal was almost always to stop Obama and Senate Democrats from getting things done, to prevent us from having achievements we could point to. But Obama wouldn't be on the ballot in 2016, and McConnell was suddenly interested in getting some things done so that *his* majority could have something to show for itself.

But, hey, after six years, Democrats were willing—hell, eager—to go along with it. We believe in government, after all. And even if it meant Republicans got a lot of the credit, we were happy to be moving forward on long-delayed priorities like a five-year highway bill and, at long last, education reform.

At the outset, Republican HELP Committee chairman Lamar Alexander put together a totally partisan Republican bill, which ranking Democrat Patty Murray and the rest of us refused to take up. After that initial exchange, Lamar and Patty got down to business, working together on a truly bipartisan bill in an exemplary way.

I have tremendous admiration for Lamar Alexander. Time and again, he'd call a hearing, and the night before, I'd read through the testimony of the next day's witnesses, only to discover that one after another was planning to say something I knew Lamar didn't agree with. In other words, he was willing to call witnesses who offered opposing views—and he always listened carefully.*

The bill we passed in 2015 represented the 80 percent (or 64 percent) that Senate Republicans and Democrats finally realized we agreed on. Schools would still have to test every year between third and eighth grade and once in high school. But each state would control its own testing, and that would almost certainly mean fewer high-stakes tests.

Meanwhile, we would invest more in early childhood education, which Democrats liked. But not enough, which Republicans liked. But everyone got to say that we'd done *something* about early childhood education, which everyone liked, because the impact is so clear.

Inequality in education starts early, and it starts at home. A study by the University of Kansas found that by the time she is three years old, a child who grows up in a home on welfare will hear thirty million fewer words than a child who grows up in the home

---

* That, by the way, is why I was so disappointed when he took one for the team by cutting off questions after one round during the confirmation hearings for Trump nominees Betsy DeVos and Tom Price—I assume because the questions were revealing that DeVos didn't know the first thing about public education and Price had a long history of suspicious stock purchases. More on those hearings later.

of a professional family.* Words like "portfolio" and "equestrian."

We know that kids who have had a quality early childhood education are less likely to be placed in special education, less likely to be left back a grade, more likely to have better health outcomes, less likely to get pregnant in adolescence, more likely to graduate from high school, more likely to go to college, more likely to get a good job, and less likely to go to prison. The return on investment in quality early childhood education can be as high as sixteen dollars for every dollar spent.

If we really wanted to address future deficits, we would be pouring money into training early childhood educators. Didn't happen here, though.

The law we passed put more funding into after-school programs. More funding into school counselors. More funding for mental health in schools. Although not enough of any of it.

There was also more (but not enough) funding for STEM skills—science, technology, engineering, and math—which are necessary for so many twenty-first-century jobs.

When I think about after-school programs and

---

* That's not thirty million distinct different words. I don't think there are thirty million words. During their study, researchers found that children from welfare families heard on average about six hundred words an hour. Children from professional families heard twenty-one hundred words an hour.

STEM skills, I don't just think of the academic literature on school achievement. I think of First Robotics. In First Robotics, high school teams build and program robots to compete against other schools in a complex game, which changes every year—like hitting a target with a Frisbee and climbing a jungle gym. Believe it or not, there are now more high school First Robotics teams in Minnesota than boys' varsity hockey teams.

When the team from East Duluth finished tenth in the world championships a few years ago, I went up to highlight their achievement at an auto body shop where they were building their new robot. The fabrication co-captain, a sophomore named Anna Karas, introduced me to the programming co-captain, the business co-captain, and the media co-captain. Then Anna did an interview with the three Duluth camera crews that showed up for the event.

"What does it mean to you that three cameras are here today?" one of the producers asked.

"It's very in line with our media strategy," Anna answered.

I don't worry about Anna. With millions of self-replicating tireless robots as her obedient slaves, there is almost no limit to what she can accomplish in the future.

* * *

A number of my amendments didn't make it into the bill. Take, for example, my Student Non-Discrimination

Act. SNDA would give LGBT students the same rights that students have on the basis of race, disability, and gender, including the private right of action (the right to sue). There has been an epidemic of bullying of LGBT students across our country. Many LGBT kids have committed suicide. Thirty percent of LGBT students report missing a day of school in the last month because they're afraid.

For years, I tried and failed to get a Republican cosponsor. One night, I called a good Republican friend of mine.

> ME: My amendment gives LGBT kids and their parents a private right of action.
> COLLEAGUE: Well, the kids will just act more gay so they can sue.
> ME: Oh, no. No. No. That's not what would happen.
> COLLEAGUE: You just watch!
> ME [silently]: Oy.

But there's one amendment that I did get through that I am as proud of as anything I've done in the Senate.

It's not uncommon for foster children to have ten, eleven, twelve sets of foster parents during their childhood. This wreaks havoc on their education. If a child's new foster parents live in a different school district, the foster child is yanked out of school and sent to one in the new school district. Sometimes the kids fall through the cracks. Kayla VanDyke, an impressive high school senior from Minnesota who had been in seven foster homes, testified to the HELP Committee that she had missed fourth grade entirely.

For foster kids, school is often the one constant in their lives. Maybe they have a teacher they really like. Or an extracurricular activity that means everything to them. Or maybe, maybe they have these things called friends.

My amendment was simple. It allowed foster kids to choose to stay in their school if they wanted to. That meant the school district and local social services would have to find a way to pay for the transportation. At first, almost all of my Republican colleagues were against it. After all, it was a federal mandate, requiring local school districts to spend money. But after six years of talking to my colleagues one-on-one, they had come to see the wisdom of my proposal. The amendment passed overwhelmingly and became part of the new law.

I like to think that somewhere there's a foster child running cross-country, or developing a passion for history because of a great teacher, or doing homework with a good friend, because of the legislation I worked hard on—legislation that passed with a strong bipartisan majority.

And my fervent hope is that that kid will grow up to run for the Senate as a Democrat and knock off a Republican incumbent.

* * *

If we want to help kids, especially kids who don't have all the advantages that I had, and that my kids had, and that my grandkids are going to have, then one education bill isn't going to do it.

And just focusing on education itself isn't enough. For example, kids who grow up poor are far more likely to suffer what are called "adverse childhood experiences": not just the stress of living in poverty itself, but domestic violence, abuse or neglect, the incarceration of a parent, the death of a sibling—all of which affect brain chemistry and the ability to learn. If we want to improve education, we need to do a better job of helping these kids overcome these traumas—and a better job of addressing economic inequality so that fewer have to deal with trauma in the first place.

Which means we need to create more prosperity, and do it in a way where everybody gets to prosper. Which means we need to invest in our infrastructure, and in research and development, and in innovative technologies, and in our workforce, and, most of all, in our kids.

Which would be a hell of a lot easier if our political system wasn't broken. And it's going to be hard to unbreak it as long as Republicans continue to hold a lot of power.

It would be great if, someday soon, we had a Democratic president, and a Democratic House, and a filibuster-proof Democratic majority in the Senate. Or, really, any of those things. And a huge part of what all of us have to do from here on out is to fight back to win back the country, up and down the ballot. We have to organize from the grassroots on up, we have to make our case to the public, and we have to go on offense.

But in the meantime, on Capitol Hill, I still believe that the 64 Percent Rule applies. Just because we're out of power doesn't mean we abdicate our responsibility to try to improve people's lives. That's what makes us Democrats. It's what makes us worth electing in the first place.

Of course, now that Donald Trump is president, even 64 percent might be a little optimistic. I figure we're going to spend some portion of our time trying to stop him from giving Alaska back to the Russians. Let's say we spend 60 percent of our time on stuff like that instead of making progress.

Doing the math, that means we're down to, let me see, 64 percent times the remaining 40 percent... Okay, 25.6 percent. But I'm an optimist. So let's round up: 26 percent.

And, of course, our new secretary of education is

a right-wing ideologue who hates public schools. So maybe education isn't going to be in that 26 percent for a while. But something else will be. I can't think of anything right now. ISIS? Opioids? Cybersecurity? Sentencing reform? Maybe that Victor Borge stamp from a couple of chapters ago? There's plenty to choose from.

Chapter 36

My Republican Friends

Okay, maybe 26 percent is a little high. Maybe it's more like 20 percent. Or 15. Or maybe you're just a total pessimist and you think it's closer to 2 percent.

But even if 98 percent of the time we're at an impasse, there's progress to be made in that 2 percent.

Remember how my dad's quilting factory failed because the railroad wouldn't stop in Albert Lea to pick up his goods to bring to market? That's an example of something called "captive shipping." In much of America, railroads enjoy a monopoly and are able to charge farmers and manufacturers exorbitant prices to carry their products. If you don't pay, the railroad doesn't stop, and you have to move to St. Louis Park to become a printing salesman.

The Surface Transportation Board (STB) has jurisdiction over railroads. And just as George W. Bush invaded Iraq to avenge his own father, I wanted to make it easier for someone who had been the victim of captive shipping to do something about it. When I first got to the Senate, it cost $20,000 to lodge a complaint with the STB. If you're a small farmer watching freight trains zip through your community without stopping because you can't afford to pay monopoly prices to the railroad, you tend not to have $20,000 lying around.

I wanted to put pressure on the STB to lower the fee for lodging a complaint. But as is almost always the case, the odds of success were going to be far higher if I had a Republican partner.

Which is how I ended up working with David Vitter, an extremely conservative Republican with whom I almost never agreed and whose personal conduct I was, um, repulsed by.* Together, David and I got the STB to lower the fee to $350. And then we went back to voting against each other all the time.

I've worked with John Boozman from Arkansas on improving health care for veterans. I've worked with Deb Fischer from Nebraska on increasing access to rural broadband. I've worked with Bill Cassidy from Louisiana on addiction issues. I'm working right now with Thom Tillis from North Carolina on funding housing and wraparound services for people with mental illness.

---

* Google it.

They're all extremely conservative Republicans who I'm sure don't want me to say anything good about them. And make no mistake, I hope they get beat in their next elections.

But they're there right now! And just as part of my job is standing my ground against all the terrible things they want to do, part of it is looking for opportunities to find common ground, because that's how stuff gets done.

You see, there are only a hundred of us senators. And none of us can do the job without working with the other ninety-nine.

Mike Mansfield had a saying: "It only takes one senator to make a scene. But it takes more than one to make a difference."

Okay, he never said that. I made it up. But if he *had*, it certainly would have made my point. Which is that, sure, a lone senator can hold things up with a filibuster or some other procedural maneuver. But actually passing legislation takes teamwork.

Very often, the only way a bill stands a chance is if you can find a cosponsor in the other party, to make it bipartisan. Sometimes you have a regional issue that requires you to cooperate with colleagues from neighboring states, even if you and said colleagues don't see eye-to-eye on pretty much anything. For example, there's a history of flooding in the Red River Valley between Minnesota and North Dakota, so it's really important that North Dakota Republican John Hoeven and I be able to work together to fight for flood mitigation funding.

That's why we have all these unwritten rules, like addressing each other as "my esteemed colleague" even when we may in fact esteem each other very little. It's why you're not supposed to smirk or roll your eyes when someone else is giving a speech on the floor and you're presiding. That would be a real jerk move.

And it's why, as silly as it may sound, it's important that we try to *like* each other. That's right: *like* each other. Not just the Lamar Alexander types, either. In my view, you've got to build friendships with the Jeff Sessions types, too. Like, for example, with Jeff Sessions.

* * *

When I first got to the Senate, Jeff was the ranking member of the Judiciary Committee, and I made it a point to go to every hearing, no matter how perfunctory. Often we'd have a nomination hearing for a judge whose confirmation was completely noncontroversial, and it would be just the chairman (Patrick Leahy), Jeff, and me.

I wasn't just there because I had nothing else to do. I was there to prove that I had come to the Senate to work, not to be a clown. And Jeff took notice. He saw me show up for every hearing. He heard me take the responsibility of questioning nominees seriously. And even though he probably agreed with literally nothing I said, he quickly grew to like the cut of my jib.

A few weeks in, Chairman Leahy had to miss a hearing, so he asked me to fill in. I arrived early, and when Jeff got there he saw me sitting in the chairman's seat, holding the gavel.

"Well," exclaimed Jeff in his thick southern drawl. "A meteoric rise!"

"And well deserved," I replied in my nasal midwestern Jewish twang. Jeff laughed. He's been an easy laugh for me ever since. Except at his confirmation hearing.

Anyway, the point is, Jeff liked me. And here's why I like him.

A few years later, the Judiciary Committee was holding a hearing on a Dianne Feinstein bill to protect American citizens apprehended within the United States on terrorism charges from being detained indefinitely without a trial.

One of the witnesses was Steven Bradbury, a lawyer who had written one of the Bush administration memos inventing some flimsy legal rationale for torture, thus contributing to the decline of our reputation on the world stage, inflaming anti-American sentiment in the Middle East, and putting our troops in more danger.

I wasn't really interested in hearing this guy's

thoughts on due process. And I told him so. "It's very difficult for me, frankly, to rely on your legal opinion today," I said, suggesting that someone with his record had no business testifying before the committee.

It was pretty aggressive by Senate committee standards. So aggressive, in fact, that my questioning really offended some of the Republicans on the committee.

But I didn't know that until Jeff was kind enough to call me and give me a heads-up that I should probably cool it for a little while. It was a nice thing to do. I had had no idea that I was digging myself such a hole with my colleagues by teeing off on this ghoul, and I really appreciated that Jeff was gracious enough to clue me in so I could back off a bit.

When Trump won the election and nominated Jeff to be attorney general, it was time for me to return the favor by setting aside my very real concerns about his record and the Trump administration's plans for the Department of Justice and just waving his nomination through.

No. Of course not. Being a senator does mean finding a way to make friends with people you're fighting against with every fiber of your being. But it also means finding a way to fight with every fiber of your being against people you're friends with.

I rarely voted with Jeff when he was a senator. And that's fine. Senators disagree. But I knew that as attorney general he would represent a clear and present danger to the civil rights of millions of Americans. And his confirmation hearing would be my opportunity to raise that alarm. Which I did, without apology, calling him out for overstating his involvement in civil rights cases and holding his feet to the fire on Donald Trump's fearmongering about voter fraud (which, of course, is nothing more than a pretext for voter suppression). And then I voted against him.

Jeff Sessions is my friend (or was). Franni is friends with his wife, Mary. When our grandson, Joe, was born, Mary knit him a baby-blue blanket, which became his favorite.

It's hard to unfairly demonize someone whose wife knit your grandson his favorite blankie. Which is why when my job meant doing everything in my power to deny my friend this important position, I was relieved that there was so much to fairly demonize him for.

* * *

For my part, I've tried to create more opportunities for us senators to be nice to each other. For example, at any given time we have thirty or so pages working in the Senate. Pages are high school juniors—sixteen-year-old kids—who come to Washington to spend months helping out with day-to-day operations in the Senate chamber. They all live together in a dorm. And if I were the parent of one of them, I realized, I would want to know that senators were keeping an eye out for them and helping them to have a positive experience.

So Franni and I teamed up with Mike and Diana Enzi to start a tradition of throwing pizza parties and ice-cream socials for these kids. Pages are generally not allowed to initiate conversations with senators, so Mike and I give them an opportunity to ask us questions like, "Is being a senator as much fun as being on *Saturday Night Live*?" or, in Mike's case, "Is being a senator as much fun as being an accountant?"

Another initiative I spearheaded, over the repeated and grumpy objections of Harry Reid, was our annual Senate Secret Santa. I modeled it after the Secret Santa we had back in elementary school in St. Louis Park. The idea was that every kid would get a gift, but also that every kid would have to learn something about someone they maybe didn't know and do a nice thing for them. I figured it would be a fun, bipartisan thing for us to do, and because every senator who participated would get a present, no senator would get his or her feelings hurt.

One year, though, Jeff Flake, an iconoclastic Republican from Arizona, kind of hurt my feelings by giving me a crappy present: a hat bearing the logo of "PING," which is apparently a golf equipment company based in his home state.

I complained about it to Tim Kaine. "Flake gave me this stupid hat. This is the worst Secret Santa gift ever. What was he thinking?"

"Staff error," said Tim. He's really smart. And would make a great vice president. Goddammit. Now I'm depressed. Let's move on.

* * *

Not surprisingly, the quickest way to my heart is through my funny bone (which isn't the elbow, but rather the rib that lies directly over the heart).* And my favorite Republican colleagues aren't the ones whose politics are the least objectionable, but rather the ones with the best senses of humor no matter how objectionable their politics may be.

Pat Roberts has got to be near the top of the list. As I mentioned earlier, he loves Bob and Ray, but he loves Jack Benny even more, and he has a little bit of that famous Jack Benny comic timing. When I see him at an elevator or in the Senate subway, I usually greet him with a "May I help you?!" in the shrill voice of annoying character actor Frank Nelson, a regular on the Jack Benny program. Pat replies with a great Benny-esque "You again?!" And then we laugh.

No one within earshot has a clue what we're laughing about, and odds are neither do you, but we don't care. And though our politics couldn't be more different, we always jump at the chance to work on something together. For example: The regulations on drug

---

* Awww.

compounding (which is when pharmacists mix prescriptions themselves from individual ingredients) were extremely confusing, and in 2012, eight hundred Americans contracted fungal meningitis, and sixty-four died, due to unsafe drugs that shouldn't have been allowed to be distributed. Pat and I discovered that we both wanted to work on this issue, so we teamed up and closed the loopholes.

Then there was the time I needed Republican votes for an amendment to get $11 million for energy projects in Indian country, so I asked Pat. He stood with me in the well of the Senate, doing his best to urge his Republican colleagues to help me. And by "his best," I mean that Pat told them, "Leadership describes this as 'completely innocuous.'" I got the votes.

Pat's funny, but the funniest Republican in the Senate is Lindsey Graham. Most of his jokes are of the "we're in a cynical business" persuasion. For example, before our Christmas break one year, Lindsey asked me if the Frankens were going anywhere for some sun. I told him we were going to Puerto Rico.

Without missing a beat, Lindsey gave me some advice. "Do two fund-raisers: one with the folks *for* statehood, one with the folks *against* statehood. They never talk to each other."

In 2016, Lindsey ran for president, and found himself somewhere around fifteenth in a field of seventeen. Running into him in the senators' bathroom, I told him, "Lindsey, if I were voting in the Republican primaries, I'd vote for you."

Again without hesitation, he replied, "That's my problem."

* * *

Believe it or not, however, not every senator has a great sense of humor.

Tom Coburn and I did not hit it off right away. A terrifyingly conservative Republican from Oklahoma, he was known as "Dr. No," for two reasons. First, Tom's an obstetrician-gynecologist. Second, he is an adamant federalist, who believes the federal government has appropriated too much power from the states, which means he's pretty much opposed to Congress doing *anything*.

But that's not why we didn't hit it off. Our first four or five interactions were just misses. Nothing terrible. Mainly, he just didn't seem to get where I was coming from. So I approached him at a Judiciary Committee hearing to take another shot at breaking the ice. "Tom, can I buy you lunch?"

"Tell you what," he said. "Buy me breakfast."

We sat down together a couple of days later in the Senate dining room around 8 a.m. I had given some thought to how I wanted to start. "Tom," I said cheerily, "let's have fun. We can talk about anything. Politics. Our families. Our careers. But let's make sure to have fun."

"Sure." He nodded. "Fun."

"Okay," I said. "Careers. Let me ask you something. To be a doctor in Oklahoma, do you have to have *any* formal education?"

"Yes!!!" he exploded angrily. "You have to go to *medical school*!!!"

Ah. I had identified our problem. "Okay," I explained, "that was a joke."

Tom understood immediately and calmed right down.

"You see, *that's* what *I* used to do for a living. I told jokes. I was in comedy."

We did have fun for the next forty-five minutes, and he wrote me a lovely note thanking me for breakfast and for the fun, which seemed like it had been a novel experience for him. Tom retired from the Senate after 2014 with a near-perfect record of voting against everything I like.

But when I called Tom a few months ago to make sure it was okay with him if I told this story, he agreed right away. "You're a gentleman to ask, but there's a First Amendment! You can write anything you want!" Very Tom Coburn. Then we had some fun talking about grandchildren.

* * *

I should note, I like my Democratic colleagues, too. But I spend a lot more time with them. And we agree on stuff. So it's easy to like them. It's harder to make friends across the aisle.

And it's also more important. It's a lot easier to negotiate with people you trust and whom you don't personally dislike. That's why you fight as hard as you can for your principles, but you try not to be a jerk about it. It's why it's important that your word is good. It's why it's important to try to build these relationships with colleagues across the aisle, whether it's through family bonding or inside jokes or writing a country song together (which I did with Orrin Hatch).*

Unfortunately, building those bonds is harder now than it used to be. For one thing, members of Congress used to bring their families to Washington to live. Members would see each other on weekends and just hang out. Their kids used to go to school together—in D.C. or suburban Maryland or Virginia. It's hard to hate the parent of a kid who's on your kid's baseball team.

To a great degree, the 1994 election changed that. Newt Gingrich told Republicans to run against Washington. They did, and they won. He told them to keep their families in their home districts. And they did,

---

* It's called "We Stayed Together for the Kids." When Orrin and I were working on it in his office, Orrin's scheduler called my scheduler and said, "I don't know what's going on in there. They're just laughing."

and for some of them, it put some pressure on their family life. Newt, for example.

But mostly it meant that members would fly into D.C. on Monday afternoon and fly out on Thursday afternoon, a practice that has continued to this day.

Meanwhile, our schedules have gotten more packed than ever. Every minute we don't spend fulfilling the requirements of our jobs, we're expected to spend raising money. And we're also expected to spend as much time as possible in our states. Which doesn't leave a lot of time for getting to know, and therefore trust, your colleagues.

At the end of the day, the Senate is like any other workplace. You don't always enjoy all of your coworkers, but you're far better off finding a way to get along with them than you are harping on the things you don't like.

And being a successful senator is as much about being a good coworker as it is about being smart or well versed in the issues or a talented orator. If you can be a pleasure to work with, you'll get more accomplished than if you're a pill whom nobody can stand.

Which brings me to Ted Cruz.

Chapter 37

Sophistry

As I mentioned in the last chapter, there are unwritten rules of the Senate that everyone follows in order to maintain civility and foster productive working relationships. One of those unwritten rules is that you aren't supposed to repeat in public a conversation you've had with a colleague in private if that conversation makes your colleague look bad in any way.

I've decided to observe that practice in this book, with one exception: Ted Cruz.

For what it's worth, I feel fully justified in doing so, because Ted violated basic Senate protocol himself when he went to the floor and called Mitch McConnell a liar. It was the sort of thing that *just isn't done*, a breach of decorum so shocking that even *I* haven't committed it. And I *love* calling people liars!

Anyway, here's the thing you have to understand about Ted Cruz. I like Ted Cruz more than most of my other colleagues like Ted Cruz. And I *hate* Ted Cruz.

The reason I like Ted more than most of my other colleagues do is that he actually has a decent sense of humor. Ted has tried out jokes on me. They're usually pretty pedestrian—generally, I can see the punch line coming, and many are not-very-good versions of constructions I've heard before. But as politician jokes go, they're not bad at all. And Ted is a fan of comedy. I think. You're never entirely sure with this guy.

One Monday, after a week's recess, Ted came up to me on the floor to tell me that he and some friends had watched a rerun of my Stuart Smalley sketch with Michael Jordan and raved about how funny it was. I think he was being sincere, which meant it was a genuinely nice gesture.

The only problem was that at that moment I was talking to Jeff Sessions about our respective recesses. And now I had to try to explain to Jeff what Ted was talking about. Which meant I had to explain what recovery is, what affirmations are, what public-access TV is, what a *parody* of public-access TV is— and I had to do it all in about thirty seconds before Jeff lost interest. Which I of course failed to do, and Jeff just kind of faded away to talk with someone else. Great.

Anyway, Ted has a sense of humor, even if it's a lame one. And he did pay me a modest compliment, even if it was some Machiavellian ploy in service of his ambition to take over the world.

The problem with Ted isn't that he's humorless. It isn't even his truly reprehensible far-right politics. No, the problem with Ted—and the reason so many senators have a problem with Ted—is simply that he is an absolutely toxic coworker. He's the guy in your office who snitches to corporate about your March Madness pool and microwaves fish in the office kitchen. He is the Dwight Schrute of the Senate.

In a way, he's a perfect example of what I said in the last chapter about how it's not your knowledge of policy or your political talents, but rather your people skills, that determine whether you succeed as a senator.

For sure, Ted is extremely smart. Only the most brilliant young lawyers get to clerk for Supreme Court justices, and Ted got to clerk for Chief Justice William Rehnquist. And he's a truly gifted speaker who can frame an argument brilliantly. From what I've heard, when Cruz later returned to the Court to argue cases in his capacity as the solicitor general of Texas, clerks would all make a point to be present in the chamber so they could watch him do his thing.

I don't begrudge Ted that. There are plenty of senators who are smarter than I am, or have more natural political aptitude than I do. For example, my own senior senator, Amy Klobuchar. Or my friend Sheldon Whitehouse, one of the smartest people I've ever met. Or Lindsey Graham. But I like them all. Because none of them are sociopaths.

* * *

Let me explain by telling you what I consider to be the quintessential Ted Cruz story.

After the unspeakable mass shooting at Sandy Hook Elementary School, Dianne Feinstein introduced a bill to reinstate the federal assault weapons ban, which was enacted in 1994 and expired in 2004.

Now, there are plenty of things we could be doing to address gun violence that are overwhelmingly popular and aren't getting done only because Republicans have decided to refuse to do *anything* on guns, such as closing the loophole that allows people to buy guns at gun shows or on some websites without a background check. But there is a little more room for disagreement when it comes to the assault weapons ban.

I, for one, wanted to cosponsor Dianne's bill right away. But we have a very strong gun culture in Minnesota. And my advisers in the state urged caution. Why be in such a rush to back the bill?

"How am I going to feel when this happens again?" I asked. But I understood why many of my constituents felt differently. I *love* football. There is no reason to love football as much as I love football, but people live for their pastimes. And one popular pastime, especially in Minnesota, is target shooting with

AR-15s. Who am I to say that's any more or less valid of a hobby than watching football players give each other concussions?

Anyway, I wanted to treat the debate with the seriousness it deserved, so even though I'd decided to support the assault weapons ban, I made sure to listen to both sides. I even visited a gun manufacturer in St. Cloud where they made AR-15s.

It's actually a great company. They have a terrific record of hiring veterans. But they are very much central-casting pro-gun guys. The company doesn't make ammunition clips, just the AR-15s themselves, so I decided to start with something I thought we could maybe agree on. I asked why anyone would need a thirty-round magazine to go hunting, and the manager shook his head and said, "If anyone needs ten bullets to take down a deer..."

It seemed like we were finding some common ground. So why, I asked, would anyone need an assault rifle to go hunting at all? And one of the guys brought up feral pigs. Apparently they run in packs, and they're vicious. We don't have a lot of feral pigs in Minnesota, but they're evidently a real problem in parts of the South.

"Has anyone ever been killed by a feral pig?" I asked.

There was an awkward pause. Then someone said, "I heard of a guy who got bit in the leg."

That didn't really seem to me like a reason to tote around an AR-15 with a thirty-round magazine, but

I didn't want to push my luck, so I asked, "Well, are they good eating? The feral pigs?"

And one of the guys said, "If they're young."

* * *

Okay, that wasn't a story about Ted Cruz, but it *was* a story about how fraught the debate was over the assault weapons ban, and how I tried hard to take that debate seriously, and also you learned something I bet you didn't know, which is that if you're going to eat a feral pig, you should eat a young one.

Here's where Ted comes into the story. Back in Washington, Ted was taking absolutely no pains to listen to the other side. Instead, he was vehemently and theatrically opposing the bill with a series of fiery sermons on the Senate floor. And then one day he came up to me during a vote and said the following: "Anyone who is for the assault weapons ban is engaged in sophistry."

"Sophistry" is an SAT word, one I had neither seen nor heard nor spoken since I was sixteen years old. Our English teacher, Mr. Glenn, had assigned us a vocabulary book, and we were to learn three words a day, and one day "sophistry" was one of the words. Sophistry is a form of argument that is intended to be deceitful.

I don't think Ted knew that I was a cosponsor of Dianne's bill. I also don't think he knew that I knew what "sophistry" meant. Which I think is why he used the word.

But I played along. "Why am I engaged in sophistry?"

"Because," Ted said, "Clinton's own Department of Justice did a study of the assault weapons ban and concluded that it doesn't work."

"No it didn't," I replied. "Actually, what the report said was there wasn't enough data to reach a conclusion, because the study was conducted only two years after the ban was implemented."

"Just read the report," Ted sneered in his pugnacious way (I think "pugnacious" was also one of Mr. Glenn's vocabulary words).

"I'll do that," I said with an edge of, um, truculence?

After the vote, I took the Senate subway to my office and found Josh Riley, my Judiciary counsel. "Ted Cruz just told me that anyone who's for the assault weapons ban is engaged in sophistry."

Josh, I should mention, is, like Ted, a super-whip-smart graduate of Harvard Law School. "What's sophistry?" he asked.

I told Josh what sophistry is, and he nodded. "What was his basis for that?"

"He said that it was because Clinton's Justice Department did a study that concluded that it hadn't worked."

Josh frowned. "That's not true." Then he proceeded to explain to me what I had already explained to Ted—that there wasn't enough data available at the time for Clinton's Justice Department to reach a firm conclusion. Still, I asked Josh to go find the Justice Department report and put a memo together so I could be prepared the next time I saw Ted.

Josh went and found the Clinton Justice Department's Impact Evaluation, which was published in 1997, fulfilling the law's requirement that an analysis of the assault weapons ban be completed within thirty months of its enactment.

And guess what? Josh and I were entirely right, and Ted was entirely wrong. The Clinton Justice Department wrote:

> Our best estimate is that the ban contributed to a 6.7 percent decrease in total gun murders between 1994 and 1995, beyond what would have been expected in view of ongoing crime, demographic, and economic trends. However, with only one year of post-ban data, we cannot rule out the possibility that this decrease [in gun murders] reflects chance year-to-year variation rather than a true effect of the ban.

In other words, the early results suggested that the ban might be working, but that there wasn't enough data to draw a definitive conclusion. Exactly what I had told Ted.

The next time I spotted Ted on the Senate floor, I

approached him and said, "Well, I guess you owe me an apology."

"Why?"

"Well," I said, getting ready to hit him with some facts, "the last time we spoke, you said that anybody who is for the assault weapons ban is engaged in sophistry."

To which Ted replied, "No I didn't."

As in a flat denial.

Not "No? I didn't!" Or "Really? I said that?" Or "That doesn't sound like something I'd say."

It was just an unqualified, unequivocal "No I didn't."

And that's when I realized that Ted Cruz was really something special.

* * *

During the Judiciary Committee's first hearing on the assault weapons ban, Ted had engaged in his own odious brand of sophistry. First, he said this:

> The assault weapons ban that used to be in effect, according to the Department of Justice, quote, "failed to reduce the average number of victims per gun murder incident or multiple gunshot wounds victims."

A 1999 summary of the 1997 report did say that. But that's very different from saying that the ban *didn't work*. (In fact, the sentence immediately preceding the one Ted quoted said, "Evidence suggests that the ban may have contributed to a reduction in the gun murder rate and murders of police officers by criminals armed with assault weapons.")

Ted continued:

> Now, that is the assessment of the United States Department of Justice, and that is in 1994 [*sic*].*
> That was the Janet Reno Department of Justice under President Clinton that said the assault weapons ban was singularly ineffective.

No. The report said nothing of the kind. The Microsoft Word thesaurus, which is even easier for me to consult while writing than the one built into Google, lists the following words as synonyms for "singularly": "unusually," "especially," "exceptionally," "rarely," and "surprisingly." So Cruz was saying that the DOJ had called the assault weapons ban "exceptionally ineffective." Of course, not only does the report say no such thing, but it repeatedly makes the *exact opposite point*, which was that there was not yet enough evidence to draw any conclusive determination.

---

* The Clinton Justice Department's report came out in 1997, and the language Ted cited actually came from a 1999 summary of that report. That kind of mistake is very common in the Senate and in life. An *innocent* mistake, I'm sure, which is rare for someone as meticulous and/or malevolent as Ted.

Ted was being singularly dishonest. And exceptionally smarmy.

After our hearings on the assault weapons ban, we went into executive session to mark up the bill. When it came time for Ted to speak, he treated us all to a breathtakingly patronizing lecture directed at Senator Feinstein, who had been in the Senate for twenty years, compared to Ted's two months.

After helpfully reminding Dianne that the Constitution is our foundational document and that the First and Second Amendments of the Constitution are part of the Bill of Rights, Ted went in for the kill:

> And the question that I would pose to the senior senator from California is, would she deem it consistent with the Bill of Rights for Congress to engage in the same endeavor that we are contemplating doing with the Second Amendment in the context of the First or Fourth Amendment?
>
> Namely, would she consider it constitutional for Congress to specify that the First Amendment shall apply only to the following books, and shall not apply to the books that Congress has deemed outside the protection of the Bill of Rights?

You get what he was trying to say, right? The bill would have outlawed assault weapons, while leaving *other* guns legal. And Ted was suggesting that this was equivalent to selectively banning books.

If this sounds like a very private-school-debate-club way to talk about gun safety, please rest assured that it was delivered in the most private-school-debate-club tone possible. Like an actor performing a monologue in which he plays an intolerably smug, self-righteous high school debater in a blue blazer with brass buttons, but way, way overdoing it. Ted's condescension hung in the air like the stench from a cat box in an apartment with forty cats belonging to an elderly woman who had just been found dead. It was bad, is what I'm saying.

Dick Durbin jumped in. "Would the senator yield for a question?"

But Dianne wanted to respond herself. "Let me just make a couple of points in response. One, I'm not a sixth-grader." Barely containing her anger, she reminded Ted that not only had she been a member of the Judiciary Committee for twenty years, but before that, she had been the mayor of San Francisco—an office to which she had ascended when her predecessor, George Moscone, was assassinated (along with Supervisor Harvey Milk).

In fact, Dianne had been the one who discovered Harvey Milk's body. "I've seen the bullets that implode," she growled at Ted.

Dianne finished by assuring Ted that she was familiar with the Constitution and sarcastically thanking him for the lecture. There was a sort of stunned silence. Then Chairman Leahy noted that Dick Durbin had asked for the floor.

"Mr. Chairman," said Dick, "I can't add anything to that."

But Ted could! Instead of dissolving into a fine pink shame-mist, he piped up to clap back at the distinguished public servant who had just taken him to the woodshed.

"I would note," he oozed, "that the senior senator from California did not answer my question, which is: In her judgment, would it be consistent with the Constitution for Congress to specify which books are permitted and which books are not?"

"Well," I chimed in, "I've got a book that I don't think the First Amendment would permit. It's called *Ted Cruz Is a Pedophile*. That would be libel. Unless, of course, you *are* a pedophile. Which we don't know."

No, I didn't say that. But, man, I wanted to. And I kind of wish I had.

* * *

Around that time, Amy Klobuchar was preparing to speak at the Gridiron Club dinner, an annual black-tie affair held by the oldest and most prestigious organization for journalists in Washington. Traditionally, the president gives humorous remarks, as do two members of Congress, one from each party.

For the record, Amy doesn't let me write jokes for her. That way, if someone asks her if I wrote any of her jokes, she can honestly say "no." Besides, Amy's really funny, and can fend for herself. But sometimes she'll run her jokes by me, and every once in a while I'll have a suggestion on how to punch up one or two.

Now, this was in early March 2013, just a couple weeks after a Carnival cruise ship had been towed into harbor after almost a week stranded at sea because of an engine fire. The ship had been nicknamed "the poop cruise" because passengers said the hallways were flooded with human waste.

Which had inspired a joke that Amy ran by me: "When most people think of a bad cruise, they think of Carnival. But we think of Ted." I thought that was pretty good, but suggested a rewrite, which I'll get to in a moment.

The Thursday before the Gridiron, as we were taking a series of votes on the floor, I noticed Amy going around to a few senators she had written jokes about. "Ah," I thought, "Amy's getting their blessing."

Then I saw her walk up to Ted. "Hmm," I thought. "This could be interesting." So I went right over and inserted myself into a conversation triangle.

"Ted," Amy smiled, "I've written a joke about you for the Gridiron, and I wanted to get your okay."

"Sure," Ted smiled back. "What's the joke?"

"Well," Amy smiled, "here it is: 'When most people

think of a difficult cruise, they think of Carnival. But we Democrats in the Senate think of Ted.'"

I noticed, of course, that she had softened the joke a bit, changing "a bad cruise" to "a *difficult* cruise" and changing "we think of Ted" to "we *Democrats in the Senate* think of Ted."

Ted smiled. Then he offered a suggestion. "What if you changed 'a difficult cruise' to 'a *challenging* cruise'?"

Oh my God. What a putz! Now the joke isn't funny. I could tell that Amy was thinking the same thing. And so could Ted. So before Amy could respond, he smiled even more broadly and said magnanimously, "I'll tell you what. I believe in the First Amendment. You go ahead and tell your joke."

Wow, that was patronizing! I decided to step in.

"Say, Ted." I smiled. "I did a rewrite of Amy's joke, and I think it's a lot better. Want to hear it?"

Out of the corner of my eye, I could see Amy having two successive thoughts:

1. "Oh no—Al's not going to do this!"
2. "But I definitely want to be here if he does."

Ted was still smiling. "Sure!"

"Okay. Here it is: 'When most people think of a cruise that's full of shit, they think of Carnival. But we think of Ted."

And there went Ted's smile. For once, he had no words.

I nodded, turned around, and walked away.

* * *

Keep in mind, this all happened within *two months* of Ted's arrival in Washington. There are senators who take six months slowly getting to know people and getting to know the institution before they even make their first floor speech, let alone manage to convince every other senator to hate them. Ted wasted no time pissing everybody off—including his fellow Republicans.

A couple weeks before the gun debate, the Armed Services Committee had held a hearing on Chuck Hagel's nomination to be defense secretary. Now, it wasn't unusual for a Republican senator to give an Obama appointee a hard time, but Chuck Hagel was a former Republican senator from Nebraska—the Republican side of the dais was packed with senators who had known and worked with and respected Hagel for decades.

But Ted decided to deliver another Cruzian performance piece, questioning the source of payments that Hagel had received for speaking engagements after leaving the Senate and making an inflammatory insinuation: "It is, at a minimum, relevant to know if that $200,000 that he deposited in his bank account came directly from Saudi Arabia, came directly from North Korea."

Yeah. Just like it would be relevant to know if you were a pedophile, Ted. But at least I had the good taste not to say that out loud, but instead to write it in a book five years later.

Republicans were at least polite about brushing back the brash new senator, with Lindsey Graham saying Cruz's remarks were "out of bounds." Democrats and the media were less restrained, comparing Ted's intimation to McCarthyesque innuendo.

It takes a special kind of jerk to get compared to Joe McCarthy just a month into your Senate career. Although it didn't help Ted that he bears more than a passing resemblance to McCarthy himself. (Franni thinks he's the love child of McCarthy and Dracula.)

Of course, Ted had been leaving a bad taste in people's mouths his whole life. His college roommate, screenwriter Craig Mazin, had been warning people about Cruz since the moment he leapt onto the national stage in the 2012 election, and when Ted ran for president in 2016, Mazin was only too happy to share some memories of what Young Ted Cruz had been like.

"As a freshman," he tweeted one day, "I would get into senior parties because I was Ted's roommate. OUT OF PITY. He was that widely loathed. It's his superpower."

Keep in mind, this is at *Princeton*. Ted Cruz was too much of a smug jerk to fit in at *Princeton*. And then he went to Harvard Law School, where during his very first week he created a study group. Hey, that's kind of human! Except that in order to apply to be part of Ted's study group, you had to have gone to Harvard, Princeton, or Yale for college. *GQ* interviewed Ted's law school roommate, who explained, "He said he didn't want anybody from 'minor Ivies' like Penn or Brown."

If I spent a thousand years on a desert island, I couldn't come up with a more obnoxious way to show my new classmates that I was a world-class butthole.[USS]

* * *

I could fill several chapters with Ted Cruz awfulness. But I'll end with one of my favorite photographs from my time in the Senate. It was taken during an especially long and tedious executive session of the Judiciary Subcommittee on the Constitution, during which we discussed and voted on Tom Udall's proposed constitutional amendment to overturn the *Citizens United* decision.

The amendment would have simply restored the power of Congress and the states to "regulate and set reasonable limits on the raising and spending of money by candidates and others to influence elections." Such laws, of course, had existed for many years before the

Supreme Court decided to wipe them all out with a 5–4 vote.

Ted opposed this, of course, and spoke against it in pieces that added up to a good hour, making bogus point after bogus point, which was why the hearing was so long and tedious. "This amendment here today," he said at one point, "would repeal the free speech protections of the First Amendment." And, "This amendment, if adopted, would give Congress absolute authority to regulate the political speech of every single American, with no limitations whatsoever." And, later, "Any politician who put his or her name to an amendment taking away the free speech rights of every American, in my view, should be embarrassed." Stuff like that.

He also tied together his blatant disregard for the truth, his relentless appetite for grandstanding, and his cringe-worthy habit of making pop culture references in an argument that seemed designed just to irritate me, referring to the political satire on *Saturday Night Live*, specifically Tina Fey playing Sarah Palin. According to Ted, if *Citizens United* were to be reversed, Tina would not have been able to do her Sarah Palin on the show, because NBC is a corporation.

Of course, as I pointed out, Tina did Sarah Palin during the 2008 election—two years before the *Citizens United* decision. Danny Aykroyd did Carter before *Citizens United*. Phil Hartman did Reagan.

Dana Carvey did George H. W. Bush. Hartman did Clinton. As did Darrell Hammond. And Will Ferrell did George W. Bush. All before *Citizens United*.

So even if you bought Ted's bogus argument that preventing corporations from pouring billions of dollars in dark money into shadowy Super PACs was equivalent to outlawing any political speech on the public airwaves, this wasn't even a relevant example. It was just a dishonest and unpleasant man trying, and failing, to use pop culture to make a false argument. In fact, a few months later he made the same argument in a floor speech, where he added, "Lorne Michaels could be put in jail, under this amendment, for making fun of any politician."

Ted Cruz isn't just wrong about almost everything. He's impossible to work with. And he doesn't care that he's impossible to work with. And that's why, even when the choice was between Ted Cruz (who was a sitting member of the United States Senate) and Donald Trump (who was Donald Trump), establishment Republicans couldn't bring themselves to rally behind Cruz. Even if you like what he stands for, the most he'll ever be able to accomplish is being an obnoxious wrench in the gears of government (like when he led the government shutdown over the Affordable Care Act). Real senator-ing requires that you build productive relationships with your colleagues. And Ted just isn't that kind of guy.

Which reminds me, here's the picture from that hearing. When Josh Riley left the Senate, he had it printed out and framed for me as a gift. The picture, as his inscription explained, is worth a thousand words of sophistry.

Al—
Sometimes a picture is worth a thousand words of sophistry. Thanks for the memories.
Josh

And it sort of captures perfectly what it's like to work with Ted Cruz.

Chapter 38

Bulletproof

After the massacre at Sandy Hook, a number of my Republican colleagues responded by saying something on the order of, "This isn't just about guns. It's about the culture and mental health." As someone who'd been working on mental health issues since I got to the Senate, I knew that a number of these colleagues had never before expressed any interest in the subject. It was like they were checking off a box by saying the words "mental" and "health" and saying them in the right order.

Even worse, by raising mental health only in the context of gun violence, they were stigmatizing mental illness. The shooters in Newtown and Aurora and Tucson and Orlando were demented. And of course early intervention can help avert some acts of violence. But the fact is that people with mental illness are on the whole no more likely to be violent (and are actually more likely to be *victims* of violence) than the general population.

Virtually every family in America is touched by a behavioral health problem—mental illness or addiction. Addressing these issues in a smart, comprehensive, and compassionate way will relieve suffering, save families and lives, give us a more productive workforce, save tons of money in law enforcement and our prisons and in emergency room visits, and, yes, maybe prevent someone from becoming so psychotic that they shoot up a movie theater, or a nightclub, or an elementary school.

*   *   *

My friend Paul Wellstone was profoundly affected by watching his brother struggle with depression. And one of his Republican colleagues, New Mexico's Pete Domenici, was profoundly affected by his daughter's schizophrenia. So in the Senate they teamed up to try to help Americans get the care they need.

Back then, one barrier to getting that care was the exceptionally high cost of treatment. Many health insurance plans would cover surgery for a broken arm, but not medication for crippling anxiety or treatment for a drug addiction. Mental health issues were seen, at least within the health insurance market, as somehow less important, or less real—or, in any case, less worthy of coverage.

Wellstone and Domenici tried to change that by fighting for what was known as "mental health parity," which would simply require insurance plans that cover mental health services to cover them to the same extent as medical and surgical services. This extremely simple, extremely commonsense, extremely *humane* reform didn't become law until October 2008. Yup: Paul Wellstone's most meaningful legislative achievement came six years after his death.

The fight to pass the Wellstone-Domenici Mental Health Parity and Addiction Equity Act was led in the House by Democrat Patrick Kennedy of Rhode Island and Republican Jim Ramstad of Minnesota. Both are recovering alcoholics. But Patrick had the harder road to recovery.

John F. Kennedy wrote a book called *Profiles in Courage*, but to me, the family's greatest profile in courage may well be Patrick. He never let his own very public and very embarrassing struggles with addiction and mental illness keep him from fighting to help others with mental health and addiction disorders get the care they needed.

My own interest in mental health issues came partly from how much I respected Paul's work on the issue and partly because, as you may recall, I, too, had been affected by loved ones who suffered from a behavioral disease: alcohol and chemical addiction.

When I got to the Senate, I was eager to do my

part to carry on Paul's legacy and, if possible, expand upon it. First step: pushing the Department of Health and Human Services to finalize the regulations prescribed by the Wellstone-Domenici Act. It was complex, painstaking work, and I was responsible for almost none of it—it was undertaken mostly by my health care legislative staff working with HHS. And it remains a work in progress: Wellstone-Domenici is now fully implemented, and the Affordable Care Act built on its success by requiring that all policies sold through the exchange cover behavioral health services, including addiction treatment—which has been a lifesaver for many during the ongoing opioid crisis. But we are still nowhere near where we need to be in making sure that people who need treatment for mental illness and addiction can always get it.

* * *

Then came the rash of mass shootings, and the rash of national conversations about mental health. Lots of people were declaring that we needed to "do something." But nobody was really clear on what exactly we could or should do.

In frustration, I asked the president of the Minnesota chapter of the National Alliance on Mental Illness how to respond.

She gave me a one-word answer: "Schools."

She arranged a roundtable at a school in the Mounds View school district. The school had adopted an approach to mental health that seemed to be working. All the adults in the school community, from the principal and the teachers to the bus driver and the lunch ladies, had been taught what it looks like when a kid is dealing with mental health problems. If they saw a kid who seemed to be struggling, they could ask a professional (a counselor, a psychologist, a social worker, or a therapist) to check in with the student and determine whether he or she had a serious mental health issue. That professional would connect the child with mental health services in the Mounds View community.

At the roundtable, three mothers raved about what a difference this program had made for their children and their families. One in particular, Katie Johnson, made a profound impact on me. Katie told me that she was the single mother of two: a nine-year-old son and a three-year-old daughter. "My son," she said, "was completely out of control. So my life was completely out of control. I was in total despair."

One day Katie got a call from a woman who introduced herself as the "mental health advocate" for Katie's son. "She's become my best friend," Katie told me.

Katie's son was diagnosed with ADHD and Asperger's. "They treated him, and he completely turned around. Now he's doing well in school. And he's taking tae kwon do."*

Katie looked me straight in the eye with the confidence of someone who had gone through a horrific ordeal and found herself safely on the other side. After years of chaos and frustration, her son was finally on the right track, and her own life finally felt manageable. Pointing to her heart, she told me proudly, "I am now bulletproof."

"Hmm," I thought. "Let's do *this*."

There was a gun bill working its way through the Senate, so I added an amendment that would fund training for people who work in schools to identify warning signs of mental illness and help detect and treat issues as early as possible. My colleagues understood the wisdom of the idea right away, and my provision passed by a nearly unanimous vote. But as you may recall, the gun bill failed. Still, the idea stuck. Soon after, we got a hundred million dollars in new funding to improve mental health services in schools. And we've gotten more since.

This money has helped train a lot of adults in schools to intervene when a student is having trouble, and it's helped schools to hire a lot more counselors and social workers to treat those students, and it's helped a lot of kids. But not every kid. On an issue

---

* I keep track. He's now a first-degree black belt.

like mental health, there's never a big, dramatic final victory. There's never a signing ceremony where the president officially abolishes undiagnosed mental illness once and for all. Kids and adults struggle with mental illness every day, and too many of them never get the help they need.

And that's just kind of how it works. Sometimes you work your whole life to do something simple and noble and it doesn't happen until six years after your death. Sometimes it never happens at all. Sometimes you get ninety-four of your colleagues to vote for your amendment, but the bill itself fails on a cynical, partisan filibuster. Sometimes you see a BREAKING NEWS banner on the TV in your office and something awful has happened and you get the creeping sensation that the whole sad "national conversation" is about to begin again.

But sometimes you can make a little progress, and sometimes you get to see what that progress looks like.

A few days after we secured that first batch of funding, I went to Westwood Elementary School in Bloomington, Minnesota, for another roundtable. There was real excitement among the twenty-some people who had heard about the new funding for programs like the one that was working in their school. Westwood has a therapist in residence, so parents don't have to take the better part of a day to pick their child up to ferry them to and from an appointment. A ten-year-old boy told me how much his therapist, a cheerful young woman in her early thirties, had helped him. When he sees her in the hall during recess, he said, he gives her a big high five. Talk about destigmatizing!

When you're a senator and you go to these round-tables, it's often just one person after another telling you incredibly sad or depressing or inspiring stories. Me being me, I have a ritual to sort of puncture the emotion so I can switch gears and get my head into the next event. And after this roundtable, my driver, Brett, and I walked out to the car, climbed in and buckled up, and, per our ritual, I nodded at Brett and said, "Fooled 'em again!"

But this time, I added, almost to myself: "I'm a good senator."

Chapter 39

Cracks in My Soul

The Democratic Senator's Serenity Prayer

God Grant Me the Serenity to Accept the
Things I Cannot Legislate
The Courage to Legislate the Things I Can
The Wisdom to Know the Difference
And the Patience to Explain That Difference to
My Donors

Probably the most enjoyable part of public service is the fund-raising. That's because you get to spend endless hours on the phone talking with people from all walks of life—though mainly rich people, and, also, you mostly talk to their voicemail or assistants. Not only that, but when you do manage to get them on the phone, the people on the other end are *super* excited to talk to you, because they know *exactly* why you're calling: to ask them for their "support."

And if you're not sitting in a small room with your call time manager, calling people for three or four hours at a stretch, you may very well be flying across the country to speak to your supporters at the sumptuous home of a wealthy donor who wisely chose not to go into public service.

Or, even better, you might be flying back across the country in the middle of the night. Flying in the middle of the night gives you plenty of time to examine the choices you've made in your life, or to sleep, but also to write thank-you notes to donors.

Okay, let's back up. Unfortunately, unless you're very rich or not interested in winning, you need to raise money if you're going to run for office. You need the resources to put a team together, to rent office space, to buy phones and computers and printers and toner, to feed volunteers, to travel around your state, to make ads, and to put the ads on the air. So before I go any further, let me just thank everyone who has ever contributed to my campaigns. The vast majority of you are not wealthy and give five, ten, or twenty-five of your hard-earned dollars. In fact, more than 90 percent of the donations I've received are of fifty dollars or less. Without the generosity of people who *don't* own sumptuous homes, I would not be in the position I am to fight for the things we believe in.

* * *

Despite my success with direct mail and online fund-raising from small donors, I have to raise a lot of money the old-fashioned way: by picking up the phone and calling rich people. And it takes a little trial and error to discover what works and what gets you a restraining order.

My very first fund-raising call, in late 2005, was to a successful St. Paul lawyer, John Faricy. Though we had never met, John took my call because he was familiar with my work as a comedian, author, and radio host. I made my pitch for the PAC I had started, and John immediately agreed to give. How much was I looking for?

I peered down at the notes on my call sheet. "Well, I guess five thousand dollars."

John said, "Okay."

I paused and then asked, "Are you sure?" I remember this only because John told the story, to gales of laughter, at one of my fund-raising dinners in 2014.

Call time is just you and your call time manager, a young staffer who is printing out and handing you call sheets and reminding you about any special information you might need to remember. Maybe the person you're calling missed your last event because they were at their mother's funeral or at a child's hockey game. Or maybe they particularly love your work on fighting climate change. Sometimes you dial the phone; other times your call time manager does. Sometimes you have to do all the talking; sometimes the person you're calling talks. Sometimes they talk too much.

As you dial, you peruse the person's giving history—every donation they've made over the past several election cycles, not just to you, but to everyone. That's all public information, by the way.

Also on my call sheets are notes from A. J. Goodman, the former death row attorney who has been my national fund-raising director for the last eleven years. A.J. makes the best call sheets, which include reminders like: "Don't call the home. The wife hates politics." Or: "Call her cell. He's a Republican." Or: "They're divorced. No more Sharon. No more Sharon money."

Am I giving you a good sense of what call time is like? Did you tune out when I mentioned "giving history" and then perk up a bit when you saw "death row"? I don't know how interesting this sounds. But call time is less interesting than that.

It's not uncommon to have three straight hours of call time scheduled as part of your day. During my recount, I often did eight hours of call time in a day. It's brutal. But I probably hate call time less than most elected officials do.

See, when I was in comedy, I used to edit, which involves sitting in an edit room for hours on end while a skilled craftsman makes the edits that you or your cowriter or the director requests. It means reviewing all the takes for pieces of the best performances and looking for different camera angles and "sizes" (close-up, two-shot, wide) to cut around weaker performance moments. This can be more or less interesting than it sounds, depending on what you're editing and whether you're the one calling the shots. But whatever the case, I would always make a conscious decision to enjoy myself. "You're going to be in this room for five hours," I would tell myself. "You might as well enjoy it."

That's my call time philosophy, too. Just as I try to make fund-raising emails fun for the people who read them, I try to make call time fun for myself and my call time manager. And for whomever I'm calling.

Let's say I get the assistant of an attorney in Dallas. I'll say, "Hi, this is Al Franken calling for Mr. Hudnut."

"I'm sorry, but Mr. Hudnut is in a meeting."

"All right. Well, I'm calling to invite him and Sandra to a fund-raiser for me in Dallas on October 11."

"Oh, I'm sorry. Mr. and Mrs. Hudnut will be out of the country on October 11."

"Uh-huh," I say. "And will the Hudnuts' *checkbook* be out of the country?"

That almost always gets a laugh, and, often, money!

* * *

Over the course of the many hours I have spent in call time during the last decade, I have composed as a sanity maintenance device a musical entitled *Call Time: The Musical.**

The musical takes place in a call time room with me and my call time manager, a table, and a phone. The audience can hear the phone on the other end. While it's ringing, I sing (to the tune of "Don't Cry for Me, Argentina"):

Please answer the phone, Howard Goldfein
You maxed to me last cycle
Oh, won't you be home, Howard Goldfein

If there's no answer, the audience hears the Goldfeins' outgoing message—an adorable little girl saying, "The Goldfeins aren't home now."

And then I leave a charming message: "Elise, this is Al Franken. You have a very young-sounding voice. I guess Howard robbed the cradle. Listen, I'm going to be in Cleveland on Thursday, April 7, for a fund-raiser at the home of Danny and Marilyn Lasky in Shaker Heights, and I'd love for you both to come. You can call A. J. Goodman at 555-287-6543 for all the details. A.J.'s a she. A female person. She's a woman."

Then I hang up and sing *Call Time*'s signature tune: "I Left a Message."

It's the signature tune for two reasons. First, because it's

---

* Here's a place where the audiobook will be a lot more fun.

so catchy and upbeat, and second, because I sing it roughly seventy-five times over the course of the show, which lasts six hours, with no intermission unless I have to go to the bathroom. Also, it provides almost all of *Call Time*'s production value. Because while I sing "I Left a Message," the chorus members (who include six ballerinas, four jugglers, some acrobats, and several chimpanzees riding tricycles) enter, do their stuff, and sing their parts.

AL:
I left a message
On the phone
I left a message
They were not home

CHORUS:
No no no

AL:
I left a message
Oh yes I did
I left a message
I do not kid

CHORUS:
He left a message
Oh yes he did
He left a message
He does not kid
Yay!!!

Then the orchestra plays them off to thunderous applause.

Seriously, without *Call Time: The Musical*, my call time manager and I would go crazy.

* * *

You might be wondering who this "call time manager" is and how he or she can stand to do this job. After all, he or she has to sit through all these calls, too, but never gets to talk to anyone but me. On the other hand, I am raising the funds that will be used to pay his or her salary. So there's that.

But because there is a burnout rate, I've actually had several call time managers over the years. Each contributed in their own way to *Call Time: The Musical*. The Beltway sensation Brian Heenan made a key breakthrough when he started to lavish praise upon my performance with every call.

"That was a *great* message," Brian would say with absolute sincerity after I left a voicemail. "If I were her, I'd go to the fund-raiser."

Or when I'd hang up after a long call with a prospective donor, Brian would say, "On this end, from what I heard, that was a *great* conversation. I bet he maxes out."

Andy Osborne, who replaced Brian when the original cast departed, developed a running bit based on my suggestion that Rain Man would be the ideal call time manager.

"Definitely call the house: 555-681-2372. Last time you called—January 27, 2009, you called the office. Definitely called the office: 555-724-0966. The assistant, Brenda Downey, said definitely call the house."

Or...

"Definitely maxed out to you in 2008. Gary gave $2,400 on April 12, 2007, for the primary. Attended Larry David event. Definitely attended. Another $2,400 for general. Definitely June 21, 2008. Summer solstice. Mariella also gave the full $4,800, also at the Larry David event. She's a big Larry David fan. Definitely loves *Curb Your Enthusiasm*. Would definitely sleep with Larry David."

"She said that?"

"Yes. But I added 'definitely.' She just said, 'I'd sleep with Larry David.'"

"Rain Man, she was joking." No reaction from Rain Man.

* * *

Now, you'll notice I referred to Larry David. This is more than just a casual name drop like my earlier mentions of call time manager Brian Heenan and Dallas super-lawyer Mr. Hudnut. One of the things Norm Coleman attacked me for during that first campaign was that I received a lot of campaign money from the Left Coast Hollywood Elite, who are poisoning our culture and contributing to the breakdown of the American family.

And, indeed, over the years I've gotten a lot of support from people in show business, especially people I worked with over my thirty-five years in the industry.

So, as Republican lines of attack went, this was among the least dishonest. But that didn't make it any less silly.

For one thing, like many Republicans, Coleman was raising much of his money from Big Oil, and Big Pharma, and Big Insurance. So I was happy to admit that I was raising money from what I called Big Comedy. It's hard to argue that Ben Stiller has been a worse influence on our country than ExxonMobil, even if you were very disappointed with *Zoolander 2*.

But the real difference was that I had actually worked in Big Comedy. These were people I had made movies and TV shows with. These were people who know me personally. These were my friends.

Norm Coleman, on the other hand, had never been a wildcatter in the oil fields. He had never developed a lifesaving drug in the research lab of a pharmaceutical company. He hadn't spent his career before politics as an actuary in the insurance business.

I got money from Big Comedy because my friends wanted to support me. My opponent got money from

Big Oil and Big Pharma and Big Insurance because they wanted something from him.

* * *

This is why I, and many other people, have long called for public financing of elections. It's not just that all this fund-raising is a huge pain and a distraction from the work our elected officials should be spending their time doing (reading briefing books [or just books], talking to experts, crafting legislation, and meeting with constituents). The role of big money in our politics gives special interests a bigger megaphone than people who can't write big checks.

Of course, the influence of special interests is now greater than ever, thanks to the Supreme Court's 5–4 decision in *Citizens United*—and the Republicans' refusal to let us do anything to bring some transparency and accountability back to our elections.

In the Court's majority opinion, Justice Kennedy tried to reassure people that allowing corporations, unions, and wealthy individuals to spend unlimited money in elections is really nothing to worry about. "With the advent of the Internet," Kennedy wrote, "prompt disclosure of expenditures can provide shareholders and citizens with the information needed to hold corporations and elected officials accountable for their positions and supporters."

Well, in theory. Except that under *Citizens United*,

there was no requirement that these expenditures actually *be* disclosed. Which made it kind of hard for anyone to be held accountable.

Now, we Democrats tried to pass a law that would actually mandate "prompt disclosure of expenditures" by the new groups that sprung up like weeds after *Citizens United*, so that "shareholders and citizens could use that information to hold corporations and elected officials accountable for their positions and supporters." We called it the Democracy Is Strengthened by Casting Light On Spending in Elections Act, which by happy coincidence we later discovered could be shortened to the DISCLOSE Act.

Like any bill, the DISCLOSE Act would need sixty votes to pass the Senate. And at the time, we only had fifty-nine.

Which shouldn't have been a problem: Given their past statements about the importance of disclosure, you'd have thought that Republicans would have been lining up to cosponsor the DISCLOSE Act. In a floor speech, I quoted my colleagues who had voted against the McCain-Feingold campaign finance reform law that passed in 2002 on the grounds that we didn't need limits on campaign donations if we only had disclosure.

For example, there was Chuck Grassley: "We can try to regulate ethical behavior by politicians, but the surest way to cleanse the system is to let the sun shine in."

There was Lamar Alexander: "I support campaign finance reform, but to me that means individual contributions, free speech, and full disclosure."

There was Orrin Hatch: "The issue is expenditures, expenditures, expenditures; and the issue, the real issue, if we really want to do something about campaign finance reform, is disclosure, disclosure, disclosure."

Even Mitch McConnell had said, "Public disclosure of campaign contributions and spending should be expedited so voters can judge for themselves what is appropriate."

But as much as my Republican colleagues had sung the praises of disclosure and hailed Justice Kennedy's decision in *Citizens United* as wise jurisprudence, Senate Republicans secretly knew they had been handed a huge advantage thanks to the most outrageous act of judicial activism in a generation, and they weren't about to look this gift horse in the mouth.

The day of the DISCLOSE vote, it was clear that the Republican filibuster would hold. I was a bit peeved at the hypocrisy, and after casting my own futile vote to move the bill forward, I stood in the well during the rest of the vote to give my good friends a bit of friendly crap. This led to the single dumbest thing a colleague has ever said to me. Which is quite a high bar.

After watching one of the Republicans who had spoken about the importance of disclosure eight years earlier vote no on the DISCLOSE Act, I asked him, rather churlishly, "What happened to 'sunshine is the best disinfectant'?"

"I'm protecting the Constitution," he replied, equally churlishly, then moved on. Another Republican, however, felt the need to defend him, also churlishly.

"There are parts of the bill we're not comfortable with," he said.

"Okay," I replied. "Name one thing in the bill you have a problem with." My colleague blanked and, without responding, turned to the clerk, voting no.

Another Republican colleague, having overheard the last two exchanges, said to me, civilly, I admit, though I thought I could still detect a hint of churlishness, "Well, the bill treats different entities differently." This was a line of argument Republicans used often, usually claiming that Democrats wanted to place new obstacles on the political power of corporations while further empowering labor unions.

"No it doesn't," I said, having had plenty of practice knocking down this bogus claim. "It treats unions the same as corporations and the same as individuals."

Now, here it comes: the single dumbest thing a colleague has ever said to me.

"Well, let's say the *New York Times* prints an editorial. *It* doesn't have to disclose."

My jaw dropped. I gave my colleague a second to figure out why that had been a spectacularly stupid argument, but it didn't seem like he was getting it. "It's in the *New York Times*!" I explained, as unchurlishly as I could manage.

"Oh," he realized. "Right." Then he turned to the clerk and voted no.

* * *

The proliferation of money in politics is a huge problem, and as I'll explain in the next chapter, it has some pretty terrible consequences. But does this mean that elected officials are all bought and paid for? The truth, I've discovered, is a little more complicated. Campaign contributions don't buy votes. What they buy is *access*.

That's why lobbyists write campaign checks. They're not bribes. They're grease. They enable those lobbyists to come to fund-raisers, where they get to talk to you while you're trying to remember their names.

Gross, right? And it is! I hear from a lot of lobbyists. And, yes, some of them are every bit as transactional as you're imagining. But others, often the more effective ones, are actually passionate about the issue they're representing. And while lobbying—and all the money associated with it—offers lots of opportunities for corruption, lobbying *itself* isn't inherently corrupt.

Many lobbyists represent good causes, like solar energy or Alzheimer's research or a woman's reproductive rights. They may have donated to you not in order to buy your support going forward, but because you've been supporting their good cause all along. And more often than not, you're not meeting with them because of a check they wrote, but rather because you're on the same team. You're strategizing together about how to move the ball forward, and trading useful information about how to achieve a shared goal.

That doesn't mean I'm pro-lobbyist—in fact, during my first campaign, I called for a lifetime lobbying ban on former members of Congress. It didn't seem right to me that after holding the high honor of public service, you could just cash out and make millions off your access to former colleagues. And it still doesn't. I still want to ban former members of Congress from becoming lobbyists. And for that matter, I still want public financing for elections so current and prospective members of Congress don't have to spend so much time fund-raising.

But the issue looks different from the inside than it did from the outside.

In 2005, Norm Coleman voted for an energy bill

that gave subsidies to the oil and gas industry. It was easy to draw a direct line between those votes and the money he got from Big Oil. And during the campaign, I drew that line with great enthusiasm.

Norm's response was always that the same bill created the Renewable Fuel Standard (RFS), which includes the ethanol mandate. Now, the oil and gas industry doesn't have a big presence in Minnesota, but we grow a lot of corn and soybeans. And corn ethanol and other biofuels like biodiesel produced from soybean oil have been extremely important to the economy of rural Minnesota.

In other words, the RFS is good for my state. The oil and gas subsidies in the bill were bad for everyone (except the oil and gas industry and oil and gas states). But while I'm sure Norm was less bothered by those subsidies than I would have been, the truth is that, on balance, I might well have wound up casting the same vote he did.

Was it unfair for me to say that Norm was in the pocket of Big Oil? Nah. But was it entirely accurate to say that he only voted for this bill because he'd been bought off? Probably not.

In 2010, I took a trip to Israel and met with some members of the Knesset. I had never given it any thought before, but every member of the Knesset represents all of Israel. There's no member representing the northern suburbs of Tel Aviv. Our system is different. House members in Congress represent their districts. Senators represent our states. I was elected to represent the people of Minnesota.

When I'm trying to decide how to vote on a bill, whether or not something is good for my state is always at the top of my mind. But of course, it's not even close to the only consideration. Does the stuff in this bill I like outweigh the stuff I don't like? If I vote for it, can I get the senator who sponsored it to vote for something of mine? If I vote against it, can we get a better deal later? What does my staff think? What do the experts I trust say? Has Atul Gawande weighed in at all?

Every so often, we have to pass what's known as a "continuing resolution," which extends current levels of funding so we can keep the government open and functioning until we can agree on an actual budget.

Often this is a big end-of-the-year package, and may contain any number of things that are just awful—and also any number of things that are great, including one or two pieces of legislation that I myself have authored and have been fighting to pass for several years. Also, if the thing doesn't pass, the government shuts down.

Obviously, there's a point at which a continuing resolution could be so bad that I'd have to vote against it even it meant voting against stuff I liked (or even authored), or even shutting the government down. But where *is* that point? I mean, it would have to be a *really* bad continuing resolution in order for me to vote against it—unless I knew it was going to pass even without my vote, in which case maybe I could vote against it as a protest of the stuff I didn't like. Then again, on principle, shouldn't you always vote as if you were the deciding vote? I used to think that. But I gave up a while ago, and I can't even remember what the hell that was about.

The point is, there are all sorts of reasons why someone might vote for something imperfect (or worse) that have absolutely nothing to do with campaign contributions.

Former Massachusetts congressman Barney Frank once said, "I only voted once for someone who believes in 100 percent of what I believe. And that's when I voted for myself—the first time."

* * *

The fact is that being in the institution changes the way you look at how Washington works. And you have to work hard to make sure that it doesn't change who you are, something a constituent warned me about after I had been in the Senate for a year or so. The woman, who was about my age, with salt-and-pepper hair, approached me after I spoke at a reception honoring the year's best in Twin Cities theater. As she stared at me for a while, I could see concern growing in her eyes.

"I can see out of physical reality," she informed me.

"Uh-huh."

"You've seen corruption and it's affected you. It puts cracks in your soul."

That's not the kind of thing you like to hear about your soul. But she assured me that I was a loving person with a great soul. It's just that it had been badly wounded since I'd been in Washington. She wanted me to heal my soul, so it could "become green and clean and good."

I told her that I was going to get a massage the next day, and she thought that was a good start.

The massage helped. But normally what helps my soul is getting something done for people—improving people's lives, as Paul Wellstone would say.

There are plenty of potentially soul-destroying aspects of running for office and serving in the Senate. Fund-raising can certainly be one of them. But you keep your eye on the prize. And it's all worth every phone call, every plane ride, every thank-you note if you can get health insurance for twenty million people. If you meet a mom whose child is alive because you helped to make sure that people with preexisting conditions can get insured. If you can get mental health care treated the same as medical care. If you can prevent an undocumented mother from being deported and separated from her American citizen children. If you can preserve net neutrality. If you can keep a family in their home.

It's a privilege to be a United States senator. Not only because you get to make this stuff happen, but because you get to work with people who are working every day themselves to make this stuff happen: Americans of goodwill, Democrats *and* Republicans, affluent and struggling, of every color and every faith (and nonbelievers), who are working to improve our country and our world.

Now give me some money!

Chapter 40

The Koch Brothers Hate
Your Grandchildren

Give a man a fish, and you feed him for a day.
Teach a man to fish, and you feed him for a lifetime.
*Unless there are no fish.**
—Maimonides (and Al Franken)

In my 2008 campaign, we raised $23 million, which was widely (and accurately) seen as an insane amount of money. But it pales in comparison to the nearly *ONE BILLION DOLLARS* that Siegfried and Roy Koch, often referred to just as "the Koch brothers," pledged to spend (personally and through their

---

* Global climate change is destroying our oceans' coral reefs, home to our planet's most bountiful fisheries, and accelerating the rise of jellyfish blooms, which sound mysterious and beautiful but are actually deadly to fish farms.

fund-raising network) on federal, state, and local elections in the 2016 cycle.

A billion dollars isn't really that much to the Koch brothers. You can find that much in change going through their couch. Between them, they are worth more than $87 billion, much of it from fossil fuel.

And all that money didn't just buy them an invitation to a nice fund-raiser or make it so that members of Congress would take their calls. Because of the Koch brothers and their ilk, the entire Republican Party has become a party of climate denial. In the last presidential primary race, not one Republican candidate was willing to support any federal action to combat climate change.

This is, of course, nuts. In December 2015, I traveled with nine of my Democratic Senate colleagues to the COP21 Climate Conference in Paris where 196 countries signed on to an ambitious and unprecedented agreement to tackle climate change as a global community by setting limits on greenhouse gases. Before the conference, we met with a delegation from the British Parliament. Every member we met with, including the Conservatives, knew that climate change is an existential threat. Virtually everyone in the world believes that climate change is real and is caused by human beings, *except* Republicans in the United States. Especially the people who would know best: 97 percent of climate scientists agree that climate change is real and caused by human activity, and I suspect the other 3 percent are being paid by the fossil fuel industry.

Let's do a little thought experiment here. Let's say you went to your doctor for a checkup, and he told you this: "Okay. You've got to go on a diet and stop smoking. You're fifty years old. You're very overweight. And your father died of a heart attack at age fifty-one. You've really got to cut down on the carbs and start exercising."

Sounds bad. But you want a second opinion. So you go to another doctor.

"Oh, boy!" says the second doctor. "I see here your father died of a heart attack at about your age. You'd be insane not to go on a diet and start working out. And for godsakes, quit smoking!"

Not what you wanted to hear. So you schedule another appointment.

"Oh my God!" says the third doctor. "It's amazing you're still alive! It would be irresponsible of me not to send you right away to this well-being center at Duke for a ninety-day stay!"

Well, that certainly seems like a drag. So you schedule another appointment, and then another, and then another. After thirty-two opinions, you're still not happy.

But then you see the thirty-third doctor. It's taken a while to schedule all these appointments, so by now you've gained so much weight that you have to go around in one of those motorized carts.

"It's a good thing you came to me," the thirty-third doctor says. "I'm sure other doctors have been telling you to do all kinds of ridiculous stuff. Well, I'm here to tell you to keep doing exactly what you've been doing. Keep smoking! Watch a little more TV. And eat more fast food! Did you see Carl's Jr. now has this sandwich where the entire bun is made out of cheese? You see, those other doctors are in the pocket of Big Fresh Fruits and Vegetables."

Republicans know that if they concede what climate scientists, the Defense Department, the Muppets, and virtually every other country in the world know—that global warming is real, that it is man-made, and that it is the greatest current threat to global prosperity and stability—the Koch brothers will spend money against them to fund a primary challenge. This goes double for Republicans from conservative states. They know from the experience of their defeated colleagues that the Koch brothers will primary them if they stray from climate denial orthodoxy, and that the biggest threat to their reelection comes not from Democrats, but from being outflanked to the right by their own party.

A Republican friend once said to me, "The easiest person to fool is yourself." I know that there are a few of my friends on the other side of the aisle who do sincerely believe that climate change is somehow a hoax, that God wouldn't let us destroy our planet, or some such nonsense. But I think the rest of them know that sea level is rising for a reason other than God's benign and fundamentally incomprehensible whim.

That's why during hearings in the Energy Committee, when Energy Secretary Ernie Moniz would testify about research on renewable energy, energy efficiency, and energy storage technologies, my Republican friends didn't yell at him, "Why are you wasting so much money on this renewable stuff when we're the Saudi Arabia of coal?!"

No. I watched my colleagues closely, and behind their eyes, I could see them thinking, "Oh, thank God *somebody's* doing this!"

* * *

One of the reasons I was so hoping that Hillary Clinton would win the election, aside from, you know, all the other ones, is that the clearest path to combating climate change ran through the Supreme Court. Overturning *Citizens United* would help break the Koch brothers' stranglehold on the Republican Party, and without that threat, some of them might be convinced to join the rest of the Senate and the rest of the world in trying to actually address climate change.

But that doesn't look terribly likely right now.

Having successfully blockaded President Obama's Supreme Court nominee, the extremely well-qualified and widely admired Judge Merrick Garland, Republicans succeeded in preserving the right to fill that seat for the next president. Who did not turn out to be Hillary Clinton. So that's going to be a problem.

Worse, the current president, real estate developer Donald Trump, has signaled that he doesn't intend to be part of any climate change solution. This is a guy who has said that climate change is a hoax perpetrated by the Chinese. Why would they do that? And why am I even trying to find any speck of logic in anything he says?

The thing is, it's not what Trump says that matters. It's what he does. And the first thing he did on climate change was to appoint a bunch of climate deniers to key posts. He picked a guy to run the Environmental Protection Agency who made his bones as Oklahoma's attorney general by suing the Environmental Protection Agency. And to succeed nuclear physicist Ernest Moniz as energy secretary, he picked Rick Perry, who famously blanked on the name of the Department of Energy when he was trying to include it in a list of Cabinet agencies he wanted to get rid of.

Maybe the president is just a big fan of irony. But more likely these selections mean that this is now going to be even more of an uphill battle. But no less of an important one. Climate change is an existential threat. That's why the Pentagon considers global warming to be "an urgent and growing threat to our national security." And it's why the Defense Department, the institution that uses more energy than any other in the world, is ordering the top brass to incorporate measures to combat climate change into virtually everything they do: war planning, joint exercises with allies, training our troops—they're even developing algal jet fuel.

So, what can we do?

First of all, don't get discouraged. Recent advances in renewable energy, energy efficiency, and energy storage technology have changed the trajectory of our energy use. Even if it feels like Washington isn't rising to the challenge, states and cities and universities and researchers and ordinary citizens are finding ways to make progress. This is not a hopeless cause.

Also, Koch Industries isn't the only big corporation in America. Scores of Fortune 500 companies, including, oddly, ExxonMobil, whose former chief executive is now Trump's secretary of state, have endorsed the Paris accords. They understand that this isn't just an environmental issue, but an economic one. There are going to be millions of good-paying jobs created by these new energy technologies. I want them created here. These CEOs want them created here. And maybe we can convince President Trump that they ought to be created here. I hear the guy is big into

America winning? Well, staying in the Paris accords would help America win the fight to own the clean energy economy.

But if we're going to do this, our movement is simply going to have to get stronger. Those of us who've been fighting for a solution to climate change for years are going to have to redouble our efforts to mobilize the American people behind this cause. It isn't going to be a fair fight, not with *Citizens United* in place. But what choice do we have?

As for me, I'm going to keep making the case to my colleagues. It may seem kind of bleak to say that the future of our planet rests in large part on the consciences of Republican politicians. But it kind of does, at least right now. The thing is, like me, many of my colleagues have grandchildren. And grandchildren can be a powerful motivator, even if they don't have a Super PAC.

I can't speak for the Republicans I serve with, but in fifty years I don't want my three grandkids saying to me, "Grandpa, you were a senator and you knew there was climate change. Why didn't you do anything? Also, why are you still alive? You're a hundred and sixteen years old!"

Chapter 41

No Whining on the Yacht

Those of us serving in government today have many more issues to deal with than the Founding Fathers had to contend with. They didn't have to worry about antibiotic-resistant bacteria, because there weren't any antibiotics. If they got a blister and it got infected, they were dead. It was a simpler and, some would argue, *happier* time.

They didn't have to worry about cybersecurity. Then again, we don't have to worry about slavery. Then again, they didn't seem too worried about it, either.

Our Founders didn't have to deal with GMOs, or nuclear proliferation, or airline deregulation, or airline safety, or the use of portable electronic devices on airplanes. Or aircraft carriers. You get the idea. They had a very easy job, compared to mine.

It's not just that there are more issues to keep track

of than ever before. Policymaking itself has become more politicized than ever. Every single issue also now has a variety of groups advocating for one position or another. For every line in every bill, there's someone whose job it is to care about that one line in that one bill. There are people in Washington making six figures a year whose entire livelihood involves making sure that the formula for calculating depreciation on tractors doesn't change in the next five-year farm bill, or fighting to protect the Medicare reimbursement rate for a certain kind of kidney procedure, or advocating for the right of Amtrak passengers to smoke e-cigarettes onboard trains.

The late political scientist James Q. Wilson described it this way: "Once politics was about only a few things; today, it is about nearly everything." No issue is so obscure or, frankly, boring that someone can't muster a high-pressure campaign to get you to vote one way or the other on it.

This means you're constantly deluged with information—from lobbyists, from public interest groups, and from the people you represent. Email has replaced postal mail as the main form of correspondence between constituents and elected officials, and it's great that a citizen now no longer has to buy a stamp to share his or her opinion. But it also means you get a lot more correspondence than ever before—Congress receives some three hundred million emails a year—and you have no way of knowing whether the person who sent you that email feels really strongly about the issue or just spent five seconds clicking on a link they were sent by some advocacy group that generated a message automatically.

So there are a lot more issues to keep track of, and there are a lot more considerations determining how you vote on these issues, and you're under constant pressure to do not just the right thing but the politically smart thing, and also everything you say and do is covered in real time by a 24/7 press corps, and you have less time in the day to talk to your colleagues or do research or just sit and think for a friggin' second.

This sounds like I'm complaining, doesn't it? Well, I'm not. As Sherrod Brown likes to remind us, "No whining on the yacht." My job is a privilege, and every moment I spend in Washington an unadulterated delight. Did that sound sarcastic? I'm sorry. I'm writing this not long after Trump's inauguration, and it's been rough. But: No whining on the yacht. No whining on the yacht. *No whining on the yacht.*

* * *

Okay, here's a bright side. Because we live in such a complex world—and because there are only a hundred senators—each senator has a real opportunity to find an issue that is of particular appeal and really grab the ball and run with it.

For example, Elizabeth Warren spent her entire career worrying about how average people get ripped off by big banks and other corporations. So when she came to the Senate, she immediately became a leader on those issues. John Barrasso, the Republican from Wyoming, was a doctor before he came to the Senate. So he became one of the Republicans' point men on spreading disinformation about the Affordable Care Act.*

When I first came to the Senate, I was ready to seize the mantle of leadership on any issues related to sketch comedy or the Grateful Dead. But in my heart, I knew it was unlikely that I'd be called on to share any of that expertise. I decided just to focus on representing Minnesota the best I could, contributing to big debates on health care and education, building on Paul's legacy on issues like mental health, and figuring out as I went along where else to focus my time and energy.

Ironically, my experience in show business turned out to come in pretty handy after all.

In December 2009, Comcast announced its plan to buy NBCUniversal, a merger that would unite the

---

* Just an example: John would occasionally claim that because of Obamacare, the Mayo Clinic had stopped treating Medicare patients, which really irritated me, and also the Mayo Clinic, which currently treats around half a million Medicare patients.

country's biggest cable TV and broadband provider with one of the world's biggest content providers. NBCUniversal didn't just own NBC and Universal Studios. It owned twenty-some other networks, including MSNBC, CNBC, Telemundo, USA Network, and Bravo.

The proposed deal made me immediately uncomfortable, not just because of its size but because, as you may recall, I had worked in color television—and I had seen a version of this before.

In 1993, during my thirteenth season at *Saturday Night Live*, the Big Three networks (NBC, CBS, and ABC) pressured Congress to change the rules that had prevented the Big Three from owning any of the shows they aired in prime time. The purpose of the rules was to prevent the networks from monopolizing the broadcast landscape.

Opponents of repealing the rules argued that if networks could put shows in which they had a financial stake in the best time slots, they would favor their own programs over those of independent producers or demand a share of ownership as a cost of getting a show on the air. The networks swore up and down in hearings that nothing of the sort would happen. *It's in our interest to have the best shows on our networks. We want ratings. We're not going to pick an inferior show just because we own it.*

You'll never guess what happened. After the rules

were repealed, not only did the networks start putting on more and more of their own shows, but they gave shows they owned preferential treatment. Remember a little hit called *Seinfeld*, about the continuing misadventures of a bunch of misfit New York Jews? Well, *Seinfeld* itself was not owned by NBC (it first aired in 1989). But it quickly became the number one show on TV, making the Thursday night time slot following *Seinfeld* the most valuable real estate on television. And the shows that wound up in that premium location on the schedule were all owned, at least in part, by NBC.

Of course, there were a bunch of them, because they quickly wore out their welcome with audiences. At the time, I performed at a fund-raiser for the Los Angeles Free Clinic with Jon Stewart. Jon told the industry-savvy audience that NBC had just announced its next post-*Seinfeld* show: *A Guy Takes a Shit on a Desk*.

* * *

Fast-forward to 2009. *Seinfeld* is off the air. I'm a U.S. senator. I lost track of what happened to Jon. Seemed like a nice guy, though.

Anyway, you'll recall that Harry Reid had assigned me to the Judiciary Committee because, basically, he had no choice. But as it turned out, being on the Judiciary Committee gave me a platform to share my concerns about the proposed deal.

On average, an American household pays $2,700 a year for Internet, video, and phone service. Cable companies have increased their costs to consumers over the last twenty years by more than twice the rate of inflation. And historically, mergers of giant telecommunication conglomerates had led to higher costs, worse service, and fewer choices for consumers.

I also knew from experience that a new Comcast/NBCUniversal would have a huge incentive to promote the programming it owned at the expense of content it didn't. Even if a network was already being carried on Comcast, it had to worry that the new combined Comcast/NBCUniversal would want to favor its own competing channels. For example, the new Comcast/NBC would want as many eyeballs as possible watching *its* business news channel, CNBC. What would keep Comcast from putting CNBC on, say, channel 32—next to MSNBC, Fox News Channel, and CNN—and putting its business news competitor, Bloomberg News, in the nosebleed section at, say, channel 531?

Meanwhile, what about other cable companies that needed to carry NBC's programming and the content from all the other networks that Comcast would now own? Couldn't Comcast/NBCUniversal charge other cable companies more for *its* content, and wouldn't that cost be passed on to consumers?

All this raised a lot of questions, and because the

Judiciary Committee had scheduled a hearing on the merger, I would have a chance to ask them.

As the hearing approached, I got a visit in my office from Jeff Zucker—then the president of NBC—who brought along Comcast CEO Brian Roberts. The first thing Jeff said to me was, "This will be good for Lorne."

That cracked me up. "I don't represent Lorne," I said. "I represent the people of Minnesota." I know that sounds like the kind of dialogue a writer from *The West Wing* might write for an inferior sequel about the Senate. But that's what I said. Sorry.*

I was the first senator to come out against the merger, and unfortunately, I wound up having very little company. Ultimately, we lost on this one. Comcast bought NBCUniversal. But, in part because of my advocacy, the FCC and DOJ placed a number of conditions on the deal.

The new Comcast/NBCUniversal would have to put content produced by competitors in the same "neighborhood" as Comcast's own content. For example, Bloomberg TV would have to be placed in the

---

* Before the deal was approved, I ran into Zucker in New York. "You know, you're right," he told me on the condition that I not quote him until after he left NBC. Jeff is now the president of CNN, which is owned by Time Warner. As I write this, AT&T has offered $85 billion to buy Time Warner (which owns CNN), and he seems to be avoiding me.

same "cable news neighborhood" as CNBC, MSNBC, CNN, and Fox News Network.

And Comcast, which of course was the nation's largest Internet service provider, would have to create an affordable standalone broadband package for low-income customers and people who wanted to "cut the cord" on cable television and just get Internet service without signing up for an expensive bundle.

I cite these two conditions in particular because Comcast agreed to them, and then ignored them.

On the Comcast dial, Bloomberg TV was placed in a galaxy far, far away from CNBC, MSNBC, et al. As for that inexpensive unbundled package, Comcast *did* create one. It just didn't tell anybody. Hard to buy a package that you don't know exists.

* * *

SMASH CUT TO: One evening in early 2014. I'm at the dining room table, reading my briefing materials for the next day. Franni is on her laptop in the living room. "Hey," Franni shouts, "Comcast wants to buy Time Warner Cable!"

"What?!" I say incredulously.

"I'm reading here that Comcast/NBCUniversal wants to buy Time Warner Cable."

"That's nuts!!!"

Comcast was the largest cable TV provider in the country and the largest broadband provider. Time

Warner Cable was the *second*-largest cable TV and *third*-largest broadband provider. This new behemoth would not only be the dominant player in a cable market already suffering from lack of competition (do you like *your* cable service?), but it would control 57 percent of the high-speed Internet market, too. Less competition would mean higher rates and worse service for Minnesotans who already hated paying as much as they did for the service they got.

"That's crazy!!!" I said, finding another word for "nuts."

I immediately called my Judiciary counsel and told him to start working on a letter to DOJ and the FCC. This was insane! This was lunacy! This was...nuts! We had to stop this from happening.

Unfortunately, when my team got the lay of the land the next day, it looked like, once again, I would be the only senator coming out in opposition to the merger. The deal looked like a fait accompli.

Part of that was because of Comcast's lobbying might. Comcast has about a hundred lobbyists on Capitol Hill—a lobbyist for each senator, more or less. But this merger was so important to Comcast that it had hired virtually every other telecom lobbyist in town. Not to lobby *for* the deal. Comcast *paid* them *not* to lobby *against* the deal. They just took them off the playing field.

I made my case to a number of colleagues, but

didn't have much luck. Once again, for fourteen months, I was the only senator to speak out publicly against the deal.

But over the next year, alongside a coalition of allies like Public Knowledge, Consumers Union, and Common Cause, I continued to fight the merger. We rallied the public, and the FCC received nearly a million comments and petition signatures from people opposed to the deal. And this time, the good guys won. After meeting with regulators and being told that the jig was up, Comcast withdrew the proposed merger. One of the big reasons for the rejection? Comcast's failure to comply with conditions on the NBCUniversal deal.

In other words, I got conditions put on Comcast's first big, problematic acquisition. They failed to comply with them. I pointed this out when they tried to make another bigger, problematic-er acquisition. And that helped sink the deal.

* * *

Over the years, I've found myself doing a lot more work on issues of media consolidation and the rights of consumers when they interact with the most powerful companies in their lives, many of which don't offer products like cars and refrigerators but rather services like cable TV and broadband Internet.

We've won some enormous victories, like protecting

net neutrality—an issue on which *four* million Americans took action by submitting comments to the FCC. We're going to need to keep fighting, though, because net neutrality is in real danger now that Donald Trump is in the White House and an avowed enemy of net neutrality is running the FCC—and because media consolidation continues to represent a real threat to the free flow of information in America.

These issues affect every one of us, every day. And while I certainly didn't expect that being a senator would mean spending so much time working on this stuff, it's become one of the most rewarding things I do.

All thanks to a career in comedy and Harry being stuck with an empty seat on Judiciary.

Chapter 42

I Win Awards

When I first got to the Senate, I scheduled a few appointments with my new colleagues, just to spend a little time getting to know them and getting their take on how to be a good senator.

One of the first was with Chris Dodd, who had represented Connecticut in the Senate since 1981 and been a leader within the Democratic Party since the age of the real giants of the Senate, the Ted Kennedy and Mike Mansfield types. And nine-foot-tall Ed Muskie.

Chris was running a little late for our meeting, so I cooled my heels in his outer office. Looking around, I noticed that the entire room was jam-packed with awards he'd received during his long and distinguished career. Plaques hung on every inch of wall space. Wooden plaques, acrylic plaques, plaques of slate and granite. And the shelves! Every possible surface was covered with awards. Crystal awards. Glass awards. Stainless steel awards. Lucite awards of all shapes and sizes. Cubes, stars, eagles! I was blown away. And a little depressed. "Oh my God," I thought. "I will never get this many awards. I'd have to be here for thirty years! How old will I be then? Eighty? No, older! Ugh." It was a stupid emotional hole to fall in, but I fell in it nevertheless.

Chris arrived, greeted me brightly, and escorted me to his office—past more and more shelves of awards. After we sat down in his office, I tried to listen to his advice, but the awards on his wall and bookshelves started to close in and mock me.

"How was the meeting?" Drew asked when I returned.

"Aw, man," I said, still in a funk. "He has *so many* awards."

Drew tried to reassure me. "Don't worry about that. You'll get plenty of awards."

I thought he was just trying to cheer me up, but it turns out he was right. Apparently, when you're a senator, people just throw awards at you on a regular basis.

Sometimes it's a trade association or a well-meaning public interest group giving you an award just for voting their way on something. Sometimes an organization will give you one of their big awards in the hope that you'll agree to speak at their annual dinner so they can get a lot more people to come. I used to get a big sack of cash for a speech like that. Now I get a Lucite plaque.

* * *

In any event, I quickly began to amass quite a collection of awards in my own office, a collection that has continued to grow over the years. I will say that some of them do mean a lot to me, like the awards I've won from Consumer Watchdog for my leadership on consumer rights, or from the Humane Society after my service dogs bill, or from the National Law Center on Homelessness for my work on the Violence Against Women Act.

Sometimes, however, an organization will go out of its way to make sure I understand that an award it's giving me means very little. I was very excited when I found out that the Minnesota Farm Bureau was presenting me with their Friend of Farm Bureau Award. The Farm Bureau is a pretty conservative organization, almost always endorsing the Republican in political campaigns, as they did Norm Coleman in 2008. The Farmers Union, the progressive farm organization, had endorsed me.

One out of five jobs in Minnesota is tied to agriculture. We're the number one producer of turkeys. Number two in pork. The Green Giant is from Le Sueur, Minnesota. You've probably heard of General

Mills—Betty Crocker is a Minnesota native. And so is the Pillsbury Doughboy, who served our nation so deliciously in World War I.

So even though I wasn't on the Agriculture Committee, it was essential that I learn about farming, something I started during the campaign by visiting farms all around the state. I learned quickly that farmers aren't just farmers. They're mechanics, veterinarians, marketers, economists, and meteorologists.

In the Senate, I had to master the very arcane world of ag policy. And even though I still had some disagreements with the Farm Bureau on things like the estate tax and clean water regulation, I fought for the interests of all our farmers.

So when Kevin Paap, president of the Minnesota Farm Bureau and a farmer with a six-hundred-acre corn and soybean operation near Mankato, came to my office to present me with my first Friend of Farm Bureau plaque, I was thrilled. "Kevin," I said, "this really means a lot to me. I really appreciate it. It's a tremendous honor."

He could tell that I meant it. "Oh," he said, matter-of-factly, "this is only about how you voted." What he was really saying was: *Don't get us wrong—we still don't like you.*

I remind Kevin about that conversation every chance I get, and we laugh about it. We've become pretty good friends. In October 2012, Kevin invited me out to his farm to harvest the last five acres of his corn crop. Kevin dubbed those last five acres the "Franken Five."

Harvesting the corn was incredibly easy because Kevin uses GPS technology to plant and harvest. The combine shoots a golden arc of grain into a truck that runs alongside, and when you reach the end, you just turn the thing around, line it up, and go. It took all of about a half hour.

On the way to the grain elevator, Kevin worried aloud that my corn might be a little dry since it was harvested so late and that he'd get less for it. I had this horrible thought that the "Franken Five" might become synonymous with the worst five acres on your farm. "I pulled one over on that guy—sold him my Franken Five! Hahaha!" Stuff like that. Fortunately, my corn had the perfect moisture content. That's just the kind of senator I am.

The Farm Bureau still doesn't support me, and a lot of its conservative members aren't big fans of mine. But I've won a few of them over in two important ways. First, I do my homework and have delivered on the issues where we agree. Second, I have a joke I tell every time I speak to an ag audience.

It goes like this. "You know," I say, "I grew up in St. Louis Park. I was a suburban kid. I knew nothing about agriculture growing up. In fact, when I was eight years old, if you'd asked me where food comes from, what do you think I would have said?"

And the audience always shouts, "The grocery store!"

And I say, "No. I would have said, 'A *farm*!' Because I wasn't a total idiot." Big laugh, every time. Well, until recently. Every farmer in Minnesota has heard it by now.

* * *

Speaking of my comedic genius, in December 2015 the Writers Guild of America East announced that I would receive its prestigious Evelyn F. Burkey Award, which recognizes a person or organization "whose contributions have brought honor and dignity to writers." Previous recipients of the award had included Edward Albee, Arthur Miller, Joan Didion—and now me, the distinguished author of "Porn-O-Rama."

I decided to point out in my acceptance speech that it didn't say the recipient of the Evelyn F. Burkey Award had *always* "brought honor and dignity to writers." Just on balance.

Today, there are too many awards to fit in my office. But when I told my staff I was writing this chapter, they warned me: *People might stop giving them to you.*

"Well, first of all," I told them, "no, they won't. People understand jokes. Take it from me, an Evelyn F. Burkey Award–winning writer."

They rolled their eyes.

"Second of all, if they do stop giving me awards, that's really kind of fine. We've run out of space anyway. But they won't."

To inquire about giving Sen. Franken an award, please contact Brynna Schmidt at (202) 224-5671.

Chapter 43

We Build a DeHumorizer™

As I hope I've made abundantly clear, senators don't get a lot of opportunities to be funny in public. Remember when Jeff Blodgett, Wellstone's campaign manager, told me to try writing a five-minute speech with no jokes in it, and I thought he was crazy? Well, it turns out that you really *can't* tell a joke in a speech on the Senate floor. Why? Because *no one is there.* The Senate chamber is usually empty except for the speaker, a few staffers, and the presiding officer, who's reading press clippings instead of listening to you. But viewers at home don't know that: C-SPAN is on a tight single of you, the speaking senator. To the viewer, it looks like you could be addressing a packed house. But if you were stupid enough to tell a joke, viewers would hear no reaction. Nothing. Which means your joke died a terrible death.

Still, like in any profession, humor can be a way to create connections that could blossom into friendships.

Or at least a little slack-cutting. Plus, it can help keep everybody sane at especially stressful moments. Which is true even when the people you work with don't necessarily have finely honed comedic sensibilities themselves.

Here's my best example of all of those things happening at once.

One day in 2015, right after the Iran nuclear agreement was announced, there was a classified briefing in a secure room with about eighty senators.

Republicans were eager to attack the deal and condemn the president for agreeing to it. Plus, we were talking about issues of war and peace, life and death. So it was kind of a tense meeting, and it got even more tense as we heard impressive presentations from Secretary of State John Kerry, Energy Secretary Ernest Moniz, Treasury Secretary Jack Lew, and our lead CIA expert on Iran, whom I will call "Mr. Quimby."

The Senate majority leader, whom I will call "Mitch," was in charge of the meeting, and you could tell he was unhappy at how persuasive the administration's representatives had been. When it came time for questions, both Republicans and Democrats asked some difficult ones, but I think it's fair to say that the Republicans (all of whom ended up voting against the agreement) were particularly on edge, and some of their questions were downright hostile. The briefers, for their part, handled these tough questions extremely well. Which only seemed to make the Republicans crankier.

Eventually, it was my turn. I wanted to ask about something that Iran's Supreme Leader had said about the deal. But I was also sensing that the tension in the room was reaching a boiling point. So when "Mitch" called on me, I decided to at least attempt to lighten things up just a little bit.

"Yes," I said, "I have a question about the Supreme Leader. Who I like to call the Supreme Being."

Now, please understand, I consider this barely a joke. But for whatever reason, probably the high degree of tension in the room, it got an *enormous* laugh. Even Mitch McConnell laughed out loud! Try to imagine what that looks and sounds like! You can't!

"Mr. Quimby" explained why he thought the Supreme Leader—"or Supreme Being, if you will" ("Mr. Quimby" enjoyed the joke, too)—had said what he said. And we moved on.

But the weird thing was, the joke—again, as slight as it was—did the trick. The tension drained out of the room. Leaving the briefing later, I was still a little puzzled. Frankly, my jokes are often underappreciated in the Senate. But this one, if anything, was overappreciated.

On the subway back to my office, a Republican senator who hardly ever votes with me asked, "Could I use that joke in my state?"

"Sure," I said. "Be my guest."

"Why is it funny?" he asked.

"Well," I said, "I guess it's because 'Supreme Leader'

is such a weird term to us that he might as well be calling himself 'Supreme Being.'"

My colleague laughed again and nodded. Got it.

For the rest of the day, senators kept coming up to me in the halls and in hearings.

"Great joke!"

"Supreme Being!"

"That was hilarious!"

I was kind of astonished.

That afternoon, I showed up on the floor for a couple of votes and found a group of colleagues happily recalling the joke. And that's when I spotted Chuck Schumer making a beeline for me, grinning from ear to ear.

"I told the president your joke!" he exclaimed, his eyes sparkling with delight. "Supreme One!"

Huh? "Supreme *Being*," I said.

Chuck thought for a second. "Yes! Supreme *Being*!" A beat, then Chuck, still grinning, admitted, "I said 'Supreme *One*.'"

"So you told the president that the Supreme Leader might as well be called the 'Supreme *One*.'"

"Yes," Chuck affirmed, still beaming.

"Did he laugh?"

"No."

"And you told him it was my joke?"

Chuck nodded, still grinning. "Yes."

I love Chuck Schumer. He's one of the smartest, most strategic, most passionate Democrats in Washington,

which is why he's the leader of our caucus in the Senate—
I call him the Jewish LBJ. But he's also kind of a character. Running around with his archaic flip phone, barging
into conversations, talking too loud, screwing up jokes—
no matter what kind of relatives you have, Chuck will
remind you of one of them. In fact, my daughter, Thomasin, likes to say that the mere fact that he *exists*, let alone
serves in the United States Senate, is hilarious.

* * *

I get asked a lot, "Is it hard not to be funny?" (I prefer
this question to "Why aren't you funny anymore?")

And the truth is…kind of, yeah. I can't help it. Even
after all this, my instinct is still to at least try and go for
the joke. Even when it's probably a really bad idea.

For example, when I take pictures with families, I
often playfully put two kids in headlocks and squeeze
their heads together. It always gets a laugh. I did it
once to the two young sons of Chris Murphy, a rising
Democratic star who represents Connecticut in the
Senate and serves as a voice of conscience on both gun
violence and foreign policy.

Watching me squeeze his boys' heads together, Chris
said, "That's the kind of thing that would bring joy to
thousands of families, until one day it ends your career."

I still do it, by the way.

But in general, rather than trusting my ability
to sort out the funny things that would bring joy to

thousands of families from the funny things that might end my career, I've come up with a strategy to avoid falling prey to the Republicans' DeHumorizer™: I built one of my own. It's called my staff.

Every member of my staff is empowered to be the DeHumorizer™ at any given moment. Any staffer driving me, for instance, is encouraged to respond to things I say with, "Okay, that's for inside the car." Or the oft-used, "Fine. Get it out of your system."

Sometimes there's a group decision, usually involving my chief of staff and our communications team. The chief has final say, though sometimes I make an appeal to Franni. I don't know why. She always sides with the staff.

Notes have been a running source of disagreement. During my second week in office I wrote my first note to a constituent. Ruth Anderson of Marshall, Minnesota, was born on July 24, 1899, was about to celebrate her 110th birthday.

I sat down at my desk and wrote on my official stationery:

Dear Ruth,
You have a bright future.

Sincerely,
Al Franken

I handed the note to Drew.
"What's this?" he asked.

"It's a joke," I said.

"You know you can't send this, right?"

"Yeah, I guess so. I don't know, I thought maybe she'd get a kick out of it." Drew pointed out that her family might not "get a kick out of it."

Senators write a lot of notes. To constituents, to people you've had meetings with, to colleagues. Drew nixed this birthday note to John McCain:

Dear John,

Hope you have a great year. Of course, any year would be better than the five you spent in the Hanoi Hilton.

                   Sincerely,
                   Al

The thing about having Drew as a DeHumorizer™ was that it freed me to write anything I wanted. If Drew rejected it, I'd just redo it. Like the birthday note I wrote for Daniel Inouye of Hawaii, who received the Medal of Honor after losing his arm to a grenade in World War II:

Dear Danny,

I hope when I'm your age, I'm just like you— healthy, with two good arms. Oh, wait!

                   Sincerely,
                   Al

Danny had a great sense of humor, and I believed that both he and McCain would have appreciated getting something a little different. But Drew was more concerned about my colleagues' staffs getting their noses out of joint.

So I'd just write the first thing that came to mind, and if the note got through Drew, I'd assume it was fine.

One day on the floor Kay Bailey Hutchison from Texas came up to me with a big grin on her face. "I just loved your birthday note! We've hung it up in our office! It's sooo funny." I had no clue what I had written. My scheduler, Tara, pulled up the copy she'd made.

> *Dear Kay,*
>   *Happy birthday!*
>   *Well, it's been quite a year! Together, we've passed health care reform, Wall St. re—wait! I thought I was sending Kay Hagan my birthday wishes.*
>   *Anyway, happy birthday!*
>
>   *All the best,*
>   *Al*

Kay *Hagan*, of course, was a Democrat who *had* worked with me to pass health care and Wall St. reform. Thus the joke which Kay Bailey Hutchison had so vastly overappreciated.

* * *

Despite what I've learned about how tough a room the Senate chamber can be, I have sometimes tried to slip in The Funny during speeches. Once, while working on a speech about the verification regime in the New START nuclear disarmament treaty with Russia, I came up with this: "A wise man once said, 'Trust but verify.' That man was quoting Ronald Reagan."

Drew said no. "Al, people love Ronald Reagan."

"Oh, c'mon!" I said. "It's a joke!"[*]

In April 2011, Arizona Republican Jon Kyl spoke on the floor of the Senate, saying that abortion services were "well over 90 percent of what Planned Parenthood does." Actually, abortion services make up approximately 3 percent of what Planned Parenthood does.

When Kyl got called out, his spokesman issued this remarkable defense: "His remark was not intended to be a factual statement."

I told Drew I wanted to go to the floor and introduce a Senate resolution saying, "Any statement made on the floor of the Senate that is *presented* as factual must be *intended* to be factual."

---

[*] Jess McIntosh, my press secretary during my first campaign (and my first year in the Senate), told me she wanted to write a campaign memoir entitled *"Oh, C'mon!" Said Franken*. Kris Dahl, my driver, threatened to write a tell-all called *In the Car*.

"No," said Drew.

"Oh, c'mon!" said Franken. "It's funny. And it makes a point."

* * *

When Drew took the chief of staff position, he told me he would have to leave after two years, because by then both his kids would be in college and he'd have to find a real job. I asked Casey Aden-Wansbury, who had already done her share of dehumorizing as my communications director, to step into the job. As it turned out, Casey became the most unforgiving DeHumorizer™ of them all.

Casey actually does have a sense of humor, but she is also one of the most frighteningly competent people I've ever met. She kind of reminds me of the Jessica Chastain character from *Zero Dark Thirty*—the obsessed CIA agent leading the bin Laden hunt. Except if Casey had been in that job, we would have shot off his face months earlier.

Casey cracked down on this funny thing I'd do whenever I arrived at the Hart Senate Office Building around 9 a.m. There'd be long lines of staff and visitors winding out the doors waiting to go through the metal detectors. Of course, we senators get to go straight through. So I'd worm my way through the line saying, "More important than you, more important than you..." This was exactly the kind of thing that brought laughter and joy to hundreds, maybe thousands. Until Yankees first baseman Mark Teixeira took offense.

Teixeira, I am sure, was there to lobby for some very worthy cause, for which I applaud him. But he tweeted, "Just walked through security at Hart Senate OB, @AlFranken let me know 'He is more important than me.'" And that was the end of that fun thing that had brightened the mornings of so many.

Casey and I had our most protracted argument over a joke in June 2015, right after the Supreme Court issued its 5–4 ruling that marriage is a fundamental right for same-sex couples. Justice Antonin Scalia issued an unhinged dissent describing the majority ruling as "a judicial Putsch." I wanted our communications department to issue the following statement:

> Senator Al Franken of Minnesota today applauded the Supreme Court's decision and described Justice Antonin Scalia's dissent as "very gay."

My staff said no. But they didn't say I couldn't put it in a book someday!

*   *   *

When I first got to the Senate, we lived in mortal fear of Capitol Hill gossip columns, which, believe it or not, exist. There are reporters at esteemed publications who just hang out in the Capitol waiting to catch a congressman failing to wash his hands after he pees or something.

You're not safe anywhere. Once, during the height of the Tiger Woods cheating scandal (cheating on his wife, not cheating at golf), I was on the Senate subway and joked to Kris Dahl, "I'm thinking of introducing some kind of Tiger Woods stamp." He chuckled. We have fun.

Later that day, Jess stepped into my office. "I got a call from 'Heard on the Hill,'" she said, "and they said you were talking about introducing a Tiger Woods stamp."

I nodded.

"Well, did you say that?"

"Yeah."

"Ugh," she said, her shoulders slumping. "Then I just won't return the call." She turned to head back to her desk.

"No," I said, stopping Jess in her tracks. "Tell them I was citing it as an example of a bad idea." Which she did. The "Heard on the Hill" story came out the next day:

STILL FUNNY

Sen. Al Franken hasn't lost his touch. An HOH tipster overheard the former comedian practicing his deadpan routine to a staffer while riding the Senate subway late last week. The Minnesota Democrat mused that someone ought to introduce legislation to create a Tiger Woods postal stamp, our spy says.

A Franken spokeswoman says her boss used the idea of a postal stamp honoring the scandal-plagued, affair-having golfer as an "example of a bad idea."

We think it's a funny one.

The student had become the master.

Chapter 44

I Get Reelected

In my first campaign in 2008, I barely survived the year's nastiest, hardest-fought, most eventful and exhausting Senate race, winning by the smallest margin in American history after an unprecedented eight-month recount and legal battle.

In my second campaign in 2014, I ran against a friendly, very successful businessman who didn't know a lot about public policy, and I beat him by ten points.

It was a terrible year for Democrats, which everybody saw coming. For one thing, it was a midterm, and, for whatever reason, we struggle to turn out voters in nonpresidential election cycles. Meanwhile, the group of senators up for reelection included a lot of the red- and purple-state Democrats who had been swept into office thanks to the Obama phenomenon and, of course, the stench from the dead, rotting corpse of the George W. Bush administration.

That meant Mark Begich had to run for reelection in Alaska, as did Mark Udall in Colorado, and Kay Hagan in North Carolina. They would all lose. And so would longtime Democratic incumbents Mark Pryor in Arkansas and Mary Landrieu in Louisiana. Meanwhile, open seats in Iowa (where Tom Harkin retired) and South Dakota (where Tim Johnson retired) and West Virginia (where Jay Rockefeller retired) and Montana (where Max Baucus had stepped down to become President Obama's ambassador to China) all flipped to the Republicans as well.

For me, election night 2014 was pretty much the exact opposite experience from election night 2008. My race was called the moment the polls closed, and we all cheered. Then I spent the rest of the night watching all my friends give somber concession speeches.

And instead of worrying that I'd screwed everything up for everyone, I kept getting asked what my secret was. How had I pulled off such a big win in such a down year?

The weekend before the election, on *Meet the Press*, the political panel was discussing who ran the best and worst campaigns of the year. Chuck Todd had the answer:

I have to give the award for best to Al Franken. Because guess who we're not talking about today. Closest Senate election six years ago, Al

Franken. Recount, all of those things. How did this guy survive? Six years of a well-run campaign. You have to give that to him.

A lot of the credit goes to Matt Burgess, who ran my reelection campaign, and the terrific staff he pulled together. In a year when a lot of Democrats were on their heels, our campaign focused on the work I'd done on things like reining in Wall Street abuse and made an aggressive argument for a more progressive economic policy, taking on hedge fund tax breaks and other elements of the "rigged system."

The reason we were able to run such a confident campaign, though, was that the people who worked in my Senate offices in D.C. and Minnesota had done such a great job. Led by Casey, my chief of staff, and Alana Petersen, who had been my state director ever since I took office, they made me look good every day, for which I have to remember to stop giving them credit.

Chuck Todd was right. As he always is.* I didn't win reelection because of what I did during the two years of the actual campaign. I won because of what I did during the six (well, five and a half) years of my first term.

It turns out that being a good senator—working

---

* Chuck's great. And I can't wait to go back on *Meet the Press* so I can blow more smoke up his butt while I promote this book.

hard, sweating the details of legislation, staying focused on the issues that matter to your state, looking for ways to find common ground with the other side even as you stand your ground on your core principles—is good politics.

That's especially true when people initially had a lot of doubts about whether you'd be a good senator or even remotely competent. "You're better than I thought you'd be," a businessman in Bemidji told me early on in my term.

"Thanks for having low expectations," I replied.

* * *

But there is something about barely winning an election that makes you take nothing for granted. And the fact is, I had started getting nervous the day after the 2012 election was over. I was officially "in cycle."

In the spring of 2013, I made a quick fund-raising trip to Florida, and while getting on the plane from Miami to Minneapolis I had a conversation that made me feel much better about my prospects.

"Are you one of my senators?" the young woman asked as we waited on the jetway.

"You a Minnesotan?" I replied.

"Ya," she said.

"Then I'm one of your senators."

"Why are you here?" she asked.

"Fund-raising. I'm running for reelection."

She nodded. "This November?"

"No, next November."

"Oh," she said. "Is Amy running then, too?"

"No, she ran last year. She won by a big margin."

"Oh. Well, I don't think you'll have any problem. Everyone says you work really hard."

Wow! If that's what had filtered down to low-information voters, then I must be in good shape. Put *that* in your model, Nate Silver.

*   *   *

Still, I didn't take my opponent lightly. Mike McFadden was a wealthy investment banker with a very telegenic family. One of his five sons, Conor, would always sit up front at our debates with a big grin plastered on his face—which I thought was intended to psych me out until I realized it was a reminder to his dad to smile. Which was really endearing. It made me think of Franni sitting in the front row at my campaign rallies, frantically tugging her ear when she thought I had gone on too long and should wrap it up, which I never did.

On paper, Mike was a strong candidate: a successful businessman, a Pop Warner football coach, a board member of a Jesuit high school for low-income minority kids, and a political novice who could credibly claim to be an outsider in a year when people were pretty sick of Washington insiders. Like, I guess Mike would say, me.

But one thing he had going against him was his name: McFadden. You see, before me, there was Norm Coleman, who's Jewish. Norm had succeeded Paul Wellstone—also a Jew. Paul had beaten Rudy Boschwitz—Jew. My campaign slogan: "Minnesota isn't ready for a gentile in this seat!" At least that was my slogan at the Jewish Federation dinner.

Mike made some rookie mistakes, such as telling a reporter that it would be fine with him if the Keystone Pipeline were made with Chinese steel. There's a reason Minnesota's Iron Range is called the *Iron* Range. Mike's comment didn't sit well with Rangers who had lost jobs to dumped Chinese steel. As someone who had once been a rookie myself, I felt just terrible watching him step in it like that. No, actually I enjoyed the hell out of it.

Given Mike's lack of familiarity with government and the nuances of campaigning and my own work on the granular details of public policy, there was every reason for me to be supremely confident about our upcoming debates. But for some reason, debate prep seemed more difficult than it had six years earlier. The format of one-and-a-half-minute answers followed by thirty-second rebuttals seemed so artificial to me, and, my brain now packed with material from hundreds of nightly briefing binders, I kept giving wonky, almost listless answers that wandered all over the place.

The day before my first one-on-one debate with

Mike, I got a call from President Obama. I'm sure he was calling around the country, checking in on all our 2014 Senate candidates, but it was a nice gesture.

"How's it going?" the president asked.

"Oh, good," I said. "I'm ahead by ten or so."

"Great!"

"But, you know, Mr. President, I got a debate tomorrow, and for some reason, I'm really nervous."

"Uh-huh," he responded, as if he knew exactly what I was talking about.

"For some reason, I'm having a hard time learning my responses."

"Is it because the whole thing seems so phony to you?"

"Yes!"

"It's like you're learning lines for a play?"

"Yes! But it's like I'm at war with my own answers."

"Because they're not exactly what you want to say, and you want to say more?"

"Yes! Yes! Exactly!"

"Uh-huh. I've been there. Hence, Denver."*

* * *

Although Mike was a genuinely nice guy, it's hard to run in a rough-and-tumble political race without

_____

* The president, of course, was referring to his awful performance in the first 2012 presidential debate.

getting annoyed with your opponent. I didn't mind him repeating ad infinitum that I had voted with President Obama 97 percent of the time. But, man, he really hammered that talking point. At one point in a debate, after Mike had said it for the eighth time, I interrupted. "Excuse me. Could you repeat that number again? Is it 97 percent? Let me write that down or I'll forget it, sure as shootin'."

Frankly, the other thing that irked me most was one of his early web videos, in which Mike spoke directly to the camera: "A lot of people have asked me, why do I want to run for the U.S. Senate? Why do I want to put up with the attacks and insults, time away from my family?"

Yeah, why exactly *was* Mike running for the U.S. Senate? Oh, wait, I know: He was doing it because he wanted to be a United States senator!

Let me tell you a little secret about United States senators. We all *love* being United States senators. We all like having a staff of brilliant young people whose work we can take credit for. We all like having reporters ask us for our insightful takes on crucial issues. We all love being called "Senator."*

---

* In fact, when my first grandson was born in 2013, I wanted to have *him* call me "Senator." I thought it would be funny. Casey nixed it on the grounds that people wouldn't get the joke and would think I was a truly pompous jerk. But you get it, right? If so, please email her at casey.adenwansbury@DeHumorizer.org (that's a think tank she started

You'll remember that in college, after deciding not to be a real scientist, I turned to a major in behavioral science, where I learned some valuable insights into what makes people tick. Take, for example, Maslow's Hierarchy of Needs.

In 1943, Abraham Maslow formulated his influential Hierarchy of Needs theory to explain what motivates people. Usually these needs are depicted as a pyramid with five levels. The first two levels are considered "basic needs." At the bottom are "physiological needs": food, water, warmth, sleep. Next, "safety needs": basically, security.

The next two levels are considered "psychological needs." At level three, "belongingness and love needs": intimate relationships and friends. Level four, "esteem needs": feelings of accomplishment and *prestige*. In other words, being a U.S. senator. Or writing a theory of human motivation that everybody in psychology pays attention to.

After achieving your physiological (Levels 1 and 2) and psychological (Levels 3 and 4) needs, the very top of Maslow's pyramid goes to "self-actualization": achieving one's full potential, including creative activities. For example, writing a book about being a U.S. senator.

---

after leaving my office—it focuses on eliminating humor in public discourse).

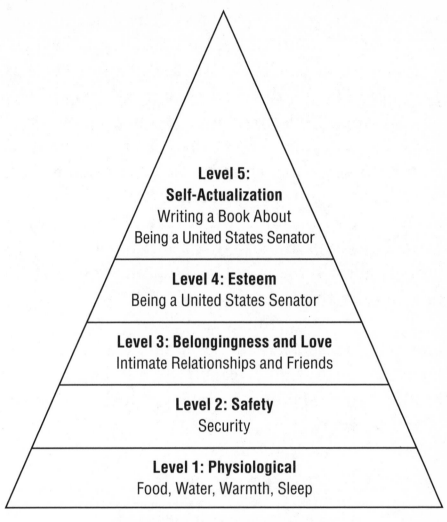

Maslow's Hierarchy of Needs

* * *

Every senator is different. Most of us are doing this to make a difference in people's lives. Most of us are also really into the self-aggrandizing part of the job. The balance between the two is different for everyone.

Some of us are more noble than others (I like to think I'm in the top quintile). But we are all human beings.

As a human being, I relished my 2014 victory as a vindication of all the good work my staff and I had done in the previous five-plus years. But the glow lasted about an hour. Pretty soon that night, my thoughts turned to worrying about a Republican-controlled Senate, our lagging economic recovery, kids living in poverty, global warming, the humanitarian tragedy in Syria, and the possibility that a real lunatic like Ted Cruz might win the Republican nomination in 2016. (Thankfully, that didn't happen!)

Then I ate something, hugged my kids and my grandson Joe, and went to sleep in my warm bed with my wife of thirty-nine years, thus fulfilling the first four levels on Maslow's hierarchy, which is a pretty lucky place to be.

Chapter 45

Lies and the Lying Liar Who Got Himself Elected President

As I watched Donald Trump campaign in 2016, I couldn't help but think back to my own entry into politics a decade or so earlier.

Like Trump, I had no previous experience in elected office. Unlike Trump, I was actually *bothered* by my lack of experience. I compensated for this by absorbing as much information in as much detail as I could. I read everything I could get my hands on. I used my radio show as a graduate education in public policy. I engaged some of the great minds of our time. Did I remember to tell you that Elizabeth Warren was a frequent guest on my show? Have I mentioned that I know Atul Gawande?

Indeed, it could be argued that in my defensiveness over not having done this before, I *slightly* overcompensated during my first run. A stump speech is supposed to be about ten minutes. It's not supposed to be a discursive forty-five-minute monologue. But there I would be, boring the hell out of forty people at some bean feed, rambling on about my belief that tidal energy could harness the power of the moon's gravitational pull to help solve our energy crisis, or how the Canadian province of Saskatchewan had led Canada to adopt its current single-payer health care system, or the precise differences between Sunnis and Shiites. Meanwhile, Franni would be madly tugging on her ear (sometimes both earlobes at the same time).

My whole thought process was that people deserved leaders who knew what they were talking about and were curious about the stuff they didn't know yet, and who they could count on being dedicated to reaching decisions based on mastery of the subject matter. I figured it was especially incumbent on me, an entertainer, to prove that I knew stuff. You know, as a sign of respect for the voters.

So you can imagine my frustration when Trump, an entertainer (sort of)[*], quickly showed not only that he had no knowledge about the details of public policy, but that he had no interest in *learning* the details of public policy. In fact, he was actively scornful of learning.

---

[*]Not only does it offend me that he's the president, it offends me that he's considered an entertainer.

"I know more than the generals," he would say. No, idiot*—you don't. You don't even know what the nuclear triad is! Hint: "triad" means three! It's three of something! C'mon, dude.

To be fair, though, maybe president is more of a "big picture" job. You know, you can *hire* people who know stuff, like your son-in-law, or some creepy white supremacist.

So I let that one go.

But I had another uncomfortable moment of déjà vu when I heard that the *New York Times* had published a story about some issue with Trump's taxes. "Gosh," I thought. "I feel for the guy. I hope he didn't pay taxes to the state where he was living instead of the states where he gave some speeches." I recalled from personal experience how embarrassing that could wind up being.

Then the story finally loaded on my laptop. Oh. He had taken a *billion-dollar write-off.* That was kind of different. And as it turned out, he had used what the *Times* described as "a tax avoidance maneuver so legally dubious his own lawyers advised him that the Internal Revenue Service would most likely declare it improper if he were audited."

---

* To be clear, I would never call the president of the United States an idiot. I simply have too much respect for the office. This is a reference to Candidate Trump.

Speaking of audited, Trump had broken with four decades of tradition by refusing to release his tax returns on the grounds that they were currently under audit. He had also refused to provide any evidence that he was being audited, and the IRS was forbidden by law from confirming or denying his story. Also, you can totally release your tax returns even if you're being audited.

On top of that, he was the defendant in a fraud suit over his fake university (which he would later end up settling for $25 million), and it looked like his family foundation was little more than a scam, and he had left a long trail of unpaid creditors and stiffed workers in his wake everywhere he had ever gone.

But I didn't see anything about a missed workers' comp payment. So, understandable that the press let most of that slide.

Still, there was the whole "moral turpitude" thing.

As you may recall, my history of indecorous statements and off-color jokes had created some question about my fitness for public service. How could a comedian who had once written about having sex with a robot—in *Playboy* magazine, no less—be trusted to honor the dignity of high office? Republicans sure seemed worried about that back when I was running. In fact, so did a number of Democrats. And, frankly, so did I. You'll recall the existential crisis I had in Rochester the night before the DFL convention in 2008.

Well, imagine my surprise when, in October, I heard a tape on which Donald Trump bragged about hitting on a married woman under the guise of taking her furniture shopping. I was so shocked by this that I missed the part right after that where he talked about grabbing women by the crotch.[USS] If I had written a sketch where a character said that, I would have been toast. But guess what happened the next day. He didn't drop out of the race!

"Huh," I thought. "The world sure has changed since 2008."

* * *

All that aside, the thing that bothered me most about Trump's campaign was the lying.

I don't know why dishonesty has always gotten under my skin. My parents taught me to tell the truth, but come on, whose parents didn't? Well, okay, maybe Trump's. The point is, I don't know where exactly my particular obsession with lies and lying liars came from. And I admit, it's a little weird.

Part of it may be that I've always been an incredibly literal person. Here's an example. When Tom Davis and I would go pitch stuff in Hollywood, and the studio executive would say, "I love it!" I would invariably assume that he said that because he loved what we had pitched.

"He loved it!" I would exult to Tom in the parking lot. "We're definitely gonna sell this thing!"

Tom was always skeptical, and almost always right. Even when a studio exec would say, "Not only do I love it, I want to buy it!" that rarely, if ever, meant a sale. No matter how many times that would happen, I never failed to get excited the *next* time it would happen. I never, ever learned.

The first time I ever heard of Rush Limbaugh was in the early 1990s, when I was researching something for an *SNL* sketch and stumbled upon a clip from the TV show Rush had back then. At the time, George H. W. Bush was under fire for questioning Bill Clinton's patriotism because Clinton had protested the Vietnam War while on foreign soil (at Oxford). In defense of Bush, Rush showed his audience a clip *from a different part of Bush's speech.* "See?" I remember him saying indignantly. "Bush didn't question Clinton's patriotism! What's everyone talking about?!"

I couldn't believe it. Who was this guy? Why would anyone just lie like that? What made him think he could get away with it? And I *could not let it go.* It made my teeth itch. I'm mad about it all over again right now. I mean, it was a totally different part of the speech! And he just presented it as if it was what everyone was complaining about! Like, with no compunction whatsoever!!! *NO COMPUNCTION!!!*

Anyway, it bugged me.

Two years later, Newt Gingrich and the Republicans took over Congress for the first time in more than forty years, which was upsetting in and of itself. What made it even worse was that this same Limbaugh character was their mouthpiece and mascot—they even made him an honorary member of the freshman class. That's when I decided that if I was going to write a book about politics, *Rush Limbaugh Is a Big Fat Idiot* would be a satisfying title. And as I dug into the research for that book, I found plenty more lies, big and small, to fixate on.

Even after the Rush book came out, I kept noticing conservatives in the media saying things that were recklessly, provably false. And every time I noticed it, it would drive me bananas. No matter how many times it would happen, it would engender the same visceral reaction every time. "You can't just lie!" I would yell, to no one in particular. "You can't!" But they did.

Even worse, not only were they lying, but there were more liars than ever before, and on more platforms. They had Fox News. They had right-wing think tanks feeding pundits to other cable networks and publishing op-eds in newspapers. They had the conservative Internet. They had this thing called Ann Coulter. They lied and lied and lied.

And the biggest lie of all was that the mainstream media had a liberal bias, because from where I sat, the mainstream media seemed like part of the problem.

They never seemed to call out the lying liars on their lies. Far from it—they would invite the lying liars to come back on the air and lie some more the next time. Not only were these people lying with total impunity, but they were getting *rewarded* for lying if they could do it entertainingly.

So I wrote a follow-up (*Lies and the Lying Liars*) about how this was poisoning our discourse. I wrote about how Fox News and the right-wing echo chamber worked, but I also explored how these lies were seeping out of the conservative bubble and into the so-called "liberal media" without being challenged. Asking whether the mainstream media had a liberal bias, I argued, was asking the wrong question. Their bias was toward getting ratings. And that meant reveling in conflict and sensationalism. And if *that* meant putting lying liars on the air, then so be it.

Two years after that, I wrote *The Truth (with Jokes)*, focused on how the Bush administration had lied us into a war, and into two gigantic tax cuts, and into giving him four more years to keep lying about economic and foreign policy as our president.

Sure, the books were about more than just the lies. And, through my radio show, I started not just exposing the bad guys but giving a platform to the good guys. And I became part of the whole progressive movement that roared into high gear after 2004. But if I'm being honest, my favorite part was always busting liars.

Even getting elected to the Senate didn't diminish the rush of catching someone saying something that wasn't true. There's a flip side to it, by the way: I get paranoid about making sure everything my office puts out is carefully fact-checked, and although we do make mistakes sometimes, I get really upset about it when we do.* And when President Obama said, "If you like your doctor, you can keep him," and that turned out not to be accurate, that bothered me just as much as any Republican falsehood.

All of this to say that I care a lot about people in politics telling the truth. And even considering all the horrible things Trump got away with during the campaign—mocking a disabled reporter, attacking a Gold Star family, referring to Mexican immigrants as "rapists" and "drug dealers," calling for Muslims to be banned from our country—I still can't believe he got away with lying so much.

Frankly, it all made me wonder whether, sadly, the war was over and the liars had won.

Back in the good old days, fact-checking politicians was a different ball game. Looking back now, it seems almost adorable that I made a decent living writing books about catching right-wing Republicans in their lies. What I did was effective, I realize now, mainly

---

* There will be something in this book that is wrong, and if I try to defend it as satire, just know that I'll be dying inside just a little bit.

because a lot of their lies had the veneer of plausibility, and because at least some of the liars liked to pretend that they were telling the truth—which was of course a lie, but which was also part of the fun.

But now we seem to have entered an era where getting caught lying openly and shamelessly, lying in a manner that insults the intelligence of both your friends and foes, lying about lying, and lying for the *sake* of lying have all lost their power to damage a politician. In fact, the "Trump Effect" yields the opposite result: Trump supporters seem to approve of the fact that he lies constantly, including to them. Like a movie that is loosely based on a true story, Trump's fans seem to feel that he is making the dull reality of politics more fun and interesting by augmenting it with gross exaggeration, and often utter fantasy.

During the campaign, Trump would give speeches that would just be one lie after another, with a personal insult or two thrown in to keep things interesting. And the media would just air these speeches in their entirety.

Here's a thought experiment. What would Trump have had to say for a network to cut off his speech and break in, with the anchor saying, "Good Lord. I'm sorry. We're just not going to show you any more of this crap." Or at least run a ticker at the bottom of the screen with some underpaid intern just Googling the numbers Trump was pulling out of his ass.

For example, when he would say that the U.S. murder rate was at a forty-five-year high (something he said constantly).

"Nope," the intern could say. "Not true. Says right here it's actually at a fifty-year low."

"Where's that from?" his boss could reply.

"The FBI's Uniform Crime Report."

"Okay. Jesus. Put that up on the screen. Wait, what did he just say about climate change being a Chinese hoax?"

But of course, even when networks finally started to occasionally fact-check him in real time, it didn't matter. Trump has deployed a variety of methods to debunk debunkings that have proven startlingly effective. The first and most common is to simply ignore the correction even when confronted with it.

This is why he's continually planting the seed that the media is dishonest. It renders statements of contrary fact highly suspect, because you tend to hear those via the media:

TRUMP SUPPORTER (skeptically): Uh-huh, the FBI's Uniform Crime Report. Where'd you hear that?

YOU: CNN.

TRUMP SUPPORTER (sarcastic): Ah, okay. CNN, right. And they always tell the truth. Come on, man! Wake up!

Another crowd-pleaser is to cite an alternate, very anecdotal authority:

TRUMP SUPPORTER (sarcastic): Oh, so you think the murder rate is at a fifty-year low, do you? Well, tell that to the parents of a college student who's just been murdered!

There's also this variant, the sort of ear-to-the-ground evidence that only a common man with a deep understanding of other common men like Donald Trump would have:

TRUMP SUPPORTER: A fifty-year low? That's not what I'm hearing. People are saying it's at an all-time high!

* * *

As Trump prepared to take office, there was a lot of talk about the different norms he had violated, was in the process of violating, or would shortly have the opportunity to violate. Stuff like refusing to divest from his businesses and place his assets in a blind trust. Or using his office to sell hotel rooms to Kuwaiti diplomats and bother foreign regulators about construction projects he wanted to get moving.

And that is all terrible. But I really think that if we don't start caring about whether people tell the truth or not, it's going to be literally impossible to restore anything approaching a reasonable political discourse. Politicians have always shaded the truth. But if you can say something that is provably false, and no one cares, then you can't have a real debate about anything.

I firmly believe that you can draw a straight line from Rush Limbaugh through Fox News through present-day websites like Breitbart and the explosion in "fake news"* that played such a big role in the 2016 campaign. And that's how someone like Trump can wind up in the Oval Office.

I know I'm sort of farting into the wind on this. But I hope you'll fart along with me. I've always believed that it's possible to discern true statements from false statements, and that it's critically important to do so, and that we put our entire democratic experiment in peril when we don't. It's a lesson I fear our nation is about to learn the hard way.

That's why my Global Jihad on Factual Inaccuracy will continue. I cling to the hope that national gullibility is a cyclical phenomenon, and that in a few short years we may find ourselves in an era of Neo-Sticklerism. And a glorious era it shall be.

---

* The flip side of the public believing that fake news is real is that they also start to believe that the real news is fake, something that Trump himself had exploited. It is a turn of events that is truly, to coin a phrase, Orwellian.

Chapter 46

I Attend a Presidential Inauguration

Senators get great seats for presidential inaugurations. Well, we stand, actually, but it's in a good spot. Standing just yards from where the new president takes the oath of office, it's a rare opportunity to have a front-row seat to history. Except that, again, you're standing.

When President Obama first took the oath of office in 2009, I, of course, was still in recount limbo. They gave me a decent seat out with the crowd. It was an actual place to sit, which was nice, considering that the nearly two million other people who had flocked to the National Mall to witness this historic moment had to stand. But it was freezing cold. Plus, I had to get there really early, and by the time the new president gave his address, I couldn't have cared less what he was saying. I just wanted to go inside somewhere and get warm.

Anyway, my point is that I was really stoked to have that special senatorial spot to watch Hillary Clinton take the oath of office in 2017. I'd campaigned hard for Hillary, who is the smartest, toughest, hardest-working person I know, with the possible exception of Atul Gawande. She would have been a great president.

But after election night, I started looking at the date of January 20 on the calendar with—what's the word? Dread? No. Something worse than that. It was really, really bad. I felt like I was looking at my own execution date—and not a relaxing, fun execution by lethal injection, but a horrible, painful execution by a faulty electric chair or being slowly strangled by a piano wire.

As that date approached, of course, things just kept getting worse and worse. President-elect Trump made it clear that he had no intention of divesting himself of his business interests. He shrugged off reports by every intelligence agency that his election had been, in part, the product of interference by the Russian government. He installed a white supremacist in the White House as his chief strategist.

He also insisted on being a complete jerk.[USS] Hillary had graciously conceded the election to him despite the fact that she had earned nearly three million more votes than he had. He couldn't even bring himself to concede the legitimacy of that popular vote.

Mind you, no one was saying he couldn't be president

if he lost the popular vote. It didn't matter. He could have let it go. But no. He was a sore winner. The president-elect actually insisted that three to five million votes had been fraudulently cast by illegal immigrants, every single one of them for Hillary Clinton. It was almost as if the incoming commander-in-chief had some sort of mental health problem. The kind of mental health problem that you would be disturbed to discover in your kid's piano teacher, let alone the president of the United States of America.

Later, when Trump demanded an investigation into those three to five million fraudulent votes, it reminded me of O. J. Simpson, who, after being acquitted of murdering his ex-wife and Ron Goldman, vowed to spend the rest of his life "finding the killer or killers."

* * *

Some sixty House Democrats decided to skip Trump's inaugural. I respected their decision. But I decided to go—the peaceful transfer of power and so on.

Standing with my colleagues on the Capitol platform, flanked by fellow senators Kirsten Gillibrand (a young, dynamic Democrat) and Mike Lee (a young, dynamic Republican), we passed the forty-five minutes before the start of the official program doing what senators do—being convivial and generally enjoying ourselves. I warned Bill Cassidy, the Louisiana Republican who stood directly in front of and a step down from me, that I very well might vomit the moment Trump said, "So help me God."

I don't know what's wrong with me, but for some reason I had expected that President Trump would use his inaugural address to pivot from the awful, divisive transition—to reach out and strike a more lofty, unifying tone. Instead, he had "crafted" a speech that was just as awful and divisive and so unartful that it seemed he had written it himself in about twenty minutes. Or, given his attention span, in forty thirty-second spurts.

His message was that all the people on the platform except for his family and the rest of his team had selfishly turned the country into a dark, perilous place, the scene of pretty much nothing but "American carnage."

After that things went downhill. Angered by accurate reports that the crowd for his inauguration was smaller than those at the two Obama inaugurals and the Women's March on Washington the day following his swearing-in, President Trump ordered his spokesman to call a press conference and lie to the media with "alternative facts," a new phrase coined by Kellyanne Conway to encourage sales of George Orwell's *1984*.

After the public learned that President Trump spent actual time calling the National Park Service to insist they release more flattering photographs of the crowds at his inauguration, it began to dawn on many Americans, including a number of my Republican colleagues, that the new leader of our country was, indeed, unbalanced.[USS]

By then, of course, it was too late. Donald J. Trump was the president of the United States. And there's a decent chance that he still will be by the time you read this book.

* * *

Even before President Trump took the oath of office, the clear majority of Americans who didn't vote for him (and a growing number of Americans who were really sorry they *had* voted for him) were trying to figure out how to fight back against him.

As it happened, I had had some experience with all this. I'd basically cut my teeth as a political activist in opposition—opposition to the Gingrich Revolution, opposition to the growth of the right-wing media, and opposition to the George W. Bush administration.

Because I'd been a satirist since I was a teenager, I had had plenty of experience in identifying hypocrisies and absurdities. I knew how to drill down into an argument to find the inconsistencies that would reveal the underlying mendacity of the object of my derision. I had learned not to be afraid to speak truth to power.

That's what my books were about. That's what my radio show was about. That's why I attracted a following of progressives long before I ever ran for office.

It's also why, when I *did* run for office, the transition wasn't always smooth. The tools I'd used to fight for the things I believed in as an author and radio host weren't always useful as a candidate, and they aren't always useful as a senator.

But they still work sometimes. And I've had a chance to prove it in the early days of the Trump administration.

As you will recall, committee hearings are often prime "scorn and ridicule" opportunities. And the first order of business in the 115th Congress was for Senate committees to consider President Trump's Cabinet nominees, many of whom were, shall we say, ripe for the picking.

I mentioned earlier how I confronted Jeff Sessions during his confirmation hearing for attorney general—where I busted him for claiming that he had "personally handled" four civil rights cases as a U.S. Attorney when, in fact, he hadn't.

I also, inadvertently, trapped him in an even more damaging lie. I had asked him what he would do as attorney general if it emerged that there had been contact between the Trump campaign and Russian officials. Sessions answered a different question, asserting that he, himself, had not met with any Russians during the campaign. Which turned out not to be true.

Pretty brilliant on my part, don't you think? See? I'm always three steps ahead.

Meanwhile, the HELP Committee was considering the nomination of Tom Price, the Georgia congressman and former orthopedic surgeon who had spent his career in Congress trying to slash Medicare, destroy Medicaid, and help orthopedic surgeons make as much money as possible.

In fact, Price had enriched himself even after leaving his orthopedic surgery practice to serve in Congress, thanks to a series of extremely suspicious investments he had made in health care stocks while he was writing legislation that affected the value of those stocks. Which I delighted in bringing up at his hearing to be secretary of health and human services.

But the moment when I was able to make the biggest impact came during Betsy DeVos's hearing to be secretary of education. And this time, it wasn't because I asked a tough question. In fact, it was because I asked a very, very easy question.

Remember back in the education chapter where I talked about how judging schools by "proficiency" created all sorts of bad outcomes? The alternative is to judge schools by "growth"—instead of measuring how many students reach a certain bar of proficiency, measure how much progress every student has made over the course of the school year.

This is a very basic and very important debate in

education policy. But when DeVos had come to my office for her pre-hearing courtesy call, my staff and I were surprised to discover that she seemed to have no understanding at all about education policy in general. So I thought it might be fun to ask her about growth vs. proficiency.

In the hearing, I made sure to give her as much context about this issue as possible before asking for her thoughts. She had none. In fact, she had no idea what I was talking about. It was a shocking moment in a hearing full of them (for example, she had no idea that disabled children's right to a quality education is protected by a federal law, and she suggested that schools might want to keep guns around in case of grizzly bear attack).

DeVos offered perhaps the worst performance by any Cabinet nominee in the history of nomination hearings. And for the first time in American history, the vice president of the United States had to make the trip down Pennsylvania Avenue to cast the tie-breaking vote on behalf of a Cabinet nominee.

* * *

As one of the forty-eight Democratic senators in the unique position of serving as a constitutional check on this president, I have opportunities to fight back against this administration that I wouldn't have had as an author and radio host.

But my job also comes with its own set of responsibilities and constraints. I have to be strategic about how to use the considerable, but not unlimited, leverage I have. I have to coordinate with forty-seven other Democrats who may have different political realities or even different political philosophies than I do. And I have to remember that the people of Minnesota didn't just send me to Washington to be part of the Democratic caucus—they sent me to Washington to be *their* Senator.

Figuring out how to balance all these considerations is never easy. And as someone who's been part of this fight from a number of different perspectives, I've learned that these judgment calls sometimes look different on the inside than they did when I was on the outside.

I can't tell you I'll always get it right. But I can tell you this: I'm going to keep fighting as hard as I can in the coming months and years to protect our children, our values, and our future from Donald Trump.

And I can tell you this, too: The work people like you are doing on the outside matters a lot on the inside.

The Women's March on Washington was one of the most inspiring things I've ever seen. But ever since the march, ordinary people with a ton of passion but limited time, money, and energy have been wrestling with the question: "What can I do now?"

Everyone has to figure that out for themselves. But here's a little perspective from the inside.

First: Keep showing up and keep speaking out. The Women's March didn't force Trump to resign. It didn't even stop any of his Cabinet nominees from going through. But it really, really mattered. It sent a clear message to the president (and to Republicans in Congress) that the American people won't surrender their rights or their core values without a fight—and it sent a clear message to Democrats that, when we stand up to Trump, people will have our backs.

Second: Keep being a pain in the butt, including to me. Phone calls make a difference. Letters make a difference. Emails make a difference. Coming up and yelling at me in the airport about how Democrats need to learn to message better makes somewhat less of a difference.

But showing up in person makes the biggest difference of all—and we've seen huge crowds at town hall meetings held by Republican officeholders in very red parts of the country. Unlike the crowds that packed town hall meetings held by Democratic officeholders in the summer of 2009, these crowds haven't been badly misinformed by right-wing talk radio and the conservative Internet. But I believe they can make just as big of a difference.

I never really had any contentious town hall meetings back in 2009. Which is not to say I avoided my constituents. It's just that I called these meetings "community forums" instead of "town halls," and the Tea Partiers never seemed to crack the code. But my fellow Democrats vividly remember how jarring it was to be confronted like that—and my Republican colleagues are about to learn the same lesson.

Third: Become an advocate. By which I mean, pick an issue that means a lot to you (immigration, mental health, clean water) and look for an organization that's doing work on that issue. Join. Give them your email address. Go to the meetings. Become a foot soldier. You'd be surprised how quickly foot soldiers in these organizations can become leaders—and you'd be surprised how much senators like me rely on them for information, for advice, and for support.

* * *

But maybe the most important thing I can convey to you is that you have got to keep your head up. If there's one thing I've learned in my political journey, it's that it can often be a really unpleasant journey.

I've had days where being in politics has felt inspiring and gratifying, a rare opportunity to move our country forward and make a positive impact on the lives of millions of people. I've also had days where it's felt like a frustrating, unjust, humiliating crapshow.[USS]

Lately, things have been trending crapshow.[USS] And while we don't yet know exactly how bad things are going to get under President Trump, I think we should probably be prepared for the worst.

The fact is that he is the president, and Republicans control Congress, and that means we're going to lose a lot of fights in the years ahead. Plus, we're going to have to watch Donald Trump be the president. Day after day after day. Insulting speeches. Insane tweets. Policies that are both insulting and insane. This is going to suck for a while.

But not forever. I still remember vividly how distraught I was after Bush got reelected in 2004. I also remember what came next.

I remember how he got up there and declared that he had a mandate to privatize Social Security, and how, even in the midst of our despair, we stopped him—and how winning that fight was the start of something big.

I remember how we recognized where our movement needed to grow and change, and how we built progressive infrastructure to make our voices stronger, and how being part of it felt vital and important and fun.

I remember how candidates stepped up to run for office all over the country, even in places where Democrats don't often win, and how much energy there was when I would go and campaign for them, and how we started to feel a wave building as the 2006 midterms drew near.

And I *definitely* remember how it felt just two short

years after that, watching President Obama and his family celebrate in that park in Chicago, and how it felt just eight short months after *that*, when I finally got the chance to become a senator and help him make a lot of people's lives better.

My story, the one you've just finished reading, is a small part of a bigger story—the story of how progressives picked themselves up off the mat and made an epic comeback.

And now we have to do it again. This comeback starts with standing up for our values and making it clear that no president has a mandate to spread bigotry or roll back the clock on progress (especially not one who lost the popular vote by three million). It continues through next year, when we have a chance to punish Republicans for enabling this disaster and take back governorships and state legislatures all across the country. That's how we can put a stop to the voter suppression that made such an impact in 2016 and redraw congressional district boundaries more fairly after the 2020 census.

Meanwhile, we can hold President Trump accountable for everything he does—and not just that, we can hold accountable every single Republican who enables him, so that when we kick him out, we can kick *them* out, too.

There's a part for you to play in the next great progressive comeback story. But only if you can keep from losing your mind or getting so discouraged that you quit before the comeback even begins.

* * *

Our political system isn't always fair. And it isn't always fun. Being part of it means making difficult compromises and painful sacrifices. For me, it's meant leaving a career I loved so I could be savagely attacked for having had that career in the first place. It's meant spending countless hours calling rich people to ask for money. It's meant long days of meetings and hearings and long nights of studying my binder to prepare for the next day's meetings and hearings.

But even if you don't run for office, in order to be part of determining what our shared future looks like, you have to be willing to give up things like time and energy and money. You have to be willing to tolerate a seemingly endless stream of injustices and disappointments. You have to endure an overwhelming amount of noise and nonsense. And the worst part is, you're not guaranteed a return on your investment.

After all, if 313 fewer Minnesotans had voted for me, you'd be reading a very different book right now, possibly entitled *The Bottomless Pit: My Losing Battle to Overcome Depression.*

That's why, even on the good days, politics is hard. And on the bad days, it can feel downright futile. I've had some of those bad days since I started this journey—like the day that bestiality ad made my mother-in-law cry, or the day I had to apologize to Mitch McConnell, or literally any day since November 8, 2016. But I have a feeling that the worst days of my political career are still ahead.

I'm sure there will be moments over the next few years where I'll wish I was back at *Saturday Night Live*, laughing like crazy in a room full of my best friends, or even just hanging out with my grandkids and giving my brain a break from the constant stream of noise that passes for our political discourse.

But I'll tell you this: I'm glad I'm here.

And I'm glad you're here, too.

Chapter 47

Being as Good as the People We Serve

Let me close by telling you a story that helps me keep *my* head up.

Something I love about my job as a U.S. senator is that I get to spend half my time back in my home state meeting with the people I represent. And as corny as it sounds, talking with Minnesotans always sends me back to Washington inspired and encouraged.

Minnesotans are good-hearted and generous and brilliant. And when I spend time in my state, I see Minnesotans training veterans for advanced manufacturing jobs. I see them making great advances in clean energy and energy efficiency that could wind up being game-changers in the fight against climate change. I see them helping their neighbors clean up after floods and tornadoes.

Seeing this stuff always makes me realize how

lucky I am to be Minnesota's voice in Washington. Even when being in politics feels exhausting, or dispiriting, or downright morally bankrupt, it's *still* a chance to do some good work for people who really, really deserve it.

And in that way, the people I represent don't just inspire me, they focus me. They make it possible to notice how screwed up our political system is without letting my frustration turn me inside out. They give me something to hold on to so that I can avoid getting discouraged—because in politics it's the people who can avoid getting discouraged who get a chance to make a difference.

Even on my worst days, the people I represent give me a purpose that can't be shaken by some obnoxious procedural delay or jaw-droppingly terrible Trump tweet. I represent incredible people. And my job is simply to be as good as they are.

* * *

Two days before the 2016 election, Donald Trump landed his gaudy plane at the Minneapolis–St. Paul airport, making his first public appearance in our state just in time to spread his trademark blend of hate, fear, and ignorance—this time targeting our Somali-Minnesotan community.

Somalis started coming to America in large numbers during a civil war in the early 1990s. Many families had spent years in refugee camps in Kenya and elsewhere in Africa. About fifty thousand Somali refugees now live in Minnesota—many of them in the Twin Cities, but not all. Many smaller cities and communities around the state have significant Somali populations.

At the time, Trump was attacking Hillary Clinton's plan to admit sixty-five thousand refugees out of the millions of people fleeing Syria in the worst refugee crisis since World War II. "Her plan," Trump told the crowd, "will import generations of terrorism, extremism, and radicalism into your schools and throughout your community. You already have it."

He wasn't talking about Syrian refugees. So far, Minnesota has admitted twenty-eight of them. He was talking about the Somalis who have been here for years, people who are an important part of our state's fabric.

"Here in Minnesota you have seen firsthand the problems caused with faulty refugee vetting, with large numbers of Somali refugees coming into your state," Trump told the rally. He was referring to an incident two months earlier in which a young Somali man wielding a knife had injured nine people at a shopping mall in St. Cloud before being killed by an off-duty cop. The assailant had come to America when he was four months old. Which makes it kind of hard to buy that the incident was a result of "faulty vetting."

The investigation is now in the hands of the feds, who have possession of the attacker's electronic devices. By all accounts, the man had gone off the deep end. Not unlike the Iowa man with a Trump-Pence sign in his yard who had murdered two police officers ambush-style just four days before the airport rally. Of course, no one was accusing Trump of stoking the anger that led to the senseless police killings in Iowa. But here Trump was, blaming the Somali community for the knife attack in St. Cloud.

"You've suffered enough," he snarled, talking about the presence of Somali people in our communities.

That's kind of how Trump's entire campaign went. His arguments were rarely rooted in fact, but they frequently carried a tinge of racism and paranoia. And that's what made it so upsetting when he won. How could *that* be what America chose? Is that really who we are? And if so, what's the point of trying?

The truth, however, is that, at least in Minnesota, that's *not* who we are.

The day after the knife attack, St. Cloud's police chief, William Blair Anderson, went on *Fox and Friends*, where perfectly named host Steve Doocy invited him to comment on Trump's concerns "about who is coming to our country."

Chief Anderson replied, "I can tell you the vast majority of all our citizens, no matter what ethnicity, are fine, hardworking people, and now is not the time to be divisive." Shortly after the attack, I went to St. Cloud to meet with Anderson and St. Cloud's fine mayor, David Kleis, a former Republican state legislator whom I've gotten to know well over the years. They assured me that the attack would not divide their cohesive community.

Look, a lot of Minnesotans voted for Donald Trump. And when I travel around Minnesota, I meet people who voted for him believing that only a true outsider could "drain the swamp" in Washington. I meet committed Republicans who were willing to hold their noses and vote for him so that the Supreme Court would stay in conservative hands. I meet people who bought into the misinformation spread about Hillary Clinton and couldn't bring themselves to vote for someone who was insufficiently attentive to proper email security protocols.

But where Donald Trump sees a state in which people suspect and resent their neighbors based on where they come from, I see a state where we look out for each other, because we believe that we're all in this together. Trump might have found a clever way to channel the resentments of the white working class, and he sure does seem good at playing the media for fools, but he's just plain wrong about what kind of people we are.

* * *

Willmar is an agricultural city of about twenty thousand in south-central Minnesota and the seat of Kandiyohi County, the largest turkey-producing county in the largest turkey-producing state in the nation. In June of last year, I took the unusual step of inviting myself to Willmar's high school graduation. Not just for the free punch and cookies, but because I wanted to introduce the senior who had been voted by the graduating class to be their class speaker.

Her name was Muna Abdulahi, and she had been one of our Senate pages during her junior year. Her principal had recommended her to my office, and my staff told me that her essay and interview had been unbelievably impressive. So, the day the new class of pages arrived in the Senate, I went down to the floor to meet her in person. Muna was easy to pick out of the group of thirty or so, being the only one wearing a hijab (headscarf) with her page uniform. I went up to her and said, "You look like a Minnesotan."

Muna nodded and smiled. As we talked, I was struck by her poise and intelligence. A few weeks later, the ambassador from Somalia came to the Capitol to meet with a number of senators and members of Congress from states with large Somali communities. I invited Muna to come along so that the ambassador could meet her and see that a Somali Minnesotan was a Senate page.

The Class of 2016 at Willmar Senior High had 236 members. Perusing the list of graduates in the program, I estimated that about 60 percent were your garden-variety Scandinavian/German white Minnesotans, about 25 percent were Hispanic, and about 15 percent were Somali, with a few Asian Americans tossed in. The valedictorian, Maite Marin-Mera, had been born in Ecuador.

As the orchestra played "Pomp and Circumstance," the graduates entered two by two, walking down the center aisle in their caps and gowns. Muna was up front, because "Abdulahi" was the first name alphabetically. She was holding hands with fellow senior Michelle Carlson, one of two Carlson twins to graduate that day.

The only way to tell Michelle and her twin sister, Mary, apart is that Mary has a slightly shorter haircut. Or maybe it's Michelle. Otherwise, they're identical— both are tall, both are brilliant (both graduated with highest honors), and both exude the same spirit of pure positivity and joy.

The whole day was like this. Maite gave a wonderful speech, and so did class president Tate Hovland (half Norwegian, half German), and both received enthusiastic ovations. I introduced Muna, who got a boisterous round of applause as she took the stage and a standing O when she finished.

When it came time to hand out diplomas, the crowd was told to hold their applause until the end. But they couldn't help themselves. The moment Muna's name was called, everyone erupted. Clapping, shouting, stomping on the bleachers—and it continued like that through each one of the 236 graduates. These kids loved each other.

The two hours I spent at that high school commencement were a tonic for the year of trash I'd been hearing about our country.

The previous year, I'd been in Willmar to help respond to an avian flu crisis that threatened the turkey industry that employs so many in Kandiyohi County. A number of producers were worried that they might lose their entire operations. But we were able to get some emergency funding to help keep them on their feet.

Were these turkey producers Democrats? Were they Republicans? No idea. Didn't care. Don't care. Will never care. Do *they* care that they have Somali refugees in their community? Yes, they do care. They want them. They need them. They need people like Muna's dad, who works in IT at the Jennie-O Turkey store.

Perhaps Donald Trump confused Minnesota with somewhere else. About a week after the election, I spoke to Gérard Araud, the French ambassador to the United States. He told me that in France, a Frenchman is someone who can tell you what village his family is from going back centuries. Immigrants never really get to become Frenchmen. It made me think back to the hideous massacre in Paris the year before.

Here in America, of course, we're all immigrants.

Except, of course, for Native Americans against whom we committed genocide. I'm a Jew, but I'm also an American. Muna is Somali, but she's also an American. On election day, I ran into her on campus at the University of Minnesota, where I was getting out the vote for Hillary. She told me that her sister, Anisa, had been voted homecoming queen.

That's who we are. In places like France, they isolate their refugees and immigrants. In America, we elect them homecoming queen.

* * *

Willmar is a great community. Minnesota is a great state. America is a great country.

Do we have enormous problems? You bet. Do Americans have the right to be angry about those problems? Yes. Are some of those Americans wrong about what the problems are? Sure. Does that make it harder to solve the problems? Oh yeah.

But one thing is for sure. Muna is not the problem. Muna is a big part of the solution. Her classmates know it. Her community knows it.

And her senator knows it, too.

If, when you read this book, the Trump presidency has gone in the direction we all fear it might, you might think it's strange for me to have ended this book on a hopeful note. But I'm an optimist. And, more importantly, I'm Minnesota's senator.

And no matter what happens in the years ahead, no matter who's president, no matter how exciting or depressing our current political environment may be, we who have the honor of serving our state and our country in the Senate always need to remember whom it is we're serving.

And how fucking great they are.

The End

Acknowledgments

First and foremost, I want to thank my wife, Franni, with whom I've been sharing this adventure for nearly forty-eight years. I am so grateful to our daughter, Thomasin, and son, Joe, for their love and counsel and their choice of spouses, Brody and Stephanie. So far, Franni and I have been blessed with three beautiful grandchildren, none of whom lifted a finger to help with this thing.

My brother helped, though. He's a world-class photographer and there are a number of his pictures in the photo inserts, which I hope you enjoyed. Thanks, Owen, for not going into physics. And a special thanks to Franni's family—all the Brysons, but especially my hero, Fran.

I'd like to thank the people of Minnesota for (barely, at least the first time) giving me the honor and privilege of serving you. For those of you who didn't vote for me either time, it's an honor and privilege to serve you, too, and while this book may not have changed your mind about me, thanks for reading it and hearing me out.

I'd also like to thank my fellow senators for their friendship, their mentorship, their partnership, and in the case of several Republicans mentioned in this book, for not getting mad about stuff I wrote.

The political journey in this book wouldn't have been possible without the hard work of a whole lot of people, few of whom ever get the recognition they deserve. I don't have room to change that here, but thank you to Stephanie Schriock and Matt Burgess for managing my campaigns, and thank you to every staffer, intern, and volunteer who has been part of those campaigns, or who has helped with my PAC, or who is part of the DFL family in Minnesota. Sorry I made it so difficult sometimes. And special thanks to A. J. Goodman for raising all that money to pay for everything.

Then there are the incredible public servants who help me do my job in the Senate. We have a tradition at our D.C. office. At our Christmas party, I raise a glass "to the best Senate office on Capitol Hill!" We drink, and then I raise my glass again: "And now, to our office!" I don't want the staff getting a swelled head. But they are the most amazing group of dedicated, brilliant, hard-working people I know. That goes double for our St. Paul office and our other offices around Minnesota. All of that comes from the top, of course.

Drew Littman, my first chief of staff, set it all in motion, putting a great team in place, and creating a culture of excellence. Casey Aden-Wansbury, my original communications director, took the helm from Drew, carried that culture forward, and built on it every day for four years. When Casey left, Jeff Lomonaco, who was my original foreign policy adviser and then legislative director, became chief of staff and provided a seamless transition. As you can tell, I am extremely proud of the remarkable continuity we have enjoyed, both in D.C. and in Minnesota, where Alana Petersen has provided extraordinary leadership as my state director from Day One.

For six years, my scheduler Tara Mazer, took incredible care of me, as has Sara Silvernail, my Minnesota scheduler. You guys are the best! Brynna Schmidt has taken over for Tara in D.C., and is filling big shoes extraordinarily well.

All of these people have been extraordinarily patient and supportive during the writing of this book. In particular, I'd like to thank Jeff, as well as Ed Shelleby, my deputy chief of staff and communications director, who have offered guidance throughout this process and talked me out of at least one possibly career-ending joke. That's legal, by the way, because

I paid them from my book advance. Which reminds me, I should thank Marc Elias and my lawyers at Perkins Coie, who also helped me on a little recount thing a few years back.

Oh, and speaking of lawyers (and my book advance), I'd like to thank Bob Barnett.

I'd also like to thank my editor, Sean Desmond, and the entire team at Twelve—from Jamie Raab, who recently completed her service as publisher, on down to Brian McLendon, Paul Samuelson, Jarrod Taylor, Rachel Kambury, Bailey Donoghue, and everyone else.

A number of friends read pages as I wrote, some reading successive drafts. These include Drew, Casey, Alana, Jeff, Ed, and Stephanie. Also Norm Ornstein, Mandy Grunwald, Diane Feldman, former staffers Hannah Katch and Josh Riley, Ben Wikler, John Markus, Jess McIntosh, Franni, and Thomasin and Joe. All were extremely helpful, though Norm kept asking for "more Ornstein, less Gawande." Thanks to them, and to Gordie Loewen, who helped with research and fact-checking.

Billy Kimball, my producer for *Indecision '92* and *The Al Franken Show* on Air America, also worked with me on three of my previous books. On this one, Billy provided always helpful and sometimes brutal critiques, sharpened some of the prose, and added some terrific jokes for your reading enjoyment.

I first met Andy Barr when he was a nineteen-year-old sophomore at Harvard, where he was one of the key members of TeamFranken, which researched *Lies and the Lying Liars Who Tell Them*. Andy has been working with me since, with some time off to finish college. After graduation, Andy joined my Air America show, then played a central role in my run for the Senate and has written with and for me during my Senate career. Andy has been indispensable in the realization of this book. Without Andy the writing in this book wouldn't have been good.

If I left anyone out, it's due to staff error.

Mission Statement

Twelve strives to publish singular books by authors who have unique perspectives and compelling authority. Books that explain our culture; that illuminate, inspire, provoke, and entertain. Our mission is to provide a consummate publishing experience for our authors, one truly devoted to thoughtful partnership and cutting-edge promotional sophistication that reaches as many readers as possible. For readers, we aim to spark that rare reading experience—one that opens doors, transports, and possibly changes their outlook on our ever-changing world.

12 Things to Remember about TWELVE

1. Every Twelve book will enliven the national conversation.
2. Each book will be singular in voice, authority, or subject matter.

3. Each book will be carefully edited, designed, and produced.

4. Each book's publication life will begin with a monthlong launch; for that month it will be the imprint's devoted focus.

5. The Twelve team will work closely with its authors to devise a publication strategy that will reach as many readers as possible.

6. Each book will have a national publicity campaign devoted to reaching as many media outlets—and readers—as possible.

7. Each book will have a unique digital strategy.

8. Twelve is dedicated to finding innovative ways to market and promote its authors and their books.

9. Twelve offers true partnership with its authors— the kind of partnership that gives a book its best chance at success.

10. Each book will get the fullest attention and distribution of the sales force of the Hachette Book Group.

11. Each book will be promoted well past its on-sale date to maximize the life of its ideas.

12. Each book will matter.